Corporate Agility

CORPORATE
Agility

A Revolutionary New Model for
Competing in a Flat World

Charles E. Grantham

James P. Ware

Cory Williamson

AMERICAN MANAGEMENT ASSOCIATION

New York • Atlanta • Brussels • Chicago • Mexico City • San Francisco •
Shanghai • Tokyo • Toronto • Washington, D.C.

This publication is designed to provide accurate and authoritative information in regard to the subject matter covered. It is sold with the understanding that the publisher is not engaged in rendering legal, accounting, or other professional service. If legal advice or other expert assistance is required, the services of a competent professional person should be sought.

Library of Congress Cataloging-in-Publication Data

Grantham, Charles E.
    Corporate agility : a revolutionary new model for competing in a flat world / Charles E. Grantham, James P. Ware, Cory Williamson.
        p.   cm.
    Includes bibliographical references and index.
    ISBN-13: 978-0-8144-0911-4
    ISBN-10: 0-8144-0911-3
    1. Strategic planning.   2. Organizational change.   3. Organizational effectiveness.   I. Ware, James P.   II. Williamson, Cory.   III. Title.

    HD30.28.G7219   2007
    658.4'012—dc22

                                                        2007025306

Printing number

10   9   8   7   6   5   4   3   2   1

C O N T E N T S

CHAPTER 8

The Well-Designed Workplace   193

CHAPTER 9

Collaborative Strategic Management   219

CHAPTER 10

Achieving Corporate Agility   239

A C K N O W L E D G M E N T S

No book about collaborative strategic management could be written by a single author—or even by a team of three. Our names may be on the cover, but this book was written by a host of senior executives, managing directors, and business professionals with whom we've worked and from whom we've learned over many, many years.

That said, we'd like to pick a few faces out of the crowd, and we want to begin by acknowledging the extensive support this project received from our many good friends at Jones Lang LaSalle and Herman Miller. We simply could not have written this book without the help of Debra Moritz and her colleagues at Jones Lang LaSalle. Nor would these pages have been written without the help of Jill Duncan at Herman Miller. Jill believed in our ideas from the very beginning and brought our project to Herman Miller's Joanie Reid, whose active sponsorship opened many doors for us. Many thanks to all of you, both for your faith in the project and for your willingness to share your experiences and your insights about corporate real estate, workplace design, human resources, information technology, and strategic management.

We'd also like to particularly thank certain members of the *Future of Work* community—Len Pilon of Herman Miller; Dan Johnson and Sasha Lacey at Accenture; Renee Leach, Chris Hood, and Ed Nolan at H-P; Kevin Kampschroer of the General Services Administration; Donna Biskys and Sue Reidy at Agilent Technologies; Brian Sherwood at Boeing; Tom Baker of Johnson Controls; Gloria Young at the City of San Francisco, Mark Lautman of Forest City Covington, and Diane Coles at Scan Health Plan.

Beyond that inner circle of *Future of Work* members, we'd also like to acknowledge Buzz Buzzanco, Loretta Penn, and Gail Blount at Spherion; Charemon Tovar at Sprint Nextel; Mark Gribbons at IA Interior Architects; and the folks at WIRED West Michigan. We're also grateful to Prentice

Knight and his staff at CoreNet Global for welcoming our contributions to the groundbreaking "Corporate Real Estate 2010" project back in 2002–2003 when we were just beginning our *Future of Work* community.

We'd also like to recognize two friends whose belief in our mission—way back in 2001—gave us the confidence to walk away from other endeavors and launch the Work Design Collaborative: John Igoe and Paul Bianchi. It was their conviction that human resources and corporate real estate have to be dragged—even if kicking and screaming—into the same room with information technology that motivated us to convene our first gathering of those who believe that the future of work will be radically different than anything any of us have yet imagined.

One more collection of friends deserves special mention—our monthly *Brain Blender* group. We're privileged to be a part of such a wonderfully varied and geographically distributed group, which includes Candace Fitzpatrick, Mark Gorman, John Foster, Deena Baikowitz, Terry Musch, and especially Rex Miller. Thanks for sharing your knowledge and experiences so unselfishly, and for keeping us learning, and laughing.

We also want to thank our wives—Ellen Grantham, Cindy Ware, and Maria Williamson—all of whom hung in there with us though this project's highs and lows, and as wives will, offered sound advice even when we didn't want to hear it.

To conclude, we wrote this book because the three of us share a simple goal: We want to see the future of work—where all of us will spend the rest of our professional lives—made both more productive, and more humane. We modestly offer the following stories, case studies, experiences, and research results in the service of that worthy objective.

Corporate Agility

INTRODUCTION

Early in 2002, as part of our continuing efforts at the Work Design Collaborative, we began a modest research project we called the *Future of Work*. As business consultants with backgrounds in academia—Jim at the Harvard Business School, and Charlie at the University of San Francisco—we saw the need for a new set of analytical tools that businesses could use to rationalize their real estate needs, their information technology deployment, and their human resources planning. As a result, we gathered a small group of corporate thought leaders from companies such as Agilent Technologies, Cisco Systems, Intel, PeopleSoft, Capital One, and Herman Miller and we began to survey both labor and management in an attempt to discover how new technologies, the changing workforce, and economic globalization were changing how and where people worked, and what those changes meant to the future of work in the so-called Information Economy.

The initial results confirmed what our experiences as academics, consultants, and corporate managers had long led us to suspect: Although the global economy had undergone a series of rapid, model-shattering changes, most businesses had been unable, or unwilling, to adapt their traditional management styles to new conditions. Prisoners of their outdated business practices and their assumptions about how work gets done, they found themselves losing ground to competitors who had not even been on the map a decade before. They became victims, rather than beneficiaries, of advances in information technology. And at a time when the attraction and retention of qualified, engaged employees had become an even more critical factor in a business's success or failure, they found themselves out of touch with a workforce that had undergone a dizzying transformation in attitudes, abilities, and ambitions.

Together, these factors resulted in a crippling loss of corporate agility.

1

In an economy characterized by rapid, unpredictable change, traditionally managed companies felt as though they were standing still while the new global order spun past them. The weights on those corporate ankles were easy to identify: high fixed operational costs, in other words, long-term commitments to buildings, people, and technologies, that robbed corporations of the flexibility and the agility required to compete and succeed in a period of unprecedented change in the business world.

Traditionally managed companies were paying too much for real estate and facilities, and had labor forces that were costly, inflexible, locked in to long-term contracts, and plagued by high rates of turnover. Worse, these same companies had product development cycles so lengthy and complicated that the markets themselves often changed before the *new* products ever reached them.

These Industrial-Age behemoths are often referred to as *corporate dinosaurs*, in an effort to describe just how slow and unwieldy they really are—to say nothing of being nearly extinct—and there may be even more truth and insight contained in that image than anyone ever intended. Although dinosaurs inhabited the earth for something like 150 million years, the general belief today is that they disappeared following a cataclysmic climate change caused by the impact of an enormous meteorite. The dinosaurs had become so physically large and complex, with nervous systems focused almost completely on their own internal needs—breathing, digesting food, circulation, and so on—that they were unable to adapt to the new conditions. Only smaller, fleet-footed mammals were able to survive by reacting to the changing climate, plant life, and the other remaining inhabitants of the radically changed ecosystem.

We find that a compelling metaphor for what is happening in the business world today. Those that survive will be the fleet of foot and the nimble—those organizations that create not only new products but also new markets, and do so faster than their competitors ever imagined possible. In addition to being able to advance quickly, they also will be capable of pulling back in response to unexpected changes in customer demand or interest. It's not enough to be first to market, or to double your revenue overnight; it's also important to be able to reduce your presence in one part of the globe at the same time you establish it in another. In today's business climate, only the agile survive.

How, then, does a business evolve from the dinosaur to the jaguar, and in the space of months, not millennia? After decades of research, both on our own and in conjunction with various members of the *Future of Work* community, we believe the answer is a collaborative, strategic approach to management that acknowledges and leverages the growing interdependence of human resources (HR), corporate real estate (CRE), and information technology (IT), a process we call *collaborative strategic management*. People, place, and technology, after all, are what come together to define the workplace, and it is there that businesses thrive or fail. Yet despite that simple, unassailable truth, in most businesses operating today the management of HR, CRE, and IT is disconnected, and therefore dysfunctional.

At first glance, given their dissimilarities, this is not surprising. Just think about it for a moment—are there any two professional areas more dissimilar than IT and HR? IT is all about reliably delivering data on demand, and at the lowest possible cost. IT is about machines, software codes, and electricity. It is about being 100 percent correct all the time, since one little bug, or virus, can destroy a multimillion-dollar enterprise. HR, in contrast, is about understanding and motivating human beings—highly unpredictable, emotional creatures, who often have contradictory opinions.

And the corporate real estate profession? Suffice it to say that the CRE manager lives in a world as far from IT and HR as Earth is from Saturn and Jupiter. Real estate professionals are charged with providing safe, productive, low-cost workplaces in strategically desirable locations. And they must provide that space at just the right time, anticipating the company's needs so that it's available just before it's needed, and yet can be disposed of just as soon as it isn't, and at minimal cost to the company.

Thus, each of these three functional areas has its own disciplines, its own values, and its own challenges. Yet no business can operate effectively unless HR, CRE, and IT are in sync, aligned both with one another, and with the organization's broader strategic goals. For all these reasons, businesses today desperately need a clearly defined methodology that allows them to align their HR, IT, and CRE strategies, and thus achieve that all-too-elusive corporate agility.

Three years ago, recognizing this need, all of us at the *Future of Work* redefined our community. We reshaped it into a collaborative network of thought leaders, research specialists, and business consultants committed to learning how to define, develop, and implement collaborative strategic management, and thus achieve corporate agility.

In addition to founding members Herman Miller and Agilent Technologies, the *Future of Work* community currently includes Hewlett-Packard (H-P), IBM, the General Services Administration (GSA), Boeing, the city and county of San Francisco, Accenture, Johnson Controls, Forest City Covington, SCAN Health, and Jones Lang LaSalle.

In addition, over the past few years we have worked closely with Sun Microsystems, Spherion Corporation, Cisco Systems, Capital One, Allsteel, Sprint Nextel, and Intel—among many others—in our search for both a roadmap and a compass for the future. And we've also been very fortunate to have had thought leaders such as Judy Bardwick, Sara Beckman, Peter Cochran, Lynda Gratton, Terri Griffith, and Pamela Hinds as colleagues and senior fellows working closely with us.

The pages that follow contain a collection of wide-ranging, cutting-edge ideas drawn from the pilot programs, case studies, and evolving best practices of *Future of Work* members, their clients, and industry experts. Clearly, not all of them will be relevant to every company, or helpful to every executive. Taken as a whole, however, the material contained herein will provide readers with a fund of knowledge from which they can pick and choose those concepts that can assist them in reaching their current strategic goals, as well as alerting them to conditions they may be forced to confront in the near future.

We're pleased and fortunate that the *Future of Work* community continues to attract forward-thinking corporations and industry thought leaders who believe in the power of collaborative research. The case studies, research, and recommendations that follow represent the best ideas and insights of the *Future of Work* community over the past five years, assembled here to help management around the world achieve corporate agility.

CHAPTER 1

More Corporate Agility, Less Corporate Real Estate

In the summer of 2006, senior managers from Hewlett-Packard and Sprint Nextel sat down at a Global Workplace program workshop in Dallas, Texas, sponsored by Jones Lang LaSalle's Workplace Strategies (WS) team, a relatively new but fast-growing division of Jones Lang LaSalle's Strategic Consulting Group. At the time, Hewlett-Packard's (H-P) Global Workplace team was overseeing the completion of the first phase of its Workplace Transformation program, aimed at supporting H-P's increasingly mobile workforce and significantly reducing its corporate real estate (CRE) holdings worldwide.

The growing mobility of the workforce, due more to naturally evolving workstyles than to company policy, had left the lights burning above thousands of unoccupied desks, and the company, as a result, was scrambling to *right-size* its real estate holdings. For an organization with approximately 150,000 employees and 65 million square feet of real estate—owned and leased—the logistics were daunting. What's more, H-P's merger with Compaq in 2002 had brought the company more than just increased revenues and expanded real estate holdings—it brought a fundamentally different company culture into the business equation, and presented the Global Workplace program with the additional responsibility of reaffirming the *H-P way* throughout the ever-larger and more complex organization.

Despite the baffling logistics and the delicate business of balancing corporate cultures, the Global Workplace program had one critical factor working to its advantage—the unwavering support of upper-level management. They recognized the company's CRE as an asset, rather than as an expense, and their public support of the workplace program stemmed from their plan to plow part of the savings realized from the consolidation of the company's CRE back into research and development, into an expanded, better-equipped sales force, and into modernizing the company's retained real estate.

By the summer of 2006, with the program's first phase well under way, the Global Workplace team had come to Dallas to share their experiences, to learn what they could from other companies' best practices, and to discuss the opportunities for outsourcing specific program responsibilities to service providers such as Jones Lang LaSalle.

PUTTING WORKPLACE STRATEGIES IN PLACE

Sprint, a year after its own blockbuster merger with Nextel, was in the process of realizing its own vision of the future of work—the Sprint Powered Workplace. Having realized long before the merger that the competitive pressures of the wireless communications industry made the reduction of its fixed operating expenses necessary, the company had begun to look for new ways to cut costs as early as 2003. Those efforts began with its sales force, traditionally out of the office more than 60 percent of the time. The company found, just as H-P had, that much of its real estate was going unused, or was no longer meeting the workforce's changing needs.

In Sprint Nextel's case, it already had the products, services, and know-how needed to create a more mobile workforce—in fact, it had been offering them to customers for years, but just wasn't taking full advantage of those services itself. In the spring of 2005, therefore, with full executive support, Sprint Nextel embarked on an ambitious program to consolidate its real estate holdings, to make 60 percent of the sales force "Work Anywhere Employees," and to reconfigure its remaining space to better serve its evolving workforce.

A year after the program began, it had been rolled out in more than 20 of the 125 branch offices in the United States. With the bulk of the company's locations yet to be converted, however, representatives from Sprint had come to Dallas to share ideas, to learn how mobile workforce initiatives were being handled elsewhere, and to discuss the possibility of outsourcing additional components of its program.

Led by Managing Director Debra Moritz, the Jones Lang LaSalle Workplace Strategies (WS) team—a rapidly growing division of the Strategic Consulting Group (SCON)—had brought the two companies together in the belief that a comparison of their programs, and a broad review of best practices, would lead to an even more successful implementation of their programs. Despite each initiative's unique characteristics, the WS team focused on the similarities:

- Both programs had strong executive support and high expectations from their respective business units.

- Both programs had successfully matured well beyond the pilot stage.

- Both programs had very aggressive timelines.

- Both organizations were committed to developing the teams and the resources to successfully implement their programs.

- Both initiatives had a sense of urgency, but also a need to get it right.

- Both companies had a lot riding on the success of the programs.

The initial stage of the workshop focused on identifying key challenges to the programs, and the subsequent session identified general approaches to resolving them. The challenges weren't hard to identify. In their simplest form, they are grouped here with their proposed resolutions:

- Fundamental resistance to change: Communication and change management

- Managing the programs on an extended scale: Organizational structure and review

- Impact of the Programs on day-to-day operations: Accountability and training

Everyone at the workshop agreed that the most difficult change for employees to accept was the loss of an assigned workplace (desk) and/or workspace (office). Such resistance could be expected to decrease over time; however, the rate of acceptance was greatly accelerated by clearly communicating the benefits at the organizational, departmental, and individual levels—before the program began.

In order to get employees to accept change more quickly, Sprint Nextel would have to make the case to individual employees so they understood the business reasons behind the change, the effect the change would have within their department, and the way they personally would be affected. The timetable for change also had to be effectively communicated, with special care taken to explain the way in which the initial changes would occur. Equally important, employees had to understand how the program would affect customers, and the means by which the company would respond to customer feedback.

The workshop participants all agreed that this process couldn't be left to chance. Change management teams, with dedicated resources and personnel, had to be in place at the onset of the program, and had to include representatives from HR, IT, and CRE in order to be effective. As the process of change continued, it was also important to encourage peer-to-peer exchange, and to advertise successes within the company.

Although employees couldn't expect such changes to occur without problems, management had to respond quickly and meaningfully to employee feedback in order to maintain support for the program and ensure employee buy-in. What's more, just as in any chain of command, there was bound to be some degree of disconnect between management objectives and employee performance, and management had to be patient in order to overcome the inevitable obstacles to change.

It is one thing, of course, to undertake such changes in a single office, and another to roll them out across an entire enterprise. For companywide efforts, workshop participants agreed that the organizational structure had to be reevaluated in light of the proposed changes, planning and delivery of services had to be streamlined, and the goals of the program had to be carefully aligned with the company's infrastructure functions. Once again, before any enterprisewide rollout began, customer reaction had to be anticipated. And since any miscommunication at the beginning would be repeated over and over again throughout the process, it was considered especially important to plan the transformation carefully, considering each stage in the process.

Although the rollout wouldn't be perfect, employee anxiety could be reduced and lost time could be minimized.

Finally, considering the impact on day-to-day operations, the following observations were made:

1. *Operations accountability was deemed to be critical.* Responsibilities had to be clearly defined—and monitored—throughout the process. Ideally, an integrated program office, consisting of upper-level executives in HR, IT, and CRE, would be created to provide beginning-to-end project support and accountability. The program could not succeed without both strong executive sponsorship and champions at every level of the business.

2. *Employees had to be individually assessed well before the rollout began.* Training programs would need to be tailored to each employee's specific needs, as determined by those assessments.

3. *As the plan was rolled out, service offerings had to evolve continually.* This was especially important for IT services. As the workforce became more and more distributed, service offerings would have to adapt.

4. *Constant adjustments to the organizational structure had to be made as the program continued.* This, all present agreed, would be management's most difficult challenge.

Although management by objective was prevalent in both the Sprint Nextel and H-P cultures, mid-level managers accustomed to seeing their direct reports every day could not help having difficulty supervising employees they could not see.

Employees, too, were bound to experience difficulties becoming members of a distributed workforce. Experience had taught those at the workshop that even valued employees who had been working for the company for years, and whose positions were secure, would not be able to avoid the sense that by being out of sight, they would be out of mind. In other words, adjustments would have to be made on the parts of both labor and management in order to maintain communication and productivity, and to create a new concept of trust.

The reconfiguration of the retained office space would require training for both *dedicated workers,* who would use the space every day, and *mobile workers,* who would use it only occasionally. By making design changes uniform across all branches, however, the company could offer those workers whose jobs involved greater amounts of travel a comfort zone—no matter where they touched down, they would at least find the same general layout, amenities, and services in the company offices.

In order to identify initial missteps, aggressive postoccupancy monitoring had to occur after every step in the process, at its conclusion, and every so often after the program had been officially implemented.

JONES LANG LASALLE

The WS team from Jones Lang LaSalle was no stranger to these processes. Although it had set up the workshop to provide recommendations, to review the best practices of industry thought leaders, and to promote the company's WS services, the process was one with which it was intimately familiar. Only a year earlier, Jones Lang LaSalle had begun the expansion of its own WS program into its Chicago headquarters, and it was not yet complete as the team sat down with H-P and Sprint Nextel in Dallas.

A global real estate services and money management firm, Jones Lang LaSalle offers local, regional, and global services in more than a hundred markets, in fifty countries, on five continents. The company has approximately 22,000 employees. Its range of services includes leasing, property management, project and development services, valuations, capital markets, buying and selling properties, corporate finance, hotel advisory, space acquisition and disposition (tenant representation), facilities management, outsourcing, and strategic consulting.

In addition, through LaSalle Investment Management, Jones Lang LaSalle provides money management services on a global basis for both public and private assets. Since the company went public in 1997, growth has been fueled by the expansion of the company's client base, the expanding range of its services and products, and a series of strategic acquisitions and mergers.

Jones Lang LaSalle's own WS pilot program was motivated by the same primary goal that had caused H-P and Sprint Nextel to reorganize their businesses—the reduction of fixed operating costs. Almost as important, however, was management's desire to increase agility and innovation by encouraging greater cooperation between its business units, which had been scattered throughout the four floors occupied by the company in its headquarters in Chicago's Aon Center. Formerly known as the AMOCO building and located just a few blocks from Chicago's Lake Shore Drive, the building had been home to LaSalle Partners before its merger with Jones Lang Wootton.

The pilot WS program had its beginnings in Jones Lang LaSalle's Leading Edge Series—seminars devoted to specific CRE topics attended by industry thought leaders. Through the exposure to new ideas and case studies the company began to better understand the potential impact of workplace strategies on its own strategic goals, as well as to see greater opportunities to link its overall business strategy and its real estate portfolio more closely. (This, in a certain sense, was similar to the epiphany Sprint Nextel experienced when it realized that as a corporation it had failed to take complete advantage of the services and products it offered its own customers.) Jones Lang LaSalle's subsequent companywide reorientation—called "No Barriers/No Boundaries"—was both figuratively and literally an attempt to knock down the walls between the company's core business units.

Convinced that the lack of communication between these units was causing the company to miss opportunities to offer clients a greater variety of its services—a lose/lose proposition for both Jones Lang LaSalle and its clients—management turned to the reorganization of its new space in the Aon Center. The new design, an Open Office Environment, was intended to increase cooperation by greatly reducing the number of offices and corridors, and encouraging collaboration through random, spontaneous contact. The approach began to yield results almost immediately. Listen to this story, sent via e-mail by senior management to all Aon Center employees:

> It didn't take long for employees to enjoy the benefits of the new floor plan. Just ask Dan Ryan. It started with Dan and some of his Markets colleagues, in their new space on 47, finalizing a new business presentation. At stake was the leasing and management of 225 W. Wacker in Chicago for JPMorgan, one of our core investment clients nationally. Twenty minutes before they were due to leave the office for the airport, the team realized they were missing some valuable documentation. "Ordinarily," Dan says, "it would've been next to impossible to get those materials in the time frame available to us. It would've taken us days just to ascertain who was available to help us." But, thanks to the reorientation and the new open floor plan, all Dan had to do was look up and see Melissa Latchem passing

by. He quickly enlisted her help gathering some information. Similarly, Elvia Rodriguez was nearby and was able to provide further information with additional input from Elaine Melonides and Steve Steinmeyer, who also agreed to pitch in. To make a short story even shorter, within 20 minutes the team had in its hands all the information they needed to solidify the presentation. They not only made the flight, they won the assignment— our first piece of JPMorgan business in Chicago, ever.

"What the experience underlined, for me," Dan says, "was the kind of spontaneity and teamwork the new space makes possible. Now, when you find yourself in a crunch, you don't have to run around looking for help. Your colleagues are right there with you, and everyone's motivated to help each other."

This is probably as good a place as any to note that Jones Lang LaSalle, unlike many of its competitors, does not pit its employees against one another by awarding bonuses or commissions based on individual efforts. In businesses where the rewards for success accrue to the individual, rather than to the department as a whole, employees are as likely to conceal their work from their colleagues as they are from their competitors. As a result, any sense of team or community is lost, as is the possibility of productive collaboration.

That sense of community, of course, is exactly what Jones Lang LaSalle wanted to generate with its No Barriers/No Boundaries, Open Office Environment, and WS initiatives. And while there are certainly occupations, and perhaps even whole industries, that thrive on internal competition, it's equally true that there are great advantages to be had from collaboration, and that the nature of the workplace has much to do with whether, and how, that occurs.

Achieving the right balance of individual and team rewards is one of the toughest challenges faced by business executives and HR professionals. And that balance is particularly difficult to find in professional services firms such as Jones Lang LaSalle. On the one hand, focus too much on individual rewards and you get individuals hoarding billable work and ignoring input from colleagues. On the other hand, if there is too much emphasis on teamwork, the star performers can become discouraged, feeling that they are carrying the rest of the team and would do better on their own. The fact that such a fundamental HR challenge comes to the fore in what started as a cost-reduction move underscores our fundamental theme of the need for *collaborative* strategic management of CRE, HR, and IT.

Buoyed by the initial, favorable results of the Open Office Environment, the Strategic Consulting group pressed for a pilot WS program in Jones Lang LaSalle's Chicago headquarters. It presented an outline of the additional benefits that could be gained through such a program, and the effect it would have on the company's ability to sell WS services to existing clients. Senior management approved.

Although Jones Lang LaSalle was unable to implement as comprehensive a plan as it would have liked—for reasons we will address further in this narrative—it was able to include the following elements in its initial plans:

- Multiple spaces for different tasks—both private and public space—with a significant increase in collaborative space, conference rooms, multiuse spaces, and so on

- Increased local mobility

- Workplace attributes keyed to task requirements, not to function or job title

- Touchdown spaces for teleworkers and visitors

- Low-height systems furniture

The pilot project, while not a full-blown WS implementation, allowed both the Strategic Consulting Group and upper-level management at Jones Lang LaSalle to see the program's potential. In addition, the program's implementation provided valuable insight into the challenges such organizational shifts present, and perhaps just as importantly, served to demonstrate to potential clients that Jones Lang LaSalle's professionals practiced what they preached.

Before attempting to further expand the scope and scale of the program, however, senior executives at Jones Lang LaSalle felt they needed to better understand the risks and obstacles that lay ahead, as well as their organization's potential for change. For that analysis they called on us at the Work Design Collaborative.

We had long believed that the first step in any company's transformation of its workplace and its workforce was a readiness assessment. Accurately assessing a company's readiness and capacity for change not only greatly increases the likelihood of a program's successful implementation, but—even more importantly—it helps avoid the disruption of day-to-day operations during the process of change. Toward that end, and as the first component of our *Workplace/Workforce Transformation Program*—about which we will have much more to say in Chapter 9—we developed the *Organizational Assessment System* (OAS). In short, you can consider this a mechanism for collaborative strategic management, and through its use, corporate agility.

The OAS was designed to provide decision makers with a reliable, quantifiable assessment of their company's readiness to transform their workplace and their workforce. Its purpose is to measure the following factors:

- How well the goal of the transformation has been articulated, and how well it has been communicated to the task force in charge of the change

- How much human capital exists, and how additional capital can be added or developed

- How the proposed changes will deliver value to the corporation and to its customers

- How close its information systems are to state of the practice

- How well its planning and improvement processes operate

- Whether or not the physical facilities exist to support the proposed changes

Figure 1-1 presents results from our initial assessment of Jones Lang LaSalle's ability to undertake a companywide transformation of its workplace and workforce. The outermost ring of the diagram represents the highest possible readiness for change in each of six categories. The light gray shape inside it indicates industry norms, and the darker gray shape superimposed on it represents our assessment of Jones Lang LaSalle's readiness for change. Clearly, there were challenges to be overcome. Although the company's information systems and planning capabilities were in a sufficient state of readiness and most key personnel were in place, facilities, direction, and overall agility would need to improve if the program were to succeed.

Jones Lang LaSalle responded quickly to these recommendations, and began to revise its plans accordingly. This reevaluation was made easier by the fact that it already had the most critical element of the plan in place—the support of upper-level management. In addition to that support, the company

Figure 1-1

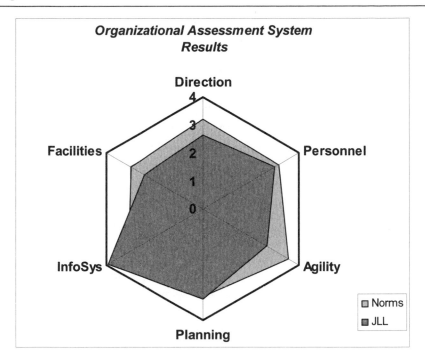

enjoyed another advantage as it began to redesign its workplace: The changes were being considered at the beginning of a classic leasing event—in this case, the renewal of its lease in Chicago's Aon Center.

Although preliminary discussions of its workplace redesign had begun more than a year earlier, the program could not move beyond the planning stages until Jones Lang LaSalle had decided where, and how, it would reestablish its headquarters. Before making that decision, management surveyed employees in the Aon Center, asking whether they preferred to stay in their location—favored by city dwellers—or whether they wished to move to a West Loop location, preferred by rail service users. The wishes of their employees aside, Jones Lang LaSalle also felt that it was important to lease space in a building under its management, a consideration that limited the choices somewhat.

As it turned out, there was companywide support for the continued occupancy of the Aon Center, and the company decided on a novel approach to the new lease—the *re-stacking* of its office space over time. In order to do this, the executives began by leasing an additional floor—the as-yet unoccupied forty-seventh—over the short term, so that the redesign could begin without unduly disrupting its daily operations. (The intent was to build out one floor at a time, moving each floor's occupants up as the floor above them became available.)

Despite the favorable set of business circumstances, and Jones Lang La-Salle's expertise in workplace strategies and project development, the WS program encountered an unforeseen obstacle, albeit one that challenges nearly every company's attempt at reorganization. Almost as soon as work on the new space had begun, the project lost its executive sponsor. Not only was momentum lost, but leadership support for the plan, a critical factor in its success or failure, was also compromised. Under the new leadership of Bill Thummel, however, the program was put back on track, and in the spring of 2006 the first employees moved into the newly designed space on the forty-seventh floor of the Aon Center.

As it turned out, the departure of the program's first head actually had unintended benefits. The new executive sponsor, mindful of the natural human resistance to change and sensitive to the additional difficulties caused by the departure of his predecessor, decided to scale back on the initial degree of redesign. As well, the slowdown in the program's implementation had allowed Jones Lang LaSalle's own WS team additional time to survey employees, thus arriving at a better understanding of how quickly, and in what order, the changes could best be implemented.

SPRINT NEXTEL

Sprint Nextel had begun its own mobile workforce initiative in the spring of 2005. At the time, the company had 16 million square feet under lease in the United States, with 3.5 million square feet of that space devoted to sales. With the greater part of the sales force already accustomed to working on the road, and vacancy rates in some sales spaces as high as 30 percent, it wasn't difficult to decide where to begin.

Now underway for more than two years, and expanded across the entire Sprint Nextel enterprise, the program the company developed is a textbook example of the competitive advantages to be gained by reducing fixed operating costs. Furthermore, by outsourcing as many of the variable costs as possible during the rollout—change management, design, and project development, to name but a few—Sprint Nextel avoided having to expand its payroll in some areas in order to reduce its workforce in others.

Once the decision had been made to initiate the program, Sprint Nextel used a form of General Electric's Work-Out process to speed its decision-making. GE describes the process as follows:

> The aptly named Work-Out process involves identifying an area in need of improvement and bringing people together from all sides of the process (design marketing, production, sales, etc.) to identify a better method. The Work-Out team meets outside of its normal work environment to discuss the issues and develop recommendations.
>
> Team recommendations are presented to the responsible managers, who must accept or reject proposals on the spot. Ideas that require further study are reviewed for a period of time agreed on by the team (usually less than a month) before a final decision is made. The process encourages responsive leadership and greater employee participation, which increases the rate of change throughout the organization.[1]

In Sprint Nextel's case, the Work-Out was convened in Kansas City, where the participants (upper-level managers from Sales, CRE, IT, and HR) were given just three days to resolve the various issues involved, and to make specific recommendations. Once the group began work, it was understood that there was no going home without a proposal.

The group's immediate goal, made possible by recent technological advances that allowed Sprint Nextel employees to work anywhere there was a cellular signal, was the reduction of nearly 2 million square feet of space, or more than half of that occupied by the U.S. sales force. In order to achieve that goal, Sales agreed to give up one-to-one seating—that is, one salesperson to every desk—and to adopt a three-to-one ratio instead. In return, part of the savings in real estate would be diverted to pay the costs of the IT necessary to support the newly mobile workforce. As well, significant design changes in the remaining sites were proposed to make customers more at home, to make use of the space more flexible, and to fit the varied demands of the new workforce. As soon as they had completed their work, top-level Sprint executives were called in for a town hall meeting, and after reviewing the recommendations, the Sprint Powered Workplace was born.

The executive thumbs-up, far from allowing anyone to take a breath, meant that the Work-Out team now had a 100-day window to come back with a specific plan for putting the program into motion, including timetables, new site designs, cost estimates for the necessary new IT and for the reconfiguration of those spaces that were to be retained, as well as the change management programs necessary for the plan's successful implementation.

Chief among the latter was the assessment of current employees—excepting certain job classes such as office support and engineering—in order to select those most likely to fit the new mobile job profile. New hires, of course, would also have to be assessed using the new methods in order to determine their compatibility with the program.

The design changes in those sites that were to be retained had to both reflect and reinforce the new paradigms, but without causing significant defections from the workforce, or from Sprint Nextel's customer base. Recognizing that the loss of assigned workspaces would leave employees without a place to hang family pictures, and sensitive to the need to build a space that customers found welcoming, the design team opted for a redesign that followed the layout of a contemporary house—that is, a reception area meant to set the visual tone of the new space as customers came through the front door; a living area (for relaxed conferences); an office area (or IT lounge); and a kitchen.

Finally, the team had to decide which of the many tasks associated with the rollout would be performed in-house, which would be outsourced, and how work between the two would be coordinated. As the rollout began, management was well aware that it could not simply decide who was fit for what job, outfit them with the necessary IT tools, and then push them out the door. Neither could management presume that existing, or prospective, customers would be unaffected by the ongoing changes. Therefore, change management programs had to take into account the inevitable employee—and customer—confusion, and thus the potential for dissatisfaction, and function so that everyone's concerns were addressed as the rollout went forward.

The mobilization of the sales force also required new methods of knowledge management, data entry, and data storage. The original plans called for a paperless environment, or a digitized enterprise, but program managers quickly realized that such a goal—at least so early in the rollout—was untenable. Therefore, Sprint Nextel addressed the knowledge management needs of its newly mobile workforce through a combination of outsourcing (i.e., support functions like postal meters and copiers), and technological solutions (i.e., flash drives that can be uploaded whenever mobile employees touched down in the office).

Finally, specific, verifiable goals—for CRE cost avoidance, and for retraining and outfitting employees with the necessary IT—had to be prepared and carefully monitored as the rollout proceeded. In Sprint Nextel's case, by the time company representatives sat down at Jones Lang LaSalle's Global Workplace workshop in Dallas, the *pilot* programs had already proven so successful—with more than 20 of Sprint's 118 domestic sites already converted—that the company had begun the process of rolling out the program across the whole of the enterprise. After taking into account the additional investments in IT, the savings were projected to total more than $100 million.

HEWLETT-PACKARD

H-P's Workplace Transformation program, officially launched in the spring of 2006, was but the latest in a long line of company workplace strategy initiatives that stretched back to European *telework* programs of the 1980s. The Workplace Transformation program was fueled by senior management's desire for a more profitable use of the company's real estate assets, but it was also an acknowledgment that worker mobility within the company was increasing on its own, and management needed to get back in front of the mobility curve.

Such mobility at H-P was hardly surprising, given that Dave Packard dubbed his leadership style *management by walking around.* Today his employees have extended his technique to their own efforts.

H-P includes in its definition of the *mobile workforce* not only those employees who consistently use multiple locations in which to work, but also those who use multiple spaces within a single location. The number of employees whose work patterns fit that definition is on the rise due to a number of factors, including the continual advance of enabling technologies, cost pressures, global competition, and attitude shifts in the workforce regarding the life/work balance. As a result, instead of attempting to confine the individuals in its workforce to a single workstation, or even to a single area within the floor plan, H-P now considers the whole floor the workplace.

This recognition of different kinds of mobility is often overlooked in conversations about distributed work. Once considered, the fact that there are different kinds of mobile workers, with distinctively different work patterns and needs for support, is patently obvious. But it is so frequently ignored that we feel compelled to point it out. There are at least four distinct kinds of mobile workers (and there are just as many kinds of distributed workers, which we'll discuss at a later point):

1. Those who move among multiple locations within a single building—from one office or cubicle to another, or to conference rooms, etc.

2. Those who move around from one building to another within a relatively well-defined local area such as a corporate campus or a city

3. Those who travel widely, generally to different cities, states, and/ or even countries—the *road warriors*

4. Those who are on the go within a regional area, such as outside sales professionals, often using a car as a mobile office

As is the case with many companies, upper-level management at H-P was at first surprised to find just how mobile certain segments of its workforce had become—again, both within and without their offices—and the extent to which the company's costly, traditionally configured facilities were being underutilized.

As they discovered the true size of their mobile workforce, however, and the rate of its growth, upper-level managers realized that opportunities for leveraging mobile work patterns were being missed, that problems created by greater worker mobility were being left unaddressed, and that their real estate portfolios needed to be rebalanced in order to reflect the workforce's changing needs. Not only had personnel density dropped dramatically, but the company's space was also being used less and less frequently for the purposes for which it had been designed. Figure 1-2 shows the rapid expansion of H-P's mobile workforce.

Organizational structures also had to be revisited, new means of measuring engagement had to be created, and new methods of knowledge management had to be devised. Finally, maintaining a corporate culture formerly dependent on daily visual contact and fixed workstations had to be reconsid-

Figure 1-2

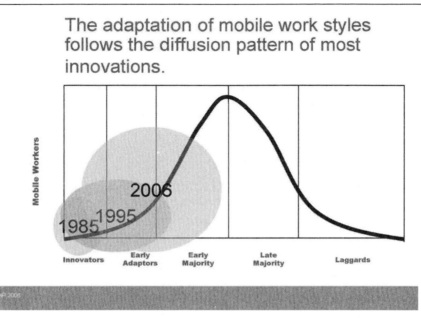

The adaptation of mobile work styles follows the diffusion pattern of most innovations.

ered in light of the new ways employees had begun to work, particularly where employees worked as part of global teams that seldom met in a face-to-face setting. Therefore, instead of being satisfied with its status as an early adaptor, management decided to accelerate the pace of change within the company and establish itself as an innovator in the field.

In order to get ahead of the mobility curve and to take advantage of the opportunities presented by a more mobile workforce, H-P established four goals for its evolving workforce and its redesigned workplaces:

1. An integrated set of space, technology, and service solutions designed to provide a productive, pleasant, and safe work environment

2. Well-utilized resources that support various work styles

3. A combination of workspaces designed to meet the differing needs of independent and collaborative work

4. Flexible, continually revisited programs able to accommodate continuous evolution in the workforce

As the percentage of true desk workers at H-P continued to decline—more than 60 percent of workers are now considered mobile based on utilization studies and are working somewhere other than "their" office space at least half of every day—a constant readjustment of the real estate portfolio was clearly required. In order to lead change rather than follow it, management began to reorient its real estate portfolio in order to effect drastic changes in utilization rates.

These changes—driven both by the continuing imperative for cost reduction and the desire to get ahead of the mobility curve—did not, of course, occur without resistance. A variety of tools, including change management programs and the IT made necessary by the redesigned workplaces, would have to be in place before the change occurred; even with them, challenges to the new order were certain to occur at all levels of the organization. Anticipating such difficulties, management began to redefine the company's concept of a productive, task-friendly working environment. The changes are summarized in Figure 1-3.

Renee Leach, director of H-P's Global Workplace Programs and Americas Region, made the point that as necessary as it is to clarify the nature of the program, it is equally important to state what it is not. Specifically, H-P's Workplace Transformation program is not:

Figure 1-3

Past	Direction
Focus on place	Focus on work
Underutilized space	Less space but better space and more effectively used
Traditional "grid" workplace design	More exciting, creative space
Enabling face-to-face engagement	More emphasis on virtual
Cost focus	Cost focus with balanced scorecard
Space, technology, and services as silos	Integrated solutions of space, technology, and services
Concern over impact of mobility on culture	Resolve to leverage benefits of distributed workforce

■ *Sending people "home" to work.*

■ *Primarily a cost-saving initiative.* Cost savings will result, but that is not the overriding purpose.

■ *A threat to H-P's corporate culture.* H-P embraces this program.

■ *Office-only solutions.* H-P's program supports both on-site and off-site work.

■ *An "alternative" approach.* It has already become the norm, and is therefore "the" global approach.

The challenge, therefore, was to rebalance asset utilization, and at the same time provide a productive work environment that did the following:

■ Leveraged the potential of the mobile work force

■ Minimized the perceived distance between coworkers

■ Maximized not the amount, but the value of face time

For these changes to occur without avoidable interruptions in day-to-day operations, change management programs would be as critical to H-P's efforts to get ahead of the mobility curve as they were in the case of the Sprint Powered Workplace. The programs were designed to follow a prescribed evolution as the program itself was rolled out. A critical part of ensuring the success of the change process was setting reachable goals, and then measuring progress toward them throughout the process of implementation (see Figure 1-4). Equally as important were postoccupancy surveys and analysis to measure the program's success, discovering ways to improve both the process of transformation and the outcomes, and, perhaps most important of all, maintaining workforce buy-in.

On that last topic it is important to keep in mind that management's willingness to consider feedback, and to respond to it, is oftentimes as important as the actions it takes. When Jones Lang LaSalle rolled out its WS program, some employees objected to the low height of the panel walls, which were topped with sections of opaque glass, believing that they didn't block acoustic distractions. For those who requested it, therefore, management had slightly higher glass sections installed atop the panels—even though growing experience showed that lower panel heights led to lower ambient noise, be-

Figure 1-4

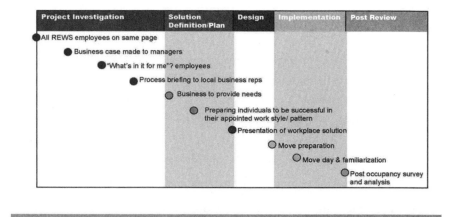

cause everyone knew their voices could be heard and were therefore more careful to lower them. Whether or not this is true in all places, the point is that in order to encourage the workforce to support the process of change, management must demonstrate that it values, and will respond to, feedback from its workforce.

To return, then, to H-P, the company's Workplace Transformation goals were as follows:

- Employee satisfaction (or 70 percent favorability rating within six months of move-in)

- Delivery excellence (quantifiable customer satisfaction)

- Operational excellence (quantifiable management satisfaction)

- Cost avoidance (through a reduction of the existing real estate footprint)

- Increased density (90 percent utilization of retained space)

This last—90 percent utilization of retained space—was an extremely aggressive goal, and was meant to do more than simply reduce costs. As important as cost avoidance is to increasing corporate agility, H-P's Workplace Transformation program was also intended to heighten the value of face-to-face interaction when employees were rubbing shoulders—in other words, to bring more buzz to the workspace through greater CRE density.

If that sounds familiar, it is: Increased collaboration was also one of the central goals of Jones Lang LaSalle's workplace strategy. Sharing these sorts of goals, experiences, and ideas was, in fact, one of the reasons that Jones Lang LaSalle's WS team put the Global Workplace workshop together. One of the clear lessons from this initial look at three very different organizations—though embarking on surprisingly parallel journeys—is that every effort to increase agility and/or to reduce cost through workplace transformation necessarily involves significant effort in all three key support areas—that is, in HR, IT, and CRE. You can't trim or enlarge one piece of the puzzle without affecting the others. In our view, the agile corporation is one whose senior executives know how to *collaborate* with their peers in order to achieve such strategies. This spirit of collaboration is not lost on a company's employees. In the case of Jones Lang LaSalle, middle management was quick to follow their leaders' example. What's more, when a prominent business magazine named Jones Lang LaSalle one of the best companies to work for, they noted that the near total absence of interior walls led to the increased availability of senior executives—and to greater employee satisfaction.

In the chapters that come we'll return frequently to these issues, but for the moment we'll turn away from workplace strategies—which are, after all, only one of the many means by which companies can reach their strategic goals—and turn to the role of corporate agility in overcoming the three major business challenges of the coming century.

CHAPTER 2

The Three Major Business Challenges:
Costs, Labor, and Innovation

No one can sketch the business world of the future with any accuracy, but one thing is certain—it will be as different from its predecessors as the factory was from the farm. And although the great drivers of change in the past century—globalization, the diffusion of technology, and shifting demographics—may not have combined to create a world that is truly flat, the playing field is unquestionably far more level than it once was.

The flow of manufacturing jobs from the traditional centers of production in Europe, North America, and the Pacific Rim to the developing economies of China, India, Central America, and South America has been well documented. But while the economic giants of the twentieth century have been able to soften the blow of that loss through the realignment of their labor forces, the long-term consequences of the transformation have not yet been fully understood. At the very least, companies with decades-long reliance on traditional product lines—whether they be automobiles, electronics, or pharmaceuticals—have begun to realize that it is not only production that has fled their shores. Accompanying those jobs, it seems, was the culture of education and innovation upon which the West was founded. As a result, forward-thinking corporate managers have been forced to rethink cost structures, management priorities, market strategies, and product development.

The workplace programs of today will age just as surely as the workforce will. It is only by continually reviewing market conditions, reexamining corporate strategies, and reallocating resources accordingly that businesses can prosper in a volatile and unpredictable global economy. Accordingly, the three major challenges facing businesses today are:

1. Reducing fixed operating costs
2. Confronting the coming talent shortage
3. Institutionalizing innovation

Of these three, the most important core function is the *institutionalization of innovation*. The case studies introduced in the first chapter—The Sprint Powered Workplace, H-P's Workplace Transformation, and Jones Lang La-Salle's Workplace Strategies—are textbook examples of forward thinking in action, and we will get back to them later in this book. As successful as they have been, however, they are but products themselves of institutionalized innovation. The key to ongoing success lies in integrating innovation into every aspect of the company.

In the pages that follow, we will address each of these challenges in turn, citing research, discussing the best practices of industry thought leaders, and featuring case studies from *Future of Work* members past and present.

We will also describe in some detail the management tools and methodologies we've developed at the Work Design Collaborative, in collaboration with members of the *Future of Work* community. Those experiences have reinforced our belief that corporate agility can be achieved only through the continuous, collaborative management of HR, IT, and CRE. We call this approach *collaborative strategic management*, or CSM for short.

That said, collaborative strategic management involves much more than the simple integration of those traditionally separate functions. CSM means putting processes and practices in place that will allow HR, IT, and CRE managers to create a unified approach to the organization's business imperatives, and to resolve them while respecting a core of shared corporate values. Seen from this perspective, CSM is as much about the why of strategy as it is the how, affecting not only strategic decision making but also plans made in the larger pursuit of corporate agility.

CSM is meant to ensure that HR, IT, and CRE work together toward common goals. It does not demand that the boundaries and differences among these three professional disciplines be eliminated. Rather, it recognizes and values those differences, and the unique contributions to the business that each of them make. It further requires that those contributions be made within a context of mutual respect, and with the understanding that all three perspectives are needed to produce an effective, sustainable, agile, organization.

CSM is *strategic* in the sense that it anticipates—in fact, even expects—continual change in the broader business environment. In that sense, it is about management *over time*, because continuous environmental change demands continuous organizational and managerial change. CSM, then, is the dynamic and ongoing process of internal decision making that is the essence of corporate agility.

Let's return now to the three major business challenges of the twenty-first century. There are various options for reducing fixed operating costs. We will examine the following:

- Corporate real estate (CRE) issues
- Nontraditional business (government agencies, nonprofit, etc.)
- Green building
- Variable-cost labor
- Outsourcing
- Employee turnover

Next, we will address the shortage of human talent—the difficulties corporations are now experiencing recruiting and retaining qualified, engaged employees. Under this heading we will examine the following:

- Shifting global demographics
- Changing attitudes in the workforce
- Benefits crunch
- Educational trends
- Politics and immigration

Finally, we will turn to the institutionalization of innovation, or the ways in which corporations must not only react to changing business conditions but also build innovation into their corporate structures, ensuring that today's solutions do not become tomorrow's problems. We will look at these case studies:

- IBM
- Herman Miller
- Johnson Controls
- Hewlett-Packard
- Jones Lang LaSalle

For now, however, let's turn to a topic that keeps the CFOs of the world awake every night—the reduction of fixed operating costs. This is the subject of Chapter 3.

CHAPTER 3

Reducing Fixed Operating Costs

Reducing fixed operating costs in order to increase corporate agility is *the* central business challenge of the twenty-first century. In an ever-more-dynamic global economy, with production routinely outsourced into the least costly labor markets, and innovation and design no longer the exclusive province of North America, Europe, and the Pacific Rim, businesses must move from a fixed-cost to a variable-cost business model in order to remain competitive and to increase their ability to react quickly to changing conditions. Human resources will soon become as scarce as petroleum, and so any company with plans for growth had better get started developing programs to attract and retain qualified, engaged employees. Without institutionalizing innovation, industry leaders today will find themselves laggards tomorrow.

Cutting costs is first on the list for a reason, however. Lower your fixed operating costs, and when market conditions unexpectedly change—as they are certain to do—you'll have resources available to throw at the sales force, or at research and development, or at services—to do, in short, whatever's necessary to make a sharp correction, and yet keep on doing business. That's what corporate agility is all about, and cutting fixed operating costs is what makes it possible. It's a little like losing weight in order to improve your racquetball game. Your goal is to improve your quickness, and to be more nimble on the court, but you can't do that without first trimming the fat.

By this we don't mean that rent, labor, support, maintenance costs, energy costs, insurance expenses, and property taxes can simply be dispensed with (although in the case of CorasWorks, a software company to be introduced in Chapter 7, that is exactly what happened, at least insofar as its real estate costs were concerned). For most corporations, however, a gradual, strategic reduction in fixed operating costs, along with the strategic use of outsourced variable cost business components—whether in labor, facilities, or management services—will enable executive management to allocate limited corporate resources more purposefully in response to inevitable shifts in the global marketplace—or, to drive the point home once more, reducing fixed operating costs increases corporate agility.

This chapter will survey the primary opportunities for reducing fixed operational costs, as well as the means by which some variable costs can be made more event-specific (i.e., becoming costs only as specific needs arise that cannot be met in a timely and efficient manner by the company's core employees). These opportunities, with no real order of importance after the first two, include the following:

- Reducing the corporate real estate footprint
- Reconfiguring corporate space
- Green building
- Choosing a location
- Labor outsourcing
- Reducing turnover costs

Here, as throughout this book, we will return again and again to the necessity of the collaborative strategic management of real estate, human resources, and information technology in order to effectively manage the following proposed changes. It is not so much that the lines between these distinct divisions have blurred over time, but that actions taken in one can have immediate and often unintended effects in the others.

Shuttering sales offices to lower costs, but without first assessing the effect of such a policy on the morale of the sales force, or without first creating the IT infrastructure necessary to support the newly mobile sales force, will certainly reduce overhead—but is also likely to result in a decline in sales, morale, and customer satisfaction. The same scenario, but with strategic collaboration between CRE, HR, and IT, will yield identical results in CRE cost avoidance, and equally important gains in employee engagement, retention, and productivity. Add personnel assessment prior to the program's inception, and change management teams during and after its rollout, and the program can save the company money *and* lead to far greater employee and customer satisfaction. Thus, as we discuss each of the topics just listed, we will constantly note the consequences of particular decisions, and the way in which the negatives can be reduced, and the positives enhanced, through collaborative strategic management.

In some sense, the local and global conditions that have caused corporate leaders to reexamine their business models have made this last job less difficult. Whereas change tended to occur from the bottom up in years past, a growing awareness of the need, and the opportunity, to cut costs strategically has finally arrived in the boardroom, and is now being communicated from executive leadership to the workforce.

Jones Lang LaSalle's Debra Moritz puts it this way:

> More and more of the workplace strategies discussions are occurring in executive suites and boardrooms. It used to be that real estate organizations within companies would push workplace strategies up the hill to get some interest and sponsorship from executives. It is now much more common for RE organizations to react to strategies being rolled down to them from C-level executives. Workplace strategies are becoming business strategies. It's becoming mainstream because executives have seen the compelling results in bottom line cost savings and improved employee engagement.

REDUCING THE CORPORATE REAL ESTATE FOOTPRINT

Of the two largest items in the traditional corporate budget—real estate and labor—the workforce is historically the first target of the axe when revenues fall. Although the labor force is certainly the easiest way to cut costs—most employees, after all, do not have contracts, and severance packages aside, can be dismissed at a moment's notice—it is also true that the loss of every employee is accompanied by a corresponding loss in a company's potential productivity, or its ability to render services.

Thus, when a company reduces its workforce, it also reduces its potential for profit. Further, it reduces the morale of those employees it retains. What's more, as the battle to recruit and retain qualified, engaged employees becomes more and more difficult in the years ahead, companies will no longer find it as easy as it has been to replace those members of the workforce they have downsized out of their organizations. This is due, in part, to well-documented shifts in demographics and employee attitudes (to be discussed at length in Chapter 4).

Moreover, if yours is a traditionally managed organization, with a one-to-one person/desk ratio and long-term CRE leases, every time you reduce your workforce you're left with excess real estate, technology, and support services, *thus driving up your costs per remaining employee.* In other words, the moment you lay someone off, you pay more to support those left on the payroll. For these reasons, while reducing the workforce is certain to remain a well-thumbed chapter of the corporate cost-cutter's bible, the reduction of corporate real estate, in comparison, has several distinct advantages.

Foremost is the issue of excess capacity. Given the increased mobility of the workforce and the changed nature of its workstyles, management has begun to realize that a great deal of its costly real estate is unused. Consider what Sun Microsystems' Eric Richert, then vice president of people and places, had to say about his company's changing real estate needs:

> Several years ago, we performed a badge swipe study of Sun corporate offices and discovered that on any given day 40 percent of our workers were not at their assigned offices—or even in their assigned buildings. We had successfully rolled out a flexible office program in the sales field, so we decided to run several pilots to test whether the program could be implemented among corporate office workers. The pilots turned out so well, that we eventually rolled the program out across the whole company.

In a company with 35,000 employees in more than 200 offices in 47 countries, the savings—and business advantages—were significant:

- Annual real estate cost avoidance of over $69 million in FY 2005
- Annual IT savings of $24 million

■   More agile organization

■   Quantifiable higher employee satisfaction

Impressive as the results of Sun Microsystems' flexible office program have been, one must turn to IBM in order to appreciate the scale of savings possible through the reduction of fixed real estate costs. IBM, with more than 320,000 employees worldwide, estimates that it has achieved annual real estate cost avoidance of *more than $450 million.*

That figure, however impressive, is but one quarter of the annual savings IBM attributes to its On Demand Workplace, a program IBM initiated more than ten years ago, and to which we will return in our discussion of institutionalizing innovation.

Although the general workforce mobility data that comes from security-badge swipes is undoubtedly useful, a series of building walk-throughs can be even more revealing. As a part of its continuing efforts at transforming its workplaces, *Future of Work* corporate member Herman Miller assembled and trained a walk-through team for each of its west Michigan sites, and then had all of them perform their walk-throughs at exactly the same time in order to improve the speed of their information gathering and the consistency of their results (see Figure 3–1).

Each set of vertical bars shows observed and actual uses of space in eight Herman Miller locations. The space in each location is divided into four categories: individual, group, community, and non-utilized. In Herman Miller's parlance *observed* numbers are those witnessed by the walk-through team, and *actual* numbers are those presumed to be in use. Note that all locations were presumed to be fully utilized, although observation showed that none of them were. It's also interesting to note the difference between the observed and actual rates of individual utilization, especially in the case of Herman Miller's Green House (GH).

As Figure 3–1 shows, there is a significant disconnect between the actual (or presumed) use, and the observed use of the facilities. Data of this nature make right-sizing the CRE portfolio much more palatable, as well as helping the interior design team reconfigure retained space so as to more efficiently support evolving workstyles.

The General Services Administration (GSA), a *Future of Work* corporate member, turned to strategic design consultant DEGW and its Time Utilization Study™ (TUS) in order to evaluate the agency's use of space before

Figure 3-1

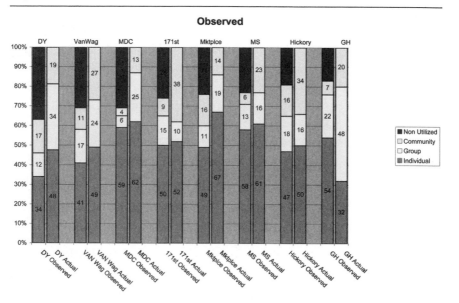

redesigning several of its regional headquarters. Operating from twelve offices in Europe, Asia, and America, DEGW developed the TUS in the late 1980s to measure the hour-by-hour occupancy rate in up to 300 distinct spaces (per evaluation route), in addition to the frequency with which certain activities (i.e., conferences, phone calls, heads-down work, etc.) occur. Handheld computers, provided by the company and operated by temporary workers, contractors, or company associates trained by DEGW, are used to compile information on work patterns, specific job functions, and the use of space by distinct business units. This leads to highly accurate measurements of the following:

- The amount of time individuals spend at their desks
- The amount of time individuals spend in and out of the office
- The breakdown of work activities
- The degree of individual versus collaborative work
- The level and extent of mobility within and across groups
- The need for conference rooms of various sizes
- The need for standard support spaces

Once completed, such an analysis shows the hour-by-hour behavior of a hypothetical workforce, and measures mobility, occupancy rates, and time devoted to specific activities (e.g., talking on the phone, talking to colleagues, working on the computer, writing by hand, handling papers, face-to-face meetings). The results, which usually surprise facilities and real estate portfolio managers, can then be used to accurately project the square footage needed per employee. As well, the data can be used to assist in the redesign of interior space to support emerging work styles, thereby increasing productivity and employee satisfaction—and, of course, reducing costs.

Whatever the method, meaningful change in a corporate real estate portfolio must begin with the accurate assessment of conditions, behaviors, and needs, and then must be followed by the right-sizing of the real estate portfolio. Seen in this light, reducing fixed operating costs by cutting back on CRE is not really a decision to cut space; it is instead a realization that the corporation has been paying for real estate it does not use—or that it no longer uses as it once did. Once that conclusion has been reached, the portfolio can be resized to fit the true needs of the workforce, and the company can turn to reconfiguring its retained space to better serve its employees and its customers. Then, as market conditions change—as they are certain to do—and changes in the workforce and workplace necessarily follow, the company will be in a far better position to sustain its strategic goals. Again, once the initial assessments have been made, management's task is much less complex—its job is then to decide which spaces to abandon, which spaces to retain, and which spaces to reconfigure.

Accenture

Accenture, a global management consulting, technology services, and outsourcing company, has one of the most well-developed mature workplace/workforce strategies program of any member of the *Future of Work* community. With approximately 140,000 employees spread out over more than 150 cities in 48 countries, Accenture has reduced its fixed costs for space through CRE consolidation, more efficient utilization, and migration to lower-cost, shorter-term leases. What's more, Accenture's workforce model is wholly distributed, and across all geographic regions. In contrast, therefore, to those companies in the process of rolling out their workplace strategy programs—however promising the initial results—Accenture is in the enviable position of being able to demonstrate that fully integrated CRE reduction strategies, combined with alternative workplace/workforce programs, actually *deliver* on those promises.

Figure 3–2 demonstrates just how dramatic the results can be. Despite increasing its global headcount by 20,000 persons in fiscal year 2006, Accenture has succeeded in steadily reducing its general and administrative costs—while its revenues continued to grow.

Founded in 1989, Accenture is one of the youngest corporate entities in the *Future of Work* community, and perhaps for that reason has had the advantage, when approaching the issues of workplace and workforce transformation, of not having to confront an entrenched, traditional business culture. This advantage is evidenced by its early experimentation, in the mid-1990s, with office seating reservations, also known as *hoteling*. (It is also worth noting, as we'll point out in greater detail later, that its workforce is atypically young, which for the moment at least relieves the company of having to deal with issues such as retirement demographics and knowledge capital risk that threaten more mature corporations.)

Figure 3-2

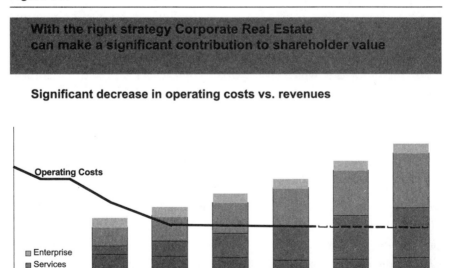

With the right strategy Corporate Real Estate can make a significant contribution to shareholder value

Significant decrease in operating costs vs. revenues

By the new millennium, Accenture had begun to allow its employees to work remotely, but it wasn't until 2002, when the company began an aggressive campaign to consolidate its CRE, that it truly began to push the workplace envelope. Aided by the rapid advance of enabling technologies, Accenture began a determined push to reduce its long-term real estate commitments, to dramatically reshape its real estate portfolio, and to expand its distributed workforce.

Today, with its virtual workforce deployed around the world, the vast majority of the company's employees perform their jobs in spaces not owned—or paid for—by Accenture. Telecommuting is now the norm, with work being done by geographically distributed teams that meet via teleconferencing, and collaborate through the use of tools like WebEx and SharePoint sites. Despite being so far ahead of the learning curve, Accenture recognizes that emerging technologies will continue to influence real estate requirements, and that as more of its workforce settles into virtual offices, the company must aggressively market legacy real estate assets to transform the portfolio's cost structure, in keeping with its evolving business strategies.

Sasha Lacey, of Accenture's CRE department, and a distributed worker himself, points to a differentiated real estate portfolio as the key to the program's success:

> Prior to 2002, Accenture's staff was accommodated either at client sites or what they describe as *large metro centers*. These centers housed a complete cross-section of the functions and services the staff delivered within a geographical area, and were typically located in a relatively prestigious part of the city. The new Accenture strategy envisages a far wider range of property types, differing location and functional characteristics, lease arrangements and standards of fit-out, which respond specifically to their varied business models.
>
> Accenture also expects that a significant proportion of work currently being performed in spaces leased by Accenture will soon take place in homes, client sites, cafes, etc., or in other words sites without cost to the company. The adoption of this strategy has already enabled our company to reduce occupation costs by more than 50 percent in some locations through right-sizing the amount of space they rent in expensive downtown locations. The new strategy also aims to shift a growing proportion of real estate costs from fixed costs to variable. The plan is that future expansion of certain business units will be accommodated through increasingly flexible

accommodations, not by increasing the fixed cost base. Additionally, Accenture monitors occupancy of [its] facilities, often finding that increased worker mobility allows a larger population to be supported out of the same office space. In this way, headcount growth doesn't necessarily mean real estate portfolio growth.

Over the past ten years, this strategy has led from a CRE model primarily based on fixed cost space to one that is dominated by variable cost, or no-cost, space (i.e., remote working, either in space owned by the employee or by the client), and guided by the following principles:

- Maximize the use of existing space before taking new space.

- Play an active and early role in all business opportunities that have real estate implications.

- Build maximum flexibility into real estate commitments so we can quickly and cost effectively expand, contract, or reconfigure as the business requires.

- Monitor utilization patterns to ensure the portfolio is always right-sized.

- Ensure our solutions are differentiated to respond to the varied needs of Accenture's businesses and workforces.

- Keep operating costs as low as possible, conserve capital, and convert to variable (vs. fixed) cost solutions wherever possible.

- Encourage the flexible work styles of our workforce with both physical and virtual solutions.

Using these guidelines, Accenture's global workplace team makes specific suggestions for its various business units, depending on conditions in its localized real estate markets (e.g., rents rising or falling) and the unit's specific business issues (e.g., impending lease expirations, higher or lower headcounts, increased seat demand, and high or low utilization of existing space). In short, this approach is the result of the company's migration from traditional to flexible workplace strategies (see Figure 3–3).

As Figure 3–3 shows, Accenture has moved from a traditional to a new, flexible workplace strategy as the characteristics of the work itself, of real estate management, and of workplace metrics have changed over time.

Figure 3-3

Accenture's workplace strategy has responded to new ways of working and incorporated thoughtful real estate management

	Traditional Workplace Strategy (Pre-1995)	New Workplace Strategy 1995–2002	Flexible Workplace Strategy (Evolving)
Work Characteristics	Process Oriented Isolated/Cellularised Static Individuals Lack of flexibility Fixed Workforce	Project Oriented Group / Interactive Community Based Increasing flexibility Mobile Workforce (emerging)	Solutions Oriented Dynamic mobile teams with physical and virtual community support Balancing physical / virtual work Mobile workforce
Real Estate Characteristics	Fixed Lease Single Location Mixed Branding Local Application (higher costs)	Consolidated Lease Office / Client Site Branded / Functional Global Standard (higher costs)	Scalable leases Diversified portfolio Flexible / functional Local interpretation of standards w/in benchmarks (reduced costs)
Metric Characteristics	~250 RSF/worksetting 118 RSF/Person ~50% Utilization	~200 RSF/Worksetting 100 RSF/Person 67% Utilization	~85–150 RSF per worksetting 65 RSF/Person (target) 85% Utilization (target)

11

The long-term move toward a more mobile workforce has been made possible through the mutual efforts of Accenture's facilities teams and its tech services and support, in a classic example of collaborative strategic management. Through such collaboration, Accenture has achieved significant cost savings not only in CRE, but also in IT costs per employee.

Although part of these savings can be attributed to a general decline in IT costs—given the decline in prices for personal computers, wireless services, and communications services—they could not have been realized without forward-thinking cooperation between CRE and IT managers before, during, and after the workforce became more mobile. Without such collaboration, services and support will continue to be provided where they are no longer needed, while those who have become part of the mobile workforce find themselves without the tools they need to do their jobs. From there it is easy to imagine the consequences: a loss of morale, increased turnover, and decreased customer satisfaction.

Change management was a critical part of Accenture's program. On paper, it's easy enough to talk of cost savings in real estate and technology services, but in the real world it's very difficult for people to give up the desk at which they've been working for years, to walk into the office far less frequently, and to do so without knowing exactly where they'll sit—and what's worse, to have to make a reservation to walk in at all. Change management, therefore, was an integral part of the process, and Accenture began that part of the process by making the business case for change.

Clearly, the company had more space than it needed, and the space it had was no longer compatible with Accenture's business strategies, or even suited to the way work was actually being done by the company's varying types of workers. To understand this last point it's important to begin by reviewing the company's broad range of services, which include management consulting, delivery of technology services, and business process outsourcing (BPO). Therefore, a one-size-fits-all workforce solution isn't possible. To support its various businesses the company has four basic types of employees:

1. *Enterprise.* These employees are typically found in corporate headquarters, without direct client contact.

2. *Consulting.* These employees are traditional business management consultants, in direct contact with clients. Therefore, they are often on the road.

3. *Services workforce.* Some Accenture employees are housed in client space to provide IT or financial services to the client.

4. *Solutions workforce.* Some employees of Accenture are engaged in applications development or systems integration, working either in Accenture's own research and development space, or in client space.

To support such a diverse workforce, Accenture uses what it calls a Facilities and Services Blueprint that takes into account the physical environment (i.e., the different places the work is actually done), the people (all of whom have different skill sets and focuses), the services to support them (either dedicated, shared, or self-enabled), the tools and technology (dependent on all of the above), and the geography and culture of each location (i.e., acknowledgment that a global workforce cannot work the same way across different cultures and in different geographic locations).

Seen this way, the workplace is not just the space in which work is done, but the combination of all of these factors. Some services workforces, for example, may be housed in spaces with dedicated seating, while others, serving multiple clients, may be highly mobile. Accenture uses six principles to integrate these disparate elements into a single workforce/workplace solution, as shown in Figure 3–4.

Beginning with the understanding that each of the company's four employee types (i.e., enterprise, consulting, services, and solutions) has differing needs, and that the facilities and services blueprint is made up of five different aspects (i.e., physical environment, people, services, tools and technology, and geography and culture), these six principles are used to facilitate the company's workplace strategy. Putting it another way, these principles promote the *how* of Accenture's workplace strategy. To better understand them, it's necessary to return for a moment to the *why*.

Accenture embarked on its workplace/workforce strategy—again, well in advance of most of its competitors—because company leadership recognized that Accenture's second-largest cost basis—after payroll—was facilities and services, and that continuing external changes in the global economy made the following internal changes necessary:

Figure 3-4

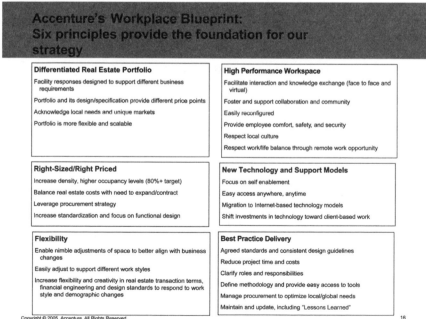

Accenture's Workplace Blueprint:
Six principles provide the foundation for our strategy

Differentiated Real Estate Portfolio
Facility responses designed to support different business requirements
Portfolio and its design/specification provide different price points
Acknowledge local needs and unique markets
Portfolio is more flexible and scalable

High Performance Workspace
Facilitate interaction and knowledge exchange (face to face and virtual)
Foster and support collaboration and community
Easily reconfigured
Provide employee comfort, safety, and security
Respect local culture
Respect work/life balance through remote work opportunity

Right-Sized/Right Priced
Increase density, higher occupancy levels (80%+ target)
Balance real estate costs with need to expand/contract
Leverage procurement strategy
Increase standardization and focus on functional design

New Technology and Support Models
Focus on self enablement
Easy access anywhere, anytime
Migration to Internet-based technology models
Shift investments in technology toward client-based work

Flexibility
Enable nimble adjustments of space to better align with business changes
Easily adjust to support different work styles
Increase flexibility and creativity in real estate transaction terms, financial engineering and design standards to respond to work style and demographic changes

Best Practice Delivery
Agreed standards and consistent design guidelines
Reduce project time and costs
Clarify roles and responsibilities
Define methodology and provide easy access to tools
Manage procurement to optimize local/global needs
Maintain and update, including "Lessons Learned"

16

- Redesign cost structures in order to remain competitive.

- Rethink cost management in order to improve delivery of services.

- Leverage facilities by introducing new models for delivering support services.

- Support aggressive growth in outsourced service offerings.

- Optimize the company's real estate portfolio.

That said, these adjustments were not meant to be ends in themselves, but were made in support of the company's workforce. For a moment, then, let's turn to the composition of Accenture's workforce, given that it is somewhat atypical compared to industry standards.

First, nearly three quarters of Accenture's employees are gen-X-ers, with the remaining quarter split almost evenly between baby boomers and millennials. For starters, therefore, the company's knowledge capital risk—at least as a result of retirement—is much smaller than it is for many other workforces. (Nearly 50 percent of the GSA's workforce, for example, will be eligible for retirement shortly after this book hits the shelves in mid-2007.) Therefore, in designing—and redesigning—facilities, support services, and operating models, Accenture has kept in mind the generational differences of its workforce. This is a good example of collaborative strategic management at work. By designing workspaces (CRE) that improve efficiency by appealing to the workforce's preferred methods of working (HR) as well as their tastes (HR), and offering them the latest in technological support (IT), a company can cut costs and increase both productivity and employee satisfaction.

To do just that, Accenture provides a scalable set of employee services, the level of which can be adjusted to meet specific workforce needs, and differences in approaches to work:

- Dedicated support for specific needs

- Shared teams to leverage expertise and experience

- Call centers to balance workload volumes (strategically positioned in low-cost delivery centers)

- Self-enablement and e-support, providing the lowest-cost, most immediate response model for anytime, anywhere workers

In addition to its wide range of employee support services, new technologies and products are constantly being incorporated into Accenture's workplace design. Toward that end, each office's reception area now offers kiosks that permit on-the-spot reservations, and in a few select locations a large, centrally located monitor displays a photograph of every employee in the office that moves—using an RFD (radio frequency device) signal—as the employee moves through the office. Accenture is also running a pilot program that provides an interface between its reservation system and its e-mail program, allowing employees to indicate their location whenever they log on. This, like the photo monitor system, makes locating its widely distributed workforce much easier.

These wide-ranging and innovative support systems, along with creative real estate deal structures, are intended to assist Accenture in achieving its aggressive goals for workplace density, reducing the support costs per employee without stifling the workforce's productivity or job satisfaction. The results speak for themselves (see Figures 3–5 and 3–6).

As you can see, through right-sizing and right-pricing its real estate port-

Figure 3-5

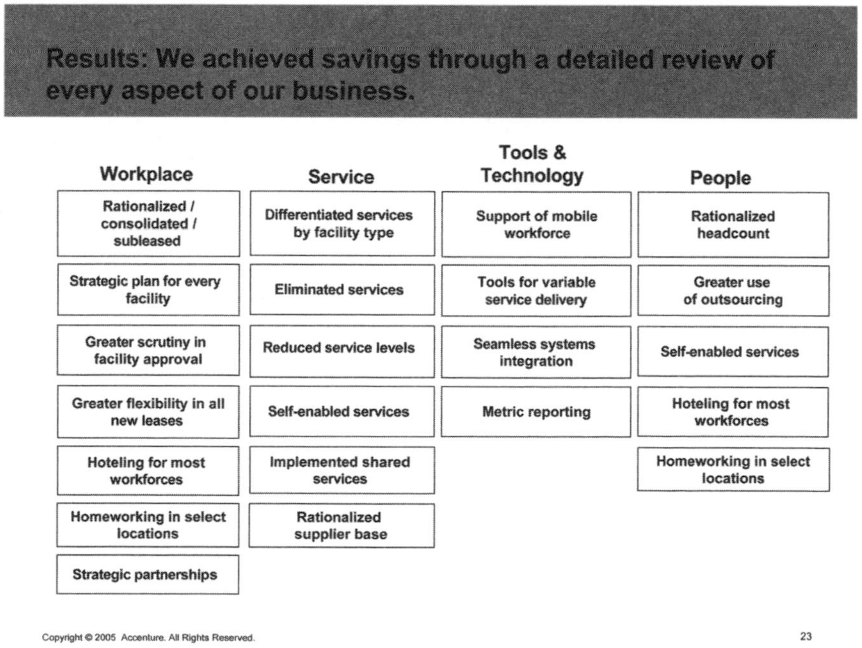

Results: We achieved savings through a detailed review of every aspect of our business.

Workplace	Service	Tools & Technology	People
Rationalized / consolidated / subleased	Differentiated services by facility type	Support of mobile workforce	Rationalized headcount
Strategic plan for every facility	Eliminated services	Tools for variable service delivery	Greater use of outsourcing
Greater scrutiny in facility approval	Reduced service levels	Seamless systems integration	Self-enabled services
Greater flexibility in all new leases	Self-enabled services	Metric reporting	Hoteling for most workforces
Hoteling for most workforces	Implemented shared services		Homeworking in select locations
Homeworking in select locations	Rationalized supplier base		
Strategic partnerships			

23

Figure 3-6

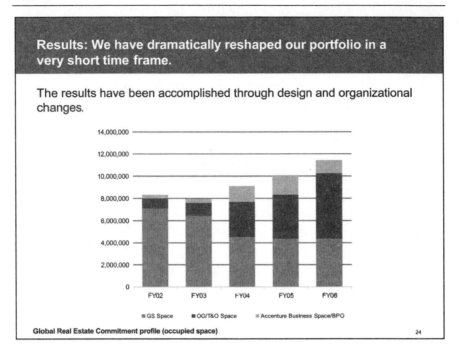

Results: We have dramatically reshaped our portfolio in a very short time frame.

The results have been accomplished through design and organizational changes.

■ GS Space   ■ OG/T&O Space   ■ Accenture Business Space/BPO

Global Real Estate Commitment profile (occupied space)   24

folio Accenture achieved cost savings and increased efficiencies across all the elements of its workplace—the physical environment, people, support services, tools and technology, and geography and culture. This, in turn, allowed the company to support growth in its Business Process Outsourcing and Global Delivery Centers, and to offset the cost of building new space.

What's more, the bulk of the savings were achieved over the space of only two years, allowing Accenture to support growth in its high-growth business units. These strategies resulted in environmental benefits as well—given that a smaller corporate real estate footprint leads to lowered energy costs and commute-related pollution—to say nothing of a more flexible workforce, which, although challenging at first, eventually leads to increased employee satisfaction, retention, and productivity—a textbook case of collaborative strategic management in action.

Not content to rest with these accomplishments, Accenture has asked itself the questions listed in Figure 3–7 in order to reach the next level of its global workplace strategy.

Figure 3-7

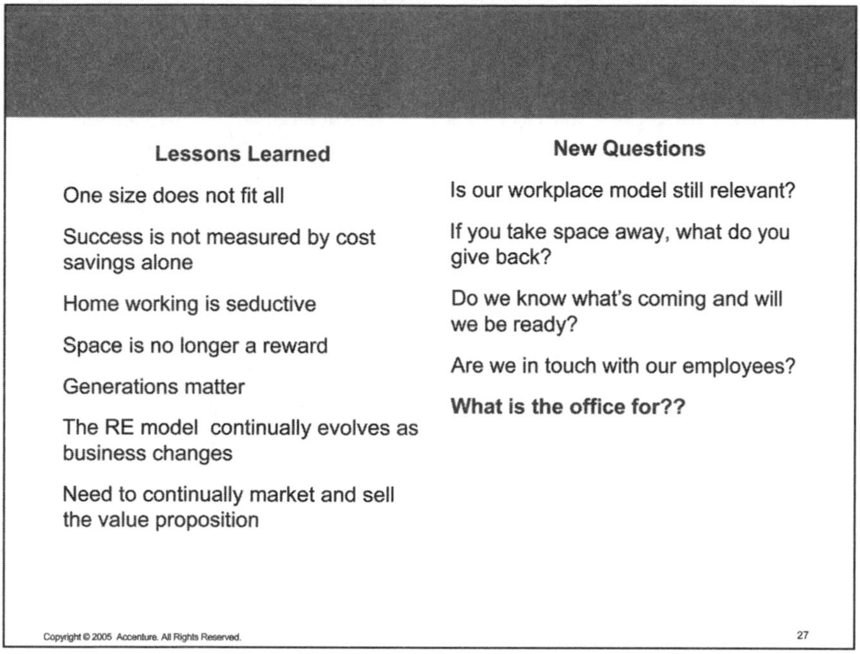
Lessons Learned
One size does not fit all
Success is not measured by cost savings alone
Home working is seductive
Space is no longer a reward
Generations matter
The RE model continually evolves as business changes
Need to continually market and sell the value proposition
New Questions
Is our workplace model still relevant?
If you take space away, what do you give back?
Do we know what's coming and will we be ready?
Are we in touch with our employees?
What is the office for??
Copyright © 2005 Accenture. All Rights Reserved.
27

Sprint Nextel

The Enterprise Location Optimization (ELO) program, nominated for a 2005 CoreNet Global Innovator's Award, is the tool Sprint Nextel uses to make decisions regarding which existing spaces to retain, and where to lease new space. Using state-of-the-art technology, Sprint Nextel's ELO program is a critical element of the company's enterprise-wide push to optimize the use of real property across all asset classes—retail stores, sales offices, call centers, corporate offices, and network technical sites—without losing sight of management's central strategic goals.

As is the case with most companies, Sprint Nextel's portfolio strategies were traditionally asset class-specific, rather than enterprisewide. Such an approach made it nearly impossible for corporate real estate to further the company's strategic objectives. What's more, within asset classes, decisions were often inconsistent and subjective, leading to variable returns on capital investment. The ELO program sought to overcome these inefficiencies in three specific ways:

1. Linking all real estate asset classes—as a whole, and individually—to corporate business strategy in order to ensure an enterprisewide perspective on real estate initiatives

2. Using an objective, fact-based, data-driven analysis to produce
   real estate portfolio decisions that further corporate strategies

3. Deploying the system within a Web portal, ensuring enterprisewide awareness of the effect of real estate decisions on long-term
   corporate strategy

In order to implement the program, it was first necessary to develop a
single repository for all real property asset information. The Sprint Enterprise
Geographic Information System (SEGIS) was created for this purpose. It now
contains records on more than 100,000 sites across all asset classes, and includes information such as size, location, lease length, and remaining financial
obligation. With this information in hand, Sprint Nextel's customer relationship management is able to focus each group's attention to its specific business
drivers, as well as to ensure that individual asset-class decisions are not made
in isolation but take into account the goals of the entire real estate portfolio,
as well as overarching corporate strategies.

Once such information has been gathered, site selection proceeds using
an application known as strategic analytical mapping, or SAM. A response to
traditional predictive analytics, which work from the bottom up—that is, first
selecting the location, and then analyzing it—SAM analyzes whole markets
using basic business information. The number of customers, both current and
perspective, revenue per customer, and real estate market data are all used to
determine which submarkets meet the defined thresholds for action (See Figure 3–8).

Once in place, the information base and the analytic tool were made
available to a much larger group within the company. SAM'S ease of use,
unlike applications that require a specialist for the programming and analysis
of data, allowed a single platform to serve hundreds of users, leading to the
broader dissemination of results from which rational, strategy-based decisions
could be made.

The program was first used in the retail sector, where the inability to
define and prioritize submarkets was hampering store delivery. Retail site
selection takes many factors into account, including proximity to prospective

Figure 3-8

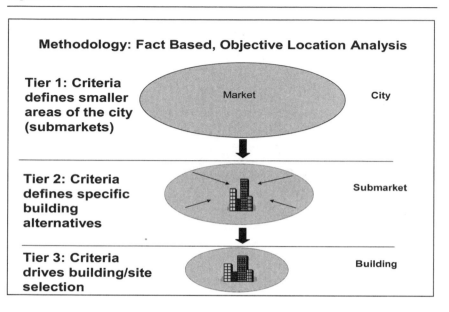

Methodology: Fact Based, Objective Location Analysis

Tier 1: Criteria defines smaller areas of the city (submarkets) — Market — City

Tier 2: Criteria defines specific building alternatives — Submarket

Tier 3: Criteria drives building/site selection — Building

customers, retail density, and the presence of competitors. Telecom retail requires the assessment of an additional factor—network infrastructure. SAM was used to analyze and prioritize the submarkets, and the ELO was then able to determine which submarkets should be targeted. Using these technologies, Sprint Nextel was able to double the number of stores—from 100 to 200—it opened in 2004.

With such promising results, the ELO program was rolled out across other asset classes as well, and was utilized in the deployment of a relatively new technology—wireless repeaters. Wireless repeaters were designed to fill in gaps of coverage where traditional towers aren't cost-effective. The placement possibilities are staggering, with literally tens of thousands of locations to choose from. Using SEGIS and SAM, the ELO program identified locations where Sprint Nextel already had infrastructure in other asset classes—such as buildings and telephone poles—in order to identify the most cost-effective solutions. Once traffic volumes and customer count had been taken into account, it was far easier to make quick, rational choices for deployment.

More important still was the use of the program to rationalize sales portfolio decisions. As leases on current locations expired, sometimes month after month, decisions had to be made regarding consolidation of spaces across the

Figure 3-9

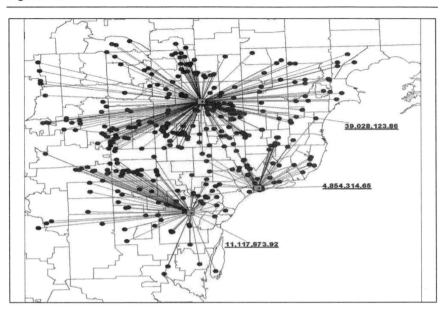

same city. This required determining which areas within the city should retain their offices, which should consolidate their offices, and where they should be consolidated, as well as what the total number of offices should be, given current activity, sales goals, and citywide economic trends.

To answer these questions, management solicited the advice of local mid-level managers in order to determine the precise factors that drive sales (drive-time information, centers of revenue in the city, etc.), as well as to prioritize those factors. The ELO program was then used to identify the optimal locations for revenue generation and real estate cost reduction, as well as the optimal number and location of sites based on the number of customers that could be served from each site. The computer-generated illustration in Figure 3–9 is representative of the program in action and shows ideal locations given the above-referenced factors.

H-P

H-P's real estate strategy, though similar in many respects to those of Accenture and Sprint, differs both as a result of its recent corporate history—mergers with Compaq, Tandem, and Digital Equipment, and the divestiture of

Agilent Technologies—as well as because of its core products and services. To recapitulate, having successfully begun its Workplace Transformation program with its sales offices, H-P's aim was to move the entire company into a smaller total number of sites, enjoying the advantages of improved scale while weeding-out space inefficiencies and underutilized space in the process. The proceeds from these savings were then to be turned back into an expanded sales force, and the renovation and reconfiguration of the company's retained space. This process, depending on your point of view, was either complicated by the fact that much of the real estate involved was owned by H-P, or made easier by the fact that many of its locations could be treated as assets rather than obligations.

Consolidation opportunities were considered first in terms of global goals, and then followed by regional and local goals, each with its own set of priorities and guidelines. Around a given city, for instance, where H-P had multiple sites, the goal of consolidation was tempered by the company's commitment to uninterrupted customer service. Other criteria included the likely commute for its site-dedicated employees, and therefore took into account the availability of public transportation. As well, when a location—or a series of locations—had a critical mass of revenue, or employee headcount, the company's consolidation strategy had to be adjusted accordingly. There were also legal reasons to consider, in the presence of government or trade commitments.

Once the primary decisions had been made about which locations to retain within a certain region or locality, the issue of renovation and/or reconfiguration had to be considered. The decisions on where and how much was mostly a matter of timing. H-P's intention was to bring the entire portfolio up to new standards over time, but clearly the tactical process of assigning priorities occurred within the constraints of the capital budget, which would be made available over time as the cost savings associated with consolidation were realized. The prioritization process also attempted to calculate the relative improvements that could be made to certain sites, compared to the costs. This calculation was intended to reveal which sites could most directly benefit from those sorts of investments designed to improve layout efficiency, productivity, and employee satisfaction.

In Melbourne, Australia, for instance, H-P had a legacy building that fit its consolidation profile in terms of size and location, but was so lacking in infrastructure potential that H-P chose instead to sell it and build on an adjacent vacant lot. The decision was made because it would have cost the company more to upgrade the mechanical systems, address the shortcomings of the floor plate efficiency, and create an energy-efficient and environmentally sustainable building than it would to build from scratch. Again, these issues become even more critical as occupancy densities are pushed to their limits, and buildings are presumed to be in full use all of the time.

That said, some infrastructure issues—in particular, IT, communications, and therefore the supply of electricity—have become easier to deal with over time. Wireless phone and data systems are making wiring infrastructure much simpler, and flexible furniture systems are making the reconfiguration of floor plans far easier than before, when old walls had to be demolished, and new walls put up in their place and rewired. Advantages in technology have also made digital data storage far easier and less expensive than paper-based systems, to say nothing of the floor space saved when information can be stored off-site, or onsite but without taking space used for the building's primary business function. Taken together, these factors make it possible to refit some legacy structures profitably that would have been untenable ten years earlier.

Moving from the abstract to the concrete—or perhaps we should say to the steel and concrete—we'll turn now to a specific H-P site in England's Thames Valley and demonstrate how the factors discussed actually came into play during H-P's continuing campaign to consolidate and reconfigure its real estate portfolio—all the while reducing cost and increasing agility.

As a result of the mergers with Compaq, Digital Equipment, and Tandem, H-P had built up a considerable space portfolio in the United Kingdom. Although the local real estate organization had successfully consolidated a number of sites in the years following the mergers, the fate of two large buildings in the Thames Valley, just west of London, had proved particularly difficult to resolve. Both had been country headquarters in their day, and had provided space for sales and service, back office hubs, and data storage and call centers. It could be presumed, therefore, that neither of the buildings' workforces would look kindly on a move.

Utilization and occupancy studies, however, made it clear that changes had to be made. Together the two buildings totaled almost 635,000 square feet, and with thousands of employees between the two of them, costs running at almost $9,000/occupant, and utilization rates hovering around 35 percent, there were really only two choices: One building would have to be closed and its employees and operations folded into the other, or both would have to be closed and a single new site, or a series of smaller sites, would have to be found to house them both.

The decision to retain the Bracknell site was the result of two factors. First, while both the Bracknell and Reading sites were situated along the M4 corridor—a major transportation route—the Bracknell site had a more contemporary appearance, and a more manageable underlying infrastructure, given the work that would be done there and H-P's current global business strategy. Second, consolidation was deemed feasible because of the high mobility of employees in both sites. For H-P, as noted before, this meant that employees in both the Reading and Bracknell sites tended to be up and moving around as they did their jobs, and whether that mobility occurred within the shell of the office building, or out in the larger business community, with only occasional visits made to the office, it was substantiated by the low-utilization numbers.

With the decision to go with Bracknell made, the workplace strategy team began to plan the consolidation of the two sites. Three overriding factors influenced the team's decisions:

1. Headcount forecasts

2. Free-address office space potential

3. Business-dedicated space

Within H-P, business-dedicated space refers to the square footage requested by individual business units to support their work. This includes space such as demonstration areas, labs, and computer rooms. Such business-dedicated space includes neither common support functions—printing, conference rooms, reception areas, etc.—nor traditional office space itself.

Historically, such spaces have presented problems for company workplace strategists. Although it might seem to those in charge of allocating space that an individual business unit could manage with less space, such presumptions often put them in the position of having to argue the merits of a particular solution with people whose expertise in the matter is unquestionably superior—even if their requests for space were not. This time, however, H-P's workplace strategists came up with a fairly straightforward solution.

A target space allocation was reverse engineered, beginning with the building's envelope, then including the total workstation needs, and finally taking into account mobility factors that led to the adoption of certain space-sharing ratios. Using this method to establish caps for each unit's business-dedicated space, each business unit was then asked to prioritize its needs within this allowed limit. The result was a series of exceptionally informative discussions that often ended up changing long-established—and therefore previously unquestioned—assumptions about business processes within the company. This led to a greater understanding of the possibilities for shared storage and laboratory space, as opposed to ownership by individual business units, that not only helped to achieve the desired targets for square footage/unit, but ultimately improved the way the businesses worked—both individually, and cooperatively.

In the Bracknell case, the demands of consolidation clearly assisted efforts to challenge long-held beliefs and encourage new thinking about how and where work was done. As long as the two separate workforces had the luxury of underutilized space, there was no imperative to search for opportunities to reduce business-dedicated space, or to more closely examine its true mobility and its implications for its business models. When pressed, however, the separate business units quickly found previously missed opportunities for cooperation, readily accepted changes in the way they worked, and in so doing demonstrated considerable agility.

The results, in terms of real estate usage and cost savings, were little short of astonishing (see Figure 3–10).

It's important to remember, though, that the resulting cost savings had already been earmarked to expand H-P's sales force, to support its increasingly mobile workforce's IT needs, and to renovate retained space—like that in the Bracknell building itself. The numbers aside, we've yet to come across a better example of forced changes leading to such improvement in business processes—and increased employee satisfaction. In adopting a change management process that threw the allocation ball back into the business units' court, management implicitly joined the process itself, giving up corner offices for small open workspaces and contributing to the growing understanding that business assets would heretofore be assigned according to need, not as a result of status or entitlement.

ADDITIONAL MEANS OF CRE COST REDUCTION

The opportunities to reduce fixed CRE costs are not limited to simple cuts in the corporate footprint, and they can also occur outside a leasing event of the

Figure 3-10

Project Metrics

	Before	After Consolidation	
Mobility	>20%	**67%**	*(across all BU's/Functions)*
Utilization	~30%	**90%+**	*(60% improvement)*
Occ.$/HC	8,900	**5,400**	*(meets global target goal)*
Total HC	2,845	**2,686**	*(WFR/cross-site moves adjusted)*
Total Ded HC		1,021	
Total Mob HC		1,665	
SQF Gross Tot	634,732	240,486	*(62% reduction)*
sqf gross/HC	223	**90**	*(60% reduction)*
sqf usable/HC	159	**62**	*(61% reduction)*
sqf off-tot/HC	131	**48**	*(63% reduction, meets standard targets)*
sqf off-Ded/HC		56	
sqf off-Mob/HC		17	
sqf BU Space	73,338	**29,194**	*(60% reduction)*

sort that led Jones Lang LaSalle to reconfigure its space in the AON Center. Debra Moritz of Jones Lang LaSalle puts it this way:

> Many companies will reconfigure and consolidate space outside a *lease event* (i.e., an expiration, option to contract, or option to cancel). The vacated space can be put on the market for sublease or the company can negotiate its way out of the contract.
>
> Today, most companies will use this as an opportunity to set up a restructuring accrual. An accrual is set up as a one-time expense to the company at the end of a reporting period. The basis of the restructuring is this: The real estate has no longer has any real value to the company, and so should be eliminated from the cost structure. As unnecessary or underutilized properties are downsized or vacated, this accrual will be used to offset the costs of the unused real estate (i.e., carrying costs, marketing costs, construction demising, cost to buy-out lease, cost difference between sublet and lease obligation, etc.). Any way it happens, the company gets an immediate cost relief on the books once a property is vacated or demised.

Chargebacks

Another opportunity for reducing fixed operating costs lies in the practice of charging groups within a corporation according to head count rather than assigned actual square footage. What division head, after all, is willing to tell his superiors that he expects no growth in the coming fiscal year, and that his group will need no additional space?

The problem, of course, arises when the request for additional space—based on intuition, not method—proves to be overly optimistic; while the assigned space may go unused, the costs of maintaining it do not disappear. Although correcting such inefficiencies in allocation may not be a cost savings measure in the traditional sense of the words—after all, the cost of maintaining the space, no matter the department to which it is assigned, must ultimately be borne by the company—a long-term advantage can be gained through accurate chargebacks to those groups that request, but do not use, costly corporate space.

Once all of the costs of assigned real estate are made part of a group's cost center, managers will find it in their interests to more accurately report their needs, thus freeing up space for growth in those divisions that are willing to pay for additional space. The ultimate benefit is a more accurate understanding of the company's true real estate needs, leading to more effective portfolio management.

Jones Lang LaSalle's solution to the worst practice of overallocation begins with AutoCAD drawings that measure all space owned or under lease, using the ANSI/BOMA standard method for measuring area in office buildings. That information is then transferred to a database, and each assignable space—workspaces, conference rooms, dedicated support areas, and so on—is added to the cost center of the division that leases it. Those areas not leased to a specific group—reception space, connecting corridors, etc.—have their costs prorated among the groups that use them, and this number, when added to each group's assigned spaces, results in a total rent assigned to each group's cost center.

In some cases, companies may choose to assign vacant, swing, and unfinished spaces to false cost centers. Through the use of such fictitious entities, real estate portfolio managers can continually track the amount of their unused space, determine how it can best be returned to active, assignable use, and thus achieve the ultimate goal of the space allocation program—the assignment of 100 percent of corporate space to specific cost centers.

Since real estate departments are not typically treated as profit centers, the chargeback rate is determined not by market rates, but by actual costs/ square foot for each site. By multiplying each group's allocation by the cost per rentable square foot, the true costs of the real estate can then be charged back to each group's cost center. These charges are normally included in the determination of that rate:

- Rent

- Utilities

- Taxes

- Insurance

- Maintenance

- Cleaning

- Security

- Building and furniture depreciation

- Risk management

- Mail/shipping/receiving

- Public conference room management

- Cafeteria management

- Other services (copiers, office supplies, etc.)

Using this system, if one of the business units legally vacates its space— that is, in keeping with company policy—the common costs per square foot will rise for those units that remain, even though no changes have occurred in the spaces they lease from corporate real estate. This inequity can be alleviated in several ways:

- The company can institute a vacancy rule allowing corporate real estate to continue charging the space to the departing business unit for a defined period—typically eighteen months—after it was abandoned, unless the departure was the result of a binding company directive.

- Corporate real estate may choose to provide an amnesty day that allows business units to give back space without being required to honor their original contracts.

■ Corporate real estate may choose to inflict a penalty—e.g., double the prevailing rate—on those business units that do not voluntarily surrender unoccupied space.

Some of these solutions may cause rather than alleviate inequities. Should one business unit succeed at using far fewer square feet per employee than the others on its floor it would be able, through an amnesty program, to force the others on the floor to subsidize its earlier miscalculation, and its better managed space. The results, whatever the means, are the same: The chargeback process encourages cost avoidance, both by insisting that every business unit pay for the space it uses, and by allowing specific business units to profit at the expense of those who use more space. Such efficiencies can be the result of the following solution.

RECONFIGURING CRE

Even if CRE successfully estimates the amount of space it needs, if the retained space is not configured to support both recent shifts in employee attitudes and workstyles, as well as technological advances, costs will remain higher than necessary. Clearly, the costly, archaic office environment designed before the advent of cordless phones, mobile headsets, fax machines, cell phones, e-mail, and the Internet cannot possibly support today's workforce. The square footage necessary for traditional workstations and the space required for staff to support them no longer matches today's business realities. Because such design is out of touch with emerging work styles, it restricts productivity, adding another layer of hidden cost, and discourages new hires.

Beyond the logic of redesigning space to support emerging workstyles, corporate space can also be used to support a company's strategic goals, as in the case of Jones Lang LaSalle's Open Office Environment. Intended to further the strategic corporate goal of greater collaboration within and among the company's business units, the low-wall design worked to increase communication and collaboration by letting everyone on the floor see and hear what their colleagues were doing. Again, while cost reduction drove the initial changes in the workplace, additional strategic benefits—support for emerging workstyles, and increased collaboration—were achieved as well.

In October of 2006, at a *Future of Work* Corporate Member Roundtable hosted by Jones Lang LaSalle at its Chicago headquarters in the Aon Center, we had the rare opportunity to see both the old space on the forty-fifth floor, and the newly designed space for the Workplace Strategies team on the forty-sixth.

The former was a claustrophobic bunker characterized by trenchlike, narrow corridors that seemed to have been excavated between drab interior walls on the right, and dark, looming, monolithic file cabinets on the left. The ceiling, although precisely the same height as the newly reconfigured space we would see afterwards on the forty-sixth floor, somehow appeared lower. There was no natural light. The workspaces were hidden behind the file cabinet walls, and visual communication between one workstation and another was all but impossible.

Here again, when management does not take advantage of the many ways in which corporate real estate can be put to work, we can speak not so much of additional costs, but of lost opportunities for both cost avoidance—in terms of employee satisfaction, and therefore productivity—and gains in revenue.

When, in our next chapter, we turn to the growing scarcity of skilled, engaged employees, interior design will be discussed as one of the most powerful lures with which management can attract prospective employees. And to the extent that a functional, comfortable, well-lit workspace increases employee satisfaction, it will figure in our discussions of reducing employee turnover, the present cost of which can easily exceed $50,000 for every upper-level employee lost to another company.[1]

Part of the problem is generational; traditional management divided its focus between places, people, and processes. Figure 3–11, part of a presentation by International Facilities Management Association (IFMA) CEO Dave Brady, illustrates the changing focus of facilities management over the past thirty years. The traditional model, in use until the 1980s, shows an approach balanced equally between people, place, and process. By the 1990s, the model had morphed to show a disproportionate focus on place. By the end of the millennium, Y2K concerns made technology an equally important concern. Now, in the post–dot.com era, the importance of place and process has been dwarfed by human resources.

The efficiencies to be gained from reconfigured space, just like the savings that come with right-sizing the real estate portfolio, have everything to do with the increasing mobility of the modern workforce and the need to support

Figure 3-11

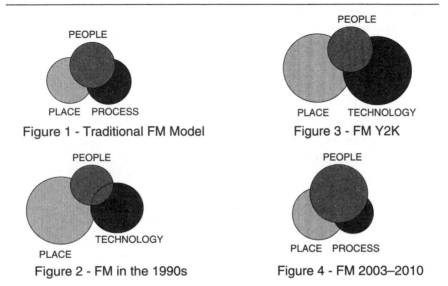

Figure 1 - Traditional FM Model

Figure 3 - FM Y2K

Figure 2 - FM in the 1990s

Figure 4 - FM 2003–2010

more mobile work styles. As we saw in Chapter 1, H-P's Workplace Transformation grew out of the realization that much of its workforce had voluntarily abandoned their desks and begun to move to where the work was. It was the company's job, consequently, to reassess its real estate needs, to reconfigure its space to support new work styles, and to equip its ever-more-mobile employees with the technology they needed to remain a productive part of the enterprise.

Examples of this approach are by no means limited to the private sector. Kevin Kampschroer, director of research, Expert Services, for the General Service Administration's Public Building Service—and a corporate member of the *Future of Work*—has much to say about the ways companies can effectively link human resources, information technology, and real estate.

In an article we co-wrote with Kevin in 2004 for CoreNet's *Corporate Real Estate Leader*, we highlighted the GSA's Workplace 20·20® program, developed to address workplace issues that challenge GSA's business performance:

> Such challenges include an aging inventory (average age of building is more than 50 years), the need for energy conservation, the adoption of sustainable design principles, and a growing trend toward a distributed workforce—incorporating both a remote workforce and outsourcing.

GSA currently manages 399 million square feet in more than 8,300 facilities. This inventory, however, no longer meets today's demands. Driving forces of extreme cost pressure on delivery of government services, a profound shift in the very nature of work, and a projected dramatic decrease in workforce numbers presage a need to develop a comprehensive strategy of Workplace Making.

The Workplace 20·20® program was the product of a collaborative work group composed of private-sector companies, including HOK, Spaulding & Slye Colliers, and DEGW, Gensler, Studios, and academic partners that included Carnegie Mellon, MIT, University of California Berkeley, Georgia Tech, and the University of Michigan, to name but a few. As Kampschroer notes, however, the complex, multipartner structure of the design process presaged the very challenges it was designed to meet in the field:

> The model required some nontraditional partnering methods such as a willingness to confront and negotiate collaborative issues and, in some cases, led to eventually screening out providers whose cultures ran counter to a collaborative partnership.

WorkPlace 20·20® comprises twelve distinct research initiatives, using the government's substantial supply of new projects to measure its effectiveness. The experiment is not a small one—each year 60,000 federal employees move into 2.5 million square meters of office space:

> The separate initiatives of WorkPlace 20·20® range from call center management to collaboration metrics to social networks, and stress the streamlining of work processes. One study, conducted in Philadelphia, looked at changing work patterns. Four hundred people were involved (thirty people in each set), and different space configurations were used to see which ones best supported new work patterns. Among the key findings were that nonlinear work processes are difficult to support with standardized real estate solutions. Further, space has the ability to affect cultural change and can either hinder organizational change or support and encourage learning efforts. Planning and design are critical steps in the process.

The mind-boggling variety of buildings managed by the GSA's Public Buildings Service—serving essentially all nonmilitary agencies from the EPA, to the FBI, to the Federal Judiciary—makes choosing a representative project difficult. Here, however, just as in the cases of Jones Lang LaSalle and Herman Miller, the Public Buildings Service first field-tested its program in its own space, specifically, its U.S. regional offices. Those pilot programs included the following:

- GSA—Auburn, Washington
- GSA—Philadelphia
- PBS—Denver
- PBS—Chicago

Each of the projects—listed in order of their dates of completion, from first to last—presented its own set of problems, and thus taken together provided an invaluable database that assisted the PBS in individually tailoring the Workplace 20·20® program to a wider variety of sites. Says Kevin Kampschroer:

> The succession demonstrates our commitment to making sure this process worked before we rolled it out across our entire portfolio, so we experimented on ourselves first (i.e., the GSA and the PBS). Each project yielded specific insights.
>
> From Auburn we learned the value of patience; that is, you might have to wait several years before new ways of working are accepted, and can affect productivity. GSA Philadelphia taught us the value of experimentation. PBS Denver taught us the value of natural light in reducing stress, and gave us confidence in our ability to make a silk purse out of a sow's ear. PBS Chicago is a case study in using redesigned space as a productivity accelerant.
>
> All have some kind of post-occupancy data, each set of which tells a part of the story, and taken together they prove the value and the viability of the Workplace 20·20® program.

For those reasons, we'll take a closer look at the most recent project on the list.

The Kluczynski Building

The John C. Kluczynski Federal Building in Chicago is home to the PBS's Great Lakes Regional Office. The Kluczynski building is one of Chicago's most revered buildings, designed by Ludwig Mies Van der Rohe in the late 1950s and completed in 1974. Therefore, the PBS team sought to increase efficiency, customer satisfaction, and employee effectiveness, while paying tribute to van der Rohe's aesthetic sensibility.

As we noted earlier in this chapter, the GSA employed the design consultancy firm DEGW as its workplace consultant for this project. As usual, DEGW began its work with an in-depth analysis of the organization and its work patterns. Interviews, focus groups, surveys, cultural analysis, and observations of the use of space revealed that workstyles were evolving rapidly, moving toward more multidisciplinary teams, multiple task performance, variable schedules, and greater focus on projects rather than individual initiatives. Together, these changes manifested themselves in the growing mobility of the workforce, both within and without the Kluczynski building. This finding was buttressed by observation data showing that offices were vacant more than 60 percent of the time.

The variety of methods used to analyze the space and its use produced some interesting, if contradictory, results. For instance, 96 percent of survey respondents stated that there were not enough conference rooms, yet direct observations revealed that conference rooms were empty 70 percent of the time. DEGW's research showed that conference rooms were used regularly between 10:00 A.M. and 3:00 P.M., but were usually empty in the early morning and late afternoon. What's more, the data showed that most meetings consisted of two to four persons in conference rooms designed for ten or more. Finally, there was no reservation system that showed which rooms were in use—and this in a building where offices and conference rooms were spread out among ten different floors within a forty-story building.

It was no surprise, therefore, that responses to a culture scorecard revealed that team leaders and professional staff perceived the atmosphere as chaotic and reactive, with unpredictable outcomes, contradictory goals, and a lack of organizational clarity.

The new design was directly based on these findings, and one of its primary goals was to produce better project integration and coordination across groups. Internal barriers were therefore reduced in order to increase informal communication, and a greater number of smaller meeting spaces was provided to support group work (the demand for which was clearly supported by the observational data). In addition, a centralized reservation system was introduced, providing improved access to these oft-used resources. Increased sharing of customer information was also encouraged through the introduction of centralized project files, and in-house employee mobility and workplace flexibility were supported with wireless technology.

The initial success of these modifications was measured by observing levels of communication and interaction both within and without the workplace, timeliness of project completion, and surveys of customer satisfaction, all of which are but part of a set of larger, continually reviewed workplace strategies with the following goals:

- Creating a more collaborative work culture geared toward achieving common organization goals

- Using the workplace to convey to customers the organization's values and expertise

- Increasing flexibility to support a variety of work processes

- Increasing the efficient use of space

- Maximizing opportunities for communication, both face-to-face and virtually

- Improving productivity for both individuals and groups

The team in charge of the redesign wanted customers and visitors to feel as if they were walking into the future when they first entered the new workspace—that is, they wanted to use the new design to brand the GSA as a forward-looking, innovative organization. This was accomplished, in part, by utilizing the design principles of the building's architect, Mies van der Rohe.

In the words of Robert Theel, chief architect of the PBS's Great Lakes Region, project architect Julie Snow translated the organization's workplace goals into visual concepts by "using simple, elegant materials to create planes of glass and curves of wood that defined the space and opened views to the outside." Having walked through both the original layouts and the redesigned spaces ourselves, we can attest to the success of the transformation.

On the older-style floors, the space is claustrophobic and gloomy, with the interior darkened by a row of offices along the perimeter wall that shuts out all natural light. The dark, high-walled cubicles somehow make the ceiling seem lower than it is, and cut off all visual contact between workspaces.

The first impression one receives upon entering the newly redesigned space is one of openness, with clear lines of sight running to the now-exposed exterior glass walls of the building, and the entire space is flooded with natural light. The low-walled workstations seem to sit far below the ceiling, though the ceiling is exactly the same height as that in the older spaces. Private offices have been moved to the building's core, workstations form a broad, varied ring around them, and glass-walled conference rooms, with blinds for privacy, now occupy the corners, providing breath-taking views of Lake Michigan and the skyline of Chicago. Interspersed along the now-clear circulation routes are a variety of meeting spaces, sized for both larger teams and smaller groups. Finally, the security system, although greatly enhanced, is artfully blended with the openness, accessibility, and overall aesthetic of the design.

A program of postoccupancy research is now underway, and the initial reports are glowing, both in terms of increased collaboration and productivity within the organization, and with respect to customer and visitor satisfaction. Low partitions are credited with promoting more natural, spontaneous communication and teamwork, and the commitment by managers to sacrifice their views has reduced traditional barriers between supervisors and staff, enhancing project acceptance. As one member of the project team put it, "Our new workplace is a striking blend of efficiency, functionality, and beauty." Had he lived to see it, it is easy to believe that van der Rohe would have agreed—with both the design and the reduced costs.

Capital One

Now let's move on to another example of collaborative strategic management at work, and turn to Capital One, a founding member of the *Future of Work*. A diversified financial services company, Capital One created its own Future of Work Environment around the growing internal mobility of its employees—that is, mobility within the walls of Capital One. The program offers employees a rich diversity of workplace settings specifically designed for a variety of tasks:

- Quiet zones
- Project rooms
- Coffee lounges
- Team neighborhoods
- Conference rooms

- Executive digs
- Anchor settings

The benefits go beyond increased productivity and greater employee sat-isfaction. In one pilot, more than 1,200 employees are now supported in a building that once housed only 600. As well, given the flexible workspace, with few assigned spaces, management can now add employees without a corresponding need for CRE to increase space. The company also has the option, given programs that allow (or even encourage) work outside the office, to hire more mobile associates.

As real as they are, these sorts of relief to the bottom line are secondary to the following three advantages:

1. *Greater business agility.* Business units can increase headcount without increasing their unit's real estate costs.

2. *Greater productivity.* Those associates working from home or "third places" save from one to three hours a day commuting, some part of which can now be devoted to their jobs.

3. *Greater associate satisfaction.* With more control over how and when they work, employee job satisfaction is higher, and turn-over is lower.

As with all change of this magnitude, it was not enough for Capital One to knock down a few walls, move the furniture, and wait for increased productivity and employee satisfaction. Change management, therefore, fo-cused on success targets and a variety of objective and subjective tools/data sources to track progress:

- Associate surveys
- Observation
- Time utilization studies
- Calendar records
- CRE costs/FTE
- Security-badge swiping
- Vacancy rates

Capital One also created a map of behavioral impacts—increased visual interaction, impromptu group meetings, and spontaneous interaction, for example—so that they could measure the impact of the program on those behaviors and diagnose problems, react to feedback, and fine-tune their solutions.

Even more important, change management teams looked at the interconnectivity of all impacts—that is, the sum of the subjective, individual impacts on behavior, and the objective cost-related measures—to determine their combined effect on the business as a whole, which is, after all, the ultimate goal of the program. As a part of that calculation, Capital One attempted to assess the effect of the program on individual productivity, as daunting a task as one can find in the world of business, and one that we will examine in greater detail in later chapters.

In short, Capital One discovered that the new program, by providing both a variety of different workspaces for specific tasks—private spaces for heads-down, high-concentration work, and open space for casual, collaborative interaction—and greater interconnectivity through mobile IT, has not only increased productivity but also lowered costs and increased employee satisfaction.

A leading national defense contractor who does business with a corporate member of the *Future of Work*—but prefers to remain unnamed—has the following to say about real estate cost avoidance in his industry:

> National security concerns increase our construction costs (and to a lesser degree our operational costs), decrease our density metrics, and limit our leasing flexibility. In addition, we have to build and operate Limited Access Areas (LAA) to varying degrees of security clearances. Once built, you don't want to abandon these CAPEX investments.
>
> Certain employees need to have space both within an LAA and in the general office area. We also need maintenance and operations staff with the appropriate clearances to clean and/or maintain the LAAs. It increases the cost, but doesn't additionally constrain their use. If an outsourcer has the required clearances, its employees can access the space. It makes no difference if they work for my company or the outsourced vendor. And we typically do outsource janitorial.
>
> Cost competitiveness and the Federal Accounting Regulations (FAR) also impact our cost structures, and the way in which our services are provided.

The tendency toward growth through acquisition in the defense industry also impacts Facilities and Real Estate Management (FRE). We tend to
accumulate lots of legacy-based operations with their own way of providing
and provisioning space. We have been in some spaces since the late 1960s,
and still have some of our original employees at work there.

Taken together, these conditions make FRE in the defense industry
exceptionally difficult to change or downsize.

Making its job even more difficult, most of this company's contracts are
government funded and subject to the budgeting processes of various congres-
sional agencies. This makes developing a leasing strategy—one that allows
them the flexibility to shrink and grow as contracts come and go—very difficult. The same executive quoted above goes on to say:

I was in a meeting today with a real estate service provider in the
greater [Washington] D.C. area that works with many companies similar
to ours. His joking observation was: What you guys need is to rent space
by the hour.

Although the particular constraints of this industry may not offer the
same opportunities for cost cutting—at least where the CRE footprint is concerned—they can be managed with an eye toward reducing fixed operational
costs, especially as individual projects begin. Our source goes on to say:

We have created an account management organization within FRE
made up of client relationship managers. Their role is to stay connected
with our varied lines of business and to know those businesses better than
those working there do themselves—at least from an FRE perspective, and
in terms of how best FRE can meet their needs. FRE has also taken the
initiative in developing a workplace strategy program for one of our divisions, in concert with HR, IT, and security, and the business owners. We
are exploring how the work is conducted, and how the workplace—from
bricks and mortar to technology, policies, procedures, and processes—can
better support the workforce.

GREEN BUILDING

Green building, or sustainable design, is yet another method of reducing fixed
operational costs, and one that bears on other issues of corporate agility as

well. As we will see in Spherion's Emerging Workforce® Study, and in Chapter 4, one of the notable differences between traditional and emergent workers is their desire to include an element of community service in their job descriptions.

This suggests that in the race to attract new talent, those companies that do their part to reduce energy consumption and greenhouse gases may enjoy a comparative advantage when seeking employees from an emergent talent pool that wish to be part of an organization that is as concerned about the environment as it is with profit.

A company's social reputation aside, as energy costs rise and sustainable architecture becomes even more practical and affordable, those companies that do not add this method of avoidance to their efforts at reducing fixed operational costs will inevitably find themselves one step further behind their competitors who do. Look at Figure 3–12, based on data from a 2005 survey by the IFMA.

Figure 3-12

Ways to make a facility greener	Now in Place	Plan to do	No Plan at this time
Using natural daylight	71 %	10 %	19 %
Purchasing recycled office products	64 %	13 %	23 %
Retrofitting lighting fixtures (other than EPA directed)	61 %	19 %	20 %
Adding light sensors	57 %	17 %	26 %
Implementing water conservation	53 %	19 %	29 %
Participating in incentive programs offered by local utilities or state/provincial agencies	47 %	17 %	36 %
Purchasing "earth-friendly" products, systems, or materials that produce as little pollution as possible in use and in production	46 %	28 %	25 %
Installing high-performance windows	42 %	15 %	43 %
Adding a green plant program (to control indoor air pollution)	38 %	13 %	48 %
Using Energy Star	34 %	23 %	43 %
Educating employees	33 %	19 %	48 %
Adding environmental criteria to vendor and product selection process	33 %	31 %	36 %
Conducting product life-cycle analysis	30 %	28 %	42 %
Using Green Lights Program (developed by the EPA)	20 %	23 %	57 %

It's interesting to note as well the means by which these savings—either active, as in the case of more efficient HVAC systems, or passive, through the use of natural light—are being realized.

Not all energy savings need come in the form of design decisions, however. As the GSA's Kevin Kampschroer notes, 30 to 40 percent of energy use is a personal decision. A large part of energy conservation, in other words, comes down to something as simple as how often the lights are turned off when no one is in the room. Instilling that sense of personal responsibility in the workplace is clearly the job of management, who can demonstrate by edict, or—much more effectively—show by example that energy conservation is a valued company behavior. We will return to this issue again and again—that is, the incalculable importance of strong executive support for change. It is not enough for upper-level managers to talk the talk; they've got to walk the walk, too.

Herman Miller

Len Pilon, corporate architect for founding *Future of Work* member Herman Miller, recalls the first days of the company coffee bar, placed smack in the center of an open office area in Herman Miller's MarketPlace (about which we will have more to say later). Employees were reluctant to be seen using the bar until upper management began to stop by themselves. By simply standing there for five or ten minutes, managers put their stamp of approval on the idea that an occasional "break" wasn't a bad idea. In so doing, they actually flipped the switch on that part of the design project. It had been designed, paid for, and put there to encourage casual collaboration between employees, but until upper-level management approved its use by their own behavior, they might as well have left it in the box.

Returning to green building, Len Pilon makes the point that reducing the corporate real estate footprint is the ultimate expression of energy conservation. An acknowledged leader in the design and manufacture of business furniture, Herman Miller has workplace strategy and green building expertise that is rooted, much like that of Jones Lang LaSalle, in its own experience with the products and services it sells. In Herman Miller's case, in fact, the company's history of environmental activism is nearly a century old.

An early innovator in employee-friendly space, Herman Miller founder D.J. DePree—the company bears the name of DePree's father-in-law, who bought controlling shares in the Star Furniture Company—declared that no employee should have to work more than seventy-five feet from a window. He also decreed that all new company properties had to devote 50 percent or more of their acreage to green space, in order to provide employees with a healthy environment in which to live and work.

Herman Miller's GreenHouse, completed in 1995 and designed by the environmentally conscious architect William McDonough, was yet another attempt on the part of the company to incorporate its environmental aesthetic into one of its own buildings. Despite the nearly 300,000 square feet of offices and light manufacturing space beneath the enormous curved glass roof of the GreenHouse, the building is stretched across the prairie of Holland, Michigan, like a slumbering giant.

The GreenHouse has been justly celebrated for its use of natural light, its abundant supply of fresh air, and its success in engineering social interaction. At its completion, the project was awarded Pioneer status by the then newly formed United States Green Building Council (USBGC).

Herman Miller, in fact, played a role in founding the USGBC, a nonprofit organization dedicated to promoting sound environmental building practices. (*Future of Work* corporate member Johnson Controls was also a founding member.) Among the organization's early initiatives was the Leadership in Energy and Environmental Design, or LEED certification process. LEED-certified buildings earn one of four designations—certified, silver, gold, or platinum—depending on the number of conditions satisfied by the building's design, construction, and management. Qualifying factors are as varied as lighting controls, water use, thermal comfort, CFC reduction, and construction waste management. In the words of the USGBC itself:

> LEED gives building owners and operators the tools they need to have an immediate and measurable impact on their building's performance. LEED promotes a whole-building approach to sustainability by recognizing performance in five key areas of human and environmental health: sustainable site development, water savings, energy efficiency, materials selection, and indoor environmental quality.
>
> The LEED rating system was created to transform the built environment to sustainability by providing the building industry with consistent, credible standards for what constitutes a green building. The rating system is developed and continuously refined via an open, consensus-based process

that has made LEED the green building standard of choice for federal agencies and state and local governments nationwide.[2]

Seven years later, in 2002, the company continued its green-building legacy with Herman Miller MarketPlace, a commercial office building in Zeeland, Michigan, that served as the company's latest statement of its evolving design principles, as well as its growing expertise in sustainable architecture. Developed by the Granger Group and leased by Herman Miller, design input was divided among the developer, the prospective tenant, and the principal architect, Integrated Architecture of Grand Rapids, Michigan. (The interiors were the work of IA Interior Architects, which was also responsible for the new Jones Lang LaSalle space in the Aon Center. We'll return to their work again in Chapter 7, when we survey the workplace of the future.)

The project was originally designed to satisfy the requirements for LEED silver designation. However, an obsessive attention to environmental details earned the building gold LEED certification, making it the seventh LEED-certified Herman Miller building. We want to remake the point here that in addition to being environmentally friendly, LEED-certified buildings save money, and therefore increase corporate agility.

H-P

H-P's approach to sustainability is more closely tied to its real estate portfolio management. H-P believes, just as Herman Miller does, that the most important environmental measure it can take is to reduce the overall size of its real estate portfolio. This reduces the company's carbon footprint, its energy consumption, use of water, coverage of nonpermeable surfaces, and so on in a way that no amount of focused reduction at a specific site can possibly hope to achieve.

H-P has recently introduced a checklist of design decisions that can be made throughout the course of a project in order to reduce its impact on the environment. Contractors are encouraged to make environmentally friendly decisions (within the payback guidelines established by the company) and to record these decisions, but this process does not typically extend to enduring the resource-heavy commitment to LEED and other certification processes, even though many of H-P's solutions conform to overall design requirements.

Again, one of the primary goals of H-P's Workplace Transformation is the creation of an employee-friendly workspace, achieved through the efficient use of its consolidated space, and enabling company growth while providing a healthier workplace for employees. Thus, by focusing on its core sites, and making its business more efficient, it also makes those sites more energy-efficient. By concentrating its efforts on the lighting and cooling plants in its more densely occupied, consolidated sites, it eliminates wasteful energy use inherent in underutilized locations. As well, H-P's guidelines for its office interiors—paint, office furniture, carpet, etc.—call for materials that emit practically no volatile organic compounds (VOC). Where possible, carpets contain recycled fiber content, and wood floors are made of sustainable wood, such as bamboo.

Electricity use accounts for 87 percent of H-P's climate change impact, and in one of a variety of attempts to reduce that use—in addition to showcasing its own sustainable technology—H-P's offices will soon feature computers with energy-efficient Liquid Crystal Diode (LCD) screens whenever possible. This change alone has the potential to reduce H-P's energy use by more than four million kWh per year, equivalent to three months of energy use at its Vancouver site.

For its mobile professionals—a large and growing percentage of H-P's workforce, as noted previously—the company is considering eliminating monitors altogether and switching to the use of laptop docking stations. Eliminating large, bulky CRTs not only saves electricity, it also eliminates dead space, allowing greater utilization of the workspace. Again, office density equals energy efficiency. H-P is installing networked printers throughout its facilities. These printers make double-sided printing easier, use less energy than desktop models, and have demonstrated a 10 percent reduction in paper consumption where they have been installed.

Small changes in routine, in a company with more than 150,000 employees, can make big differences. By setting a monitor to sleep after twenty minutes, for instance, and a hard drive after an hour, enough electricity can be saved to power the light on the desk twenty-four hours a day for a full year. The company also has an aggressive recycling program, both for paper waste and, far more importantly, for aged computer equipment.

As the H-P workforce continues to become more mobile, fewer and fewer of its employees will have dedicated desks, and that adds up to enormous savings in energy and reductions in greenhouse gases (GHG). Although it's true that many home thermostats in the world's colder regions, once automatically lowered during the workday, will now remain at higher settings while work is done in the home, the energy savings and air pollution avoidance associated with reduced commuting will more than make up the difference. H-P's telework program, for example, already saves approximately 2 million round-trip commutes in the United States and Canada, avoiding approximately 57 million miles of road travel and reducing GHG emissions by more than 24,000 tons of CO_2. The move to an even more mobile workforce is expected to decrease the CO_2 emissions from employees' cars by more than 130,000 tons—to say nothing of avoiding the consumption of almost 15 million gallons of gasoline.

Johnson Controls

Johnson Controls is a full-line service provider of heating, ventilating, and air conditioning (HVAC) in nonresidential buildings, and has been in the business for more than a century. In addition, it offers lighting, security, and fire management services, complete mechanical and electrical maintenance, and integrated facility management. At present, the company has more than a billion square feet of corporate real estate under its management.

In later chapters, we'll discuss Johnson Controls' history of innovation and its groundbreaking facilities services without facilities program, but for now we just want to touch on its sustainability initiatives and the opportunities they offer to reduce fixed operating costs and increase corporate agility.

The USGBC estimates that green building costs approximately 3 to 5 percent more than traditional construction methods (although, as we'll see in one of IA Interior Architect's stunningly successful recent projects in the northwest, it is possible to design office space that not only incorporates sustainability, but increases resident head count and *reduces* construction costs). Where such innovative design solutions are not possible, it's still not hard to see how quickly such small increases in construction costs can be recouped, what with oil and gas prices almost double what they were a year ago.

Rounding out the lengthy history of Johnson Controls' energy-savings advocacy, the company first sponsored the U.S. Energy Efficiency Forum in 1990, co-sponsored the event with the U.S. Energy Association in 1992, and has continued its co-sponsorship every year since then. It was named U.S. EPA Energy Star® Ally of the Year in 1999, and U.S. EPA Energy Star® Partner of the Year in 2001. Finally, Johnson Controls headquarters in Milwaukee was one of the first buildings to achieve a gold rating under the USGBC's LEED® certification.

The following case study is a good example of the sort of cost savings and operational efficiencies that sustainability initiatives can offer, as well as a good demonstration of the way in which outsourced services can increase corporate agility.

About six years ago Johnson Controls entered into a systemwide perform-ance contract with a regional health care provider looking to improve its healing environment by upgrading its HVAC, lighting, and security systems, but without sacrificing scarce capital urgently needed for its primary focus—providing quality health services. The performance contract—truly a partner-ship, of sorts—allowed the health care provider, whose operations include twenty-four hospitals, nine long-term care facilities, eight-assisted living facil-ities, and eleven home care and hospices, to finance most of the long-term improvements with the cost savings realized from reduced operating expenses. Each facility was allowed to customize its approach, but Johnson Controls was designated the sole provider of services for the entire system.

In order to determine the necessary extent of the individual improve-ments, feasibility studies were performed at each of the health care system's facilities. Once the results were in, the program's first stage began with a $5.2 million facilities upgrade spread across three hospitals, used primarily for energy-efficient boilers and chillers. As a result, though, of its awareness of the entire system's needs, Johnson Controls was also able to help the hospitals realize additional cost savings and improved regulations compliance through the development of a centralized waste-processing facility to serve all three hospitals.

Again, the outsourced facilities management contract allowed the client to concentrate on its core competency—providing state of the art, affordable health care—and to preserve scarce resources through cost savings and im-proved compliance. Reduced fixed operating costs, retained resources, corpo-rate agility—these are good for the environment and good for the bottom lines of both the service provider and its client.

CHOOSING A LOCATION

We are convinced that rising competitive pressures, the impending shortage of human talent, and the instinctual movement of the workforce toward distributed work will soon force changes in the way most companies look at their location strategies. No longer limited to the local labor pool, a more distributed workforce and online recruiting allows companies to throw out a wider net for new hires, but it also forces them to accept more flexible work patterns, examples of which may include employees who are in the office no more than once a month. What's more, that office may soon have more to do with where the workers are, rather than where the company is based.

Not only is space far less expensive outside major metropolitan areas, but our research shows that these days the talent everyone is seeking is more often to be found in *micropolitan* areas—that is, rural, smaller cities—in the United States, primarily because of quality-of-life concerns. It is therefore incumbent upon corporate real estate professionals to develop a comprehensive strategy of place that integrates human resource, information technology, and real estate/facilities management functions to adapt to where the talent is. In other words, location is becoming an ever more critical component of collaborative strategic management, and therefore of corporate agility.

Accenture has already put this real estate management theory into practice, choosing locations for its varied business units according to need. *Image space*, intended to brand the corporation in the eyes of its clients, is located in prestigious areas at the center of major metropolitan areas. CRE seeks long-term leases for such space, for which it is willing to spend more to lease, and more to fit out. *Hub space* is also located in the center of metropolitan areas, but its lease terms are shorter, and expenditures on interiors are more closely controlled. Satellite locations, in suburban areas, have short-term leases, and basic fit-out.

We call this approach the *strategy of place*. The work environment is ultimately about connectivity, or how a company utilizes a network of places, both virtual and physical, to enable its employees to connect with each other, and with customers and suppliers, no matter where they are. Strategy of place involves identifying who the people are that you need to hire, knowing where they are, and predicting where they will want to be in the future as they move through their careers.

We will return to this topic and discuss it at greater length in Chapter 8. Suffice it to say for now that an effective strategy of place helps to reduce fixed operating costs, and in so doing dramatically ramps up corporate agility.

OUTSOURCING LABOR COSTS

After CRE, labor and its attendant costs—benefits, taxes, insurance, and support staff—are clearly the next logical targets for cost cutting. Although a company is little more than the sum of the talent it employs, outsourcing its variable labor needs—project by project—frees up resources that can be put to work wherever market conditions, or corporate strategy, directs. This is something of a shell game—the costs of labor, after all, like the pea, do not really disappear, but just end up under another shell. However, there are still significant strategic advantages associated with outsourcing labor costs in this manner. Foremost among those advantages is the ability to incur costs according to need, rather than maintaining a workforce and the space necessary to house it, in anticipation of its use. This is, in essence, what corporate agility is all about.

Loretta Penn, vice president and chief service excellence advocate for Spherion, provides this example:

> Spherion has a client who needs an expanded sales force every year for the ninety days from late September to Christmas, and instead of adding this request to the list of everyday tasks required of HR, they give us the job. We can deliver the skilled resources quickly and efficiently because providing staffing solutions—whether temporary or permanent—is what we do. We also do it for a fixed cost, with performance guarantees built into our price, and we make improvements every year. The client gets clean beginnings and endings, with no hidden costs at the end of the season.
>
> Then every year, once it's over, we conduct a review of the process, using metrics that we develop and implement in conjunction with the client, to demonstrate how we think we can do the job better in the coming year, with their help.
>
> We also like to share best practices among our clients, so when we feel we've established a good model with one client to meet a particular staffing need, we may leverage that model by offering similar services to other companies with similar needs.

According to the Spherion® Emerging Workforce® Study, this practice is on the rise, as are employers' views of the importance of a contingent workforce. Spherion's research shows the following:

- 60 percent of U.S. companies use contingent workers as part of their workforce, and of those companies, 8 percent of their workforce is contingent.

■ 58 percent of U.S. employers surveyed agree that contingent workers are a vital part of the workforce today and believe that they will become even more important over the next ten years.

■ 80 percent of U.S. employers think cost savings and increased flexibility are important aspects of using a contingent workforce.

■ 77 percent of U.S. employers believe that a contingent workforce increases their ability to quickly adjust the size of their workforce.

■ 82 percent of medium-sized companies ($500 million to $1 billion) and 88 percent of larger companies ($1 billion or more) use contingent workers, as opposed to only 53 percent of smaller companies (less than $500 million).[3]

As we have seen over and over again, however, just because employers recognize the benefits of a certain management approach doesn't mean they'll put it into practice. According to Spherion, although nearly three quarters (72 percent) of companies agree that an integrated hiring strategy for contingent and full-time workers will result in higher workforce quality, fewer than half (45 percent) agree that their company has—or is even considering—such a strategy.[4]

Beyond remuneration itself—still the first line on the budget for most companies—there is also a significant opportunity for savings in recruitment costs, yet another task that can easily be outsourced. Effective recruitment—or hiring not just the best person available, but also the best person for the job—is another oft-missed opportunity to cut costs and increase agility.

Recruitment costs, while not fixed in the classic economic sense of the word, are nonetheless recurring expenses in every corporation's budget. If they can be quarantined through outsourcing, immediate—and lasting—savings in CRE, insurance, and benefits can be realized.

The goal here, as it is in all types of cost cutting, whether fixed or variable, is to streamline the company's fixed expenses so that during downturns or retooling the company has the resources available that it can redirect according to its changing strategic goals. This, in fact, is as good a definition of corporate agility as you'll find.

SPHERION CONTINGENT WORKFORCE CASE STUDY

In order to give our readers a better idea of just how recruitment and staffing firms provide contingent workforces for specific industries, and how the process can be used to manage costs and increase corporate agility, we asked Spherion to contribute a case study of one of its clients in the accounting and financial consulting industry. For the purposes of this book—and because Google, to our astonishment, produced no hits under this name—we'll refer to its client as AmAccount.

One of the largest providers of accounting outsourcing and financial consulting services in the world, AmAccount employs more than 22,000 people and operates in 35 countries. Spherion was asked to fill 2,400 positions, for four different AmAccount locations, in five weeks, with the understanding that, if successful, the process would be repeated every year as the tax season came to an end.

The first step was to engage the Spherion Virtual Recruiting team, who quickly developed a process to support the client's existing recruiters and then, drawing from its own ranks, assembled a team of virtual recruiters and employment specialists for each AmAccount location. Spherion was able to ramp up these teams within a week, as well as to initiate meetings and training sessions with each of the onsite recruiting contacts, in order to test drive the process. Using this collaborative approach, the two teams—virtual and local—were able to get up to speed at all of the sites and to keep the project on schedule.

Recruitment at all four sites then proceeded simultaneously, with Spherion advising the client to increase pay rates in markets where its salaries were not competitive, or where the segment of the labor force it sought was in short supply. In addition to pay, Spherion sought to leverage specific features of the positions the client needed to fill, in order to attract the maximum number of qualified candidates:

- Guaranteed five day work weeks (no weekends)
- Paid training
- Friendly work environment and inviting corporate setting
- Potential for seasonal employment the following year (depending on the candidate's performance and the company's needs)
- Possibility of a permanent position with AmAccount (depending on the candidate's performance and the company's needs)

These last two features, in addition to attracting a larger pool of applicants, were likely to affect the new hires' performances as well—a good example of how innovative, outsourced recruiting can serve more than one business strategy simultaneously.

With both the Spherion and AmAccount teams in place, a recruitment process outlined, and timetables drawn up, Spherion then turned to attracting as large a pool of qualified candidates as possible, using all the tools at its disposal. These included online posting, print advertising, online sourcing, and direct sourcing to community locations, apartment complexes, fitness and activity centers, churches, military bases, technical schools, colleges and universities, and day care sites.

The company also partnered with state employment offices to maximize AmAccount's exposure to those already in the job market, as well as those who might enter the market once the recruitment program was underway. Spherion leveraged its own National Candidate Resource Center as well—which, on average, attracts 1,000 new applications a day—to help find likely candidates in each of the four AmAccount locations.

Because it could spread such a wide net, and didn't have to rely on just one or two sources—as AmAccount would have, had it attempted to fill the positions itself—Spherion was able to reach the recruitment targets for each of the client's sites, and to do it ahead of schedule.

Filling an average of 600 positions at each of AmAccount's four sites meant sifting through more than four times as many applications—a talent pool of 9,000 potential candidates was systematically reduced to the 2,400 most qualified candidates—and it also meant that weeks might pass before the first hires actually started work. (Again, the entire recruiting process took place over five weeks.) This meant that there were bound to be candidates who, having accepted AmAccount's offer of employment through Spherion would continue to search for work until their jobs began.

Therefore, under Spherion's direction, the recruitment teams at each of the client's locations were authorized to offer paid orientation sessions to every new hire on the day they were offered, and accepted, their jobs. Then, continuing its collaboration with the client's staff, Spherion's virtual recruiting team used a multistep process that kept the new hire engaged during the remainder of the five-week period, placing scheduled calls to keep them onboard and ready to go to work while waiting for the project start dates.

Clearly, when ramping up for a project of this scale—2,400 workers recruited and hired in the space of five weeks—it's important not to jeopardize the earliest hires, especially because they are often the most qualified candidates in the labor pool. Then too, even with local teams in place to bring the new employees up to speed, training and on-boarding hundreds of new employees is something better done over time, rather than all at once, and no local employer could possibly match Spherion's experience with this process.

In fact, in cases such as AmAccount's, Spherion's virtual recruiting team is clearly its most highly leveraged asset. Positioned throughout the United States, the team offers Spherion expertise in a number of local labor pools. At the same time, these recruiting professionals can work alone or in teams, and are able to ramp up, ramp down, change focus, and turn on a dime in order to support any of Spherion's clients. Seen in a certain light they are mirror reflections of the labor force they were asked to assemble for AmAccount.

Spherion can engage as many recruiting professionals as it needs when undertaking a large project and then just as quickly turn them toward other work. And while their local knowledge can often be a great advantage—when, for instance, local businesses close and throw hundreds or even thousands of employees out of work—for Spherion's purposes it doesn't matter where the virtual team members live and work, since their work is done online.

By outsourcing jobs to Spherion, not only do clients like AmAccount avoid having to hire the workers themselves—thus avoiding the nightmarish logistics of payroll, withholding, and insurance—they are also able to avoid the headaches associated with assembling a recruiting team sizable enough to find such a large, skilled workforce. Since Spherion, not AmAccount, will technically employ all 2,400 employees, the process will have a clear beginning and end for the client, as well as a fixed cost.

The system works for the labor force as well. By availing themselves of a completely online solution, including Spherion's Candidate Resource Center, online screening tools, and virtual recruiting capabilities, the candidates can complete an application, be contacted by telephone, undergo preemployment testing, and be prequalified by the virtual recruiting team before they ever set foot on the client site. Not only is this convenient for the candidates, it also saves Spherion's staff a significant amount of time and trouble by enabling it to isolate and interview only those candidates with suitable qualifications and the greatest potential employability.

As for the interview process itself, Spherion relies on a standardized set of behavioral questions that yield valuable insight in key areas of competency. The results are then compared to the client's ideal employee profile for each of the job types it seeks to fill. The structured format of the interview ensures that all candidates are asked the same questions, thus allowing for meaningful comparison of all candidates for the job. What's more, standard criteria are used to evaluate the responses to each question, enabling Spherion interviewers to maintain objectivity.

In addition to the speed and convenience of Spherion's interview process—due primarily to the availability of its virtual recruiting teams and online applications—the company also depends on robust assessment and prescreening, soft and hard skill assessments, and job-specific behavioral interviews to evaluate the full range of a candidate's skills, knowledge, and abilities. This holistic approach allows recruiters to gain a comprehensive view of each applicant's strengths and aptitudes—thus improving their ability to identify the most suitable candidates.

Those who successfully complete the screening process are scheduled—through the virtual recruiting team—for interviews with the recruitment contact at the client's site. Thanks to Spherion's integrated systems, the candidate-screening documents, assessment scores, and notes from the virtual recruiters are readily accessible for viewing by the on-site recruiting teams. On-site recruiters then complete the application process with a face-to-face interview, and, if they wish to hire the prospect, the final employment paperwork, which includes a background check and a drug test. Contingent upon those results, an employment offer is then extended to the successful candidate.

Again, Spherion's ability to screen candidates without requiring them to present themselves on-site makes the process much more convenient for everyone. Candidates don't have to make multiple visits, arrange for transportation, or find day care, and recruiters don't have to conduct time-consuming face-to-face interviews unless the candidate has already been prescreened.

As recruiting for AmAccount continued Spherion generated dedicated reports for each client location, each recruiting team, and even each recruiter, measuring productivity, sourcing statistics, the time required to fill each position, ratios of employees submitted to those hired, and more. By these measures, Spherion's recruitment process paid off handsomely—each location exceeded its weekly targets for new starts throughout the five-week hiring campaign. In addition, throughout the contingent workforce's job contract, Spherion measured the retention rate for all 2,400 new hires.

Once the job was done, all project-related data were made available to AmAccount through Spherion's online Client Resource Center, allowing them to measure Spherion's complete performance, as well as the performance of the contract workers Spherion had hired. Access to executive summaries and customized reporting capabilities also helped the client to better understand its costs, its hiring goals, its workforce attrition, and its workforce performance.

In other words, the post-program data not only allowed AmAccount to judge the performance of the recruiting operation alone, it also provided numbers useful for strategic decision making. The process allowed management to focus on its core deliverables while Spherion handled the recruitment, training, and monitoring of the contingent workforce. In a sense, Spherion actually served as part of AmAccount's HR team, not only providing services but developing best practices that could be leveraged in the future, and providing useful data for the company's enterprisewide strategies.

In sum, this case study is as good a demonstration of the core value of outsourced labor as we've found. AmAccount realized that a large-scale staffing project—the hiring of 2,400 workers in an exceptionally short timeframe—was not one of its core competencies. Therefore it partnered with Spherion to design and implement a comprehensive program to meet its temporary needs, allowing AmAccount to ramp up for its own customers' needs without distractions, or incurring additional fixed costs.

Why did AmAccount select Spherion? Besides presenting one of the industry's most comprehensive set of recruiting tools and offering one of the largest nationwide virtual recruiting teams, Spherion already had a history of positive results with AmAccount, and at one of the very locations that figured in the larger project. Therefore, when AmAccount began the RFP process for a single-source provider of contingent labor, Spherion consistently outranked its competitors in each of AmAccount's key metrics. AmAccount was also particularly impressed with Spherion's ability to provide strategic on-site dedicated management teams for large contractor populations. In addition, Spherion had previously demonstrated its commitment to service by treating all of the client's requests with a consistent sense of urgency. In short, Spherion has developed a model that makes serving each client's needs a recurring factor in its own growth strategy—a win-win if ever there was one.

Returning to Spherion's Emerging Workforce® Study, its research indicates that it is the smaller companies ($500 million or less in revenue) that have the greatest difficulty finding qualified workers (41 percent) and keeping employment costs—recruiting and training—under control (35 percent).[5] This is partly because they tend not to use the screening tools that larger companies favor, and, as a result, spend more time and money looking for new hires:

- 44 percent of smaller companies somewhat or strongly agree that their recruiters and hiring managers interview too many people in order to find qualified candidates (as opposed to 37 percent of larger organizations).

- 39 percent of smaller companies have increased their use of screening methods, compared to 61 percent of medium-sized companies, and 66 percent of larger companies.[6]

Even if recruitment costs are outsourced, however, the money will have been poorly spent if the new hire fails to become fully engaged, or worse yet, decides to leave the company, forcing a replay of the entire, costly process. Reacting to this critical, though often overlooked, part of the hiring process, forward-thinking companies have begun to formulate employee retention strategies designed to increase job satisfaction and reduce the enormous costs of employee turnover:

- Flexible work options
- Task-friendly interior design
- Secure, state of the art tech support for both the fixed and the mobile workforces
- The opportunity to do meaningful work

It goes without saying that a satisfied, engaged employee is a much more productive employee, revealing once again the way aspects of one management challenge can affect the entire business.

Here, once more, we see the necessity and the value of the collaborative strategic management of HR, IT, and RE. Flexible work options are most often presented as a means of accommodating the workforce (HR), but they cannot become a reality without a corresponding investment in mobile communications and data processing tools (IT), and a realignment of the company's real estate portfolio (RE). And while creating task-friendly interior space based on the careful analysis of work patterns will unquestionably aid productivity, the design must also take into account real estate cost targets and if necessary concede a higher person/workspace ratio (HR). Finally, the space must serve as a palpable expression of the company's opinion of its employees, its willingness to support a variety of work styles, and its offer of meaningful work in an efficient, productive, healthy workspace.

In our next chapter, "Attracting and Retaining Human Talent," this last issue looms large indeed.

CHAPTER 4

Attracting and Retaining Human Talent

GLOBAL DEMOGRAPHIC TRENDS

Attracting and retaining qualified, engaged employees is the second of the three primary business challenges of the twenty-first century, and, unlike reducing costs, it will become more difficult decade by decade. There simply isn't enough human talent to meet the current needs of business, much less the constantly expanding global economy. The bottom line here is that in a few years—say 2010—the United States will have 10 million more jobs than it will have qualified people to fill them! Not only is that a major human resource management headache, but it also has far-reaching implications for trade and immigration policy.[1]

The primary cause of this shortage is the graying of the global workforce. Worldwide, 11 percent of the population is now more than 60 years old, and the percentage is even higher in Asia and Europe.[2] For example, 27 percent of Japan's population, and 26 percent of Italy's, is now 60 or older. In the United States, the number is now only 17 percent, but it is rising nearly as fast as college tuition. The United Nations Department of Economic and Social Affairs summarizes the data thusly:

The number of persons age 60 or over is estimated to be 688 million in 2006 and is projected to grow to almost 2 billion by 2050, at which time the population of older persons will be larger than the population of children (0–14) for the first time in human history. The majority of the world's older persons reside in Asia (54 percent), while Europe has the next largest share (22 percent).

One out of every 9 persons is now aged 60 years or over; by 2050, the United Nations projects that 1 person out of every 5, and by 2150 1 out of every 3, will be aged 60 years or over.[3]

It gets worse. The world over, only 40 percent of men over 60, and only 16 percent of women over 60, are still in the workforce. Those numbers drop dramatically in more developed countries. In America, only 30 percent of men over 60 and 19 percent of women over 60 remain in the workforce. In Europe, the numbers are lower still: Only 15 percent of the men over 60 and 7 percent of the women over 60 are still on the job. This means that the fastest-growing group in the population, with the most business experience, is abandoning the workforce and leaving behind a smaller and smaller pool of human talent to fill their jobs.

That the problem is especially grave in more developed countries, where social safety nets and incomes that permit retirement savings are more prevalent, makes the potential for economic disaster even greater. In addition to the irretrievable loss of knowledge that will accompany this exodus—a topic to which we will turn later in this chapter—as the population of older persons grows, their support will have to be borne by fewer and fewer workers. This will necessitate an ever more onerous tax burden, and put upward pressure on wages. The UN measure for this statistic is the Potential Support Ratio (PSR):

> The potential support ratio (PSR), that is, the number of persons aged 15 to 64 years per person aged 65 years or over, indicates the dependency burden on potential workers. The impact of demographic ageing is reflected in the PSR, which fell between 1950 and 2006 from 12 to 9 people in the working ages per person aged 65 years or over. By 2050, the PSR is projected to fall to 4 persons of working age per person aged 65 years or over. PSRs have important implications for social security schemes, particularly traditional pay-as-you-go systems, in which current workers pay for the benefits of current retirees.[4]

The U.S. Social Security Administration projections are equally pessimistic. As difficult a read as it is, try to get through the 2006 report of the Old Age Survivors Insurance and Disability Insurance (OASI/DI) Trust Funds:

> Under the intermediate assumptions, OASDI cost will increase rapidly between about 2010 and 2030, due to the retirement of the large baby-boom generation. After 2030, increases in life expectancy and relatively low fertility rates will continue to increase Social Security system costs, but more slowly. Annual cost will exceed tax income starting in 2017, at which time the annual gap will be covered with cash from net redemptions of special obligations of the Treasury, until these assets are exhausted in 2040. Separately, the DI fund is projected to be exhausted in 2025, and the OASI fund in 2042. For the 75-year projection period, the actuarial deficit is 2.02 percent of taxable payroll, 0.09 percentage point larger than in last year's report. The open group unfunded obligation for OASDI over the 75-year period is $4.6 trillion in present value, $0.6 trillion more than the unfunded obligation estimated a year ago. Trust fund exhaustion is sooner and the unfunded obligation increased more than would occur from changing the valuation period alone in this report largely because of a lower assumed ultimate real interest rate.
>
> The OASDI annual cost rate is projected to increase from 11.22 percent of taxable payroll in 2006, to 16.71 percent in 2030, and to 18.74 percent in 2080, or to a level that is 5.38 percent of taxable payroll more than the projected income rate for 2080. For last year's report the annual cost for 2080 was estimated at 19.12 percent of payroll. Expressed in relation to the projected gross domestic product (GDP), OASDI cost is estimated to rise from the current level of 4.3 percent of GDP, to 6.2 percent in 2030, and to 6.3 percent in 2080. In last year's report OASDI cost was estimated at 6.4 percent of GDP for 2080. Projected cost for 2080 is lower in this year's report as percentages of taxable payroll and GDP largely due to a higher assumed birth rate.[5]

The report goes on to conclude that either benefits must be reduced or payroll taxes must rise—responses that politicians of both parties will, no doubt, avoid as long as possible.

This problem could be somewhat alleviated by population growth, but there the news is no better. In 2002, the latest year for which complete data are available, the U.S. birth rate, at 13.9 per 1,000 persons, fell to the lowest level since national data have been available.[6] The report went on to conclude that the current low birth rate primarily reflects the smaller proportion of women of childbearing age in the U.S. population, as baby boomers age and Americans are living longer.[7] Although the U.S. death rate, at 8.3 per 1,000 persons[8], is still significantly lower than the birth rate—unlike those of Italy, Austria, Czech Republic, and Poland—should the birth rate continue to decline, the burden on younger wage-earners will undoubtedly increase.

With the workforce aging, the cost of Social Security obligations rising, and the birth rate at a historical low, all that remains to complete the disaster scenario is the fact that the primary historical source of the United States labor market—immigration—has become yet another casualty of the war on terror. And if you take into account the shifting global economic base and the technologies that now make it possible for anyone to work from anywhere in the world, the need for the emerging global workforce to seek work in Europe or the Americas is no longer as compelling as it once was.

Of course, it's also true that businesses need no longer bring new hires to the United States, since many jobs can be done from anywhere in the world. On the flip side, it is also no longer necessary to emigrate to the United States—or to Europe, or to Japan—to take jobs away from the local workforce.

Disputing the coming shortage of human talent has, in fact, become the equivalent of contesting global warming, but Littler Mendelson, a leading Employment and Labor Law firm, makes the interesting point that just like studies that point to the growth of some glaciers in order to refute the greenhouse effect, proof of the talent gap can be *camouflaged* by other economic factors:

> Even though the coming shortage promises to be the greatest in the history of the United States, its size and meaning is camouflaged by continuing outsourcing, reductions in force, and unemployment. It is likely that groups of employees will continue to receive pink slips and have difficulty locating comparable employment long after the skilled worker shortage becomes an indisputable crisis. It is in this seemingly contradictory economy that claims like discrimination, wrongful discharge, and retaliation will test corporate legal compliance and human resource planning.[9]

So where are we going to get the talent? We think there will be three major sources. About one third of the total will come from retirees remaining in the work force, though most likely not in a full-time capacity; one third will come from insourcing, or moving work to interior population centers within the United States; and the remaining third will come from retraining workers displaced from lower-skilled and lower-paying jobs. This is all contingent, of course, on appropriate public policies being put in place, and far-sighted corporate investment being focused on developing these new talent pools. We'll be talking more about how to do that later on.

EDUCATIONAL TRENDS

Although college graduation rates are still climbing in the United States,[10] in large part due to the growing popularity of two-year associate's degrees, the United States is no longer the undisputed international leader in educational attainment. Canada now has a higher proportion of adults holding a college degree, and among younger adults—aged 25 to 34—the United States has dropped to seventh place, behind Canada, Japan, Korea, Finland, Norway, and Sweden.[11] The *good* news is that we are still even with Belgium in that category, although it is difficult to remain optimistic about next year's results.

The United States also remains among world leaders in college participation, but lags far behind in college completion.[12] The cost of higher education, unlike graduation rates, continues to escalate rapidly, as does the number of students borrowing, and the amounts they borrow. This is an especially grim statistic when coupled with the before-mentioned predictions regarding the need for rising contributions from the working classes in order to support the aged. The day may come, in fact, when ever-greater payroll deductions prevent college students without a degree from paying off their loans before they retire.

These statistics would be somewhat less troublesome if the education Americans were receiving measured up to international standards, but there, too, the numbers are far from reassuring. Alan Wagner, author of *Measuring Up Internationally*, makes these sobering assessments of education in the United States:

Compared with other countries with advanced economies, the United States places about in the middle on direct assessments of skills and knowledge of eighth graders. Korea and Singapore are leaders on several assessments; in none of the assessments does the United States place at top levels. The United States has improved over the past five years, but not enough to place it among the leaders.

In the United States, about one-quarter of 15-year-olds fall into the lowest proficiency level on assessments of skills and knowledge. Because these young people lack even minimal capacities, they are most likely to be excluded from studies beyond high school. In Finland and Korea, less than a tenth of 15-year-olds perform at this low level. In France and Ireland, countries with average performance above but closer to that of the United States, about one-sixth of 15-year-olds demonstrate this low level of proficiency.[13]

These statistics lead Wagner to conclude the following:

In sum, although the United States continues to rank among the leaders in comparisons of performance in higher education, its leadership position has eroded. No longer the clear-cut performer in participation and completion rates, the United States has been joined by other countries that have expanded access to and completion of higher education programs. Further, comparisons of direct measures of learning show the United States as trailing the leading countries. As a result, as U.S. states strengthen higher education opportunity and outcomes, they may find that other countries also have stronger or improving performance levels.[14]

Let's face it; workforce development just isn't happening in the United States. There have been some nascent workforce development projects started by the U.S. Department of Labor, but the results won't be in for at least two more years. Still, at least it's a start in the right direction.[15] Unfortunately, as we'll discuss in more detail later, most companies in the United States have adopted a "you'd better be ready when you're called" attitude toward their knowledge workers (including middle and senior managers).

Organizations have basically abdicated almost all responsibility for workforce development and dumped it onto the backs of the workforce. As the labor pool continues to shrink, we believe that any business with plans for growth will be forced to rethink this approach—or change the business they're in.

Maybe we're just a little pessimistic. The truth is, in the next chapter we'll discuss a great example of on-the-job education when we turn to institutionalizing innovation, and IBM's eLearning program, a big part of its On Demand Workplace. For the moment though, to make amends to those few pioneering companies we've slighted—by which we mean companies that understand the value of on-the-job education to corporate agility—we'd like to offer a quick look at another innovation from Johnson Controls.

Cutting fixed operating costs may begin with reducing the CRE footprint, but reducing energy and water use lead to savings, too, and that's what Johnson Controls had in mind when it developed the Sustainable Energy Education & Communications (SEEC) program. SEEC is a ten-module lesson plan that teaches employees how to find financial, environmental, and social benefits—both at work and at home. We think it's interesting that most companies have embraced sustainability because they want to contain costs, increase employee productivity, strengthen community ties, and enhance their corporate image—seems like protecting the environment is almost an afterthought. But we're not under any illusions, either, and we too believe that the shortest way to innovation is through profitability, so this is an employee education effort we're happy to include in these pages.

"Through SEEC, employees learn how saving energy and water, keeping indoor air clean, and other sustainable strategies can save money, reduce harmful emissions and help them stay healthy—both on the job and at home," said Paul von Paumgartten, director of energy and environmental affairs for the Controls Group of Johnson Controls. SEEC can also help companies achieve innovation credits for LEED® certification from the USGBC. And it includes a customizable communications package to showcase each company's accomplishments, including LEED and ENERGY STAR® achievements. That's our kind of on-the-job education.

KNOWLEDGE MANAGEMENT

Putting aside for the moment the declining number of qualified knowledge workers available to fill the job vacancies of the future, there is yet another, perhaps even more pressing, issue concerning the present workforce—

preserving the accumulated business knowledge of the retiring baby boomers. This brain drain of business knowledge is already occurring across private corporations and all levels of government.

Gloria Young, clerk of the board and legislative administrator of the city and county of San Francisco Board of Supervisors, legislative branch of government, and a corporate member of the *Future of Work*, arrived in San Francisco in the fall of 1998. Her initial audit, completed after thirty days on the job, revealed the following deficiencies:

- No citywide policy on e-mail
- No security program in place for official records
- No inventory of computer hardware and software
- No succession policy
- No employee evaluation policy

Her initial recommendations included an improved Web page, continued efforts to prepare the city/county computer system for Y2K, automated time-card entries, continued support for a scanning project initiated to provide a complete database of the proceedings of the board for the years 1974 through 1989, improving electronic access to board agendas and supporting materials, implementing policy changes for quasi-judicial hearings, creating a customer service/mission statement that involved input from the staff, and administering a comprehensive management audit.

By far her biggest challenge, however, was capturing the knowledge held by the 30 to 35 percent of the legislative branch's employees scheduled to retire between 2000 and 2006. In her survey of the department she was astonished to find that most of the potential retirees were single points of failure, with no backups and no formally recognized work processes. There were no personal computers on their desks, and their IT awareness was all but nonexistent. Things got done because the staff had years of experience to draw on, but employees had virtually no understanding of the big picture, and therefore no ability to innovate, or even to respond to out-of-the-ordinary problems. What's worse, there had been no attempt at transferring their skills and experience to the generation of workers who would soon have to take their places.

In the years that followed, Ms. Young set out to redesign the context and rebuild the culture in which her staff accomplished their work, initiating what she called the Succession Knowledge Management Program (SKMP). She upgraded the computer systems, had specific tasks documented by formal job descriptions, and created a succession-planning program based, in part, on having the more experienced staff shadowed by those who would eventually succeed them. She also ensured that the systems, knowledge plans, and work team responsibilities were available to the organization through their internal intranet site.

For those of you in the private sector who have attempted to do your jobs while power struggles unfolded in the boardroom above you, consider Ms. Young's experience during her first four years on the job:

> The eleven-member elected board that hired me in 1998 was reelected in the 1998 elections. Within a month of that date, a board member resigned to become a director of a state board, and Willie Brown, who was mayor at the time, appointed a new member to the Board of Supervisors.
>
> In the November 2000 election a new law required that board members serve by specific districts, or in other words, run in district elections. As a result there were seven new board members elected; two of the previous board had exhausted their term limits, and five were defeated. In addition, one of the existing board members ran against Mayor Brown as a write-in and came close to defeating him.
>
> The new board was far more active within specific districts and therefore wrote legislation that touched on local as well as citywide issues. The board also sought to reduce the mayor's powers by placing ballot measures and propositions on the ballots in future elections that split responsibilities between the executive and legislative branches of city and county government.
>
> In 2003, Mayor Brown was termed out, and three members of the Board of Supervisors simultaneously ran for the mayor's seat. This had never before occurred in city history. The result was that my staff and I were working in an environment where three of our bosses were running against one another in a hotly contested mayor's race at the same time they were running the city. (Two of those board members offered me top positions if they were elected.) One was eliminated in the primary election, and two went on to the run-off election, which resulted in the election of Mayor Gavin Newsom.
>
> In addition, two long-time members of the board, who were there since

I was appointed, were elected to the State Assembly, giving the newly elected mayor the opportunity to appoint two new members to replace them. To top it all off, once elected, Mayor Newsom requested that I come to work for the executive branch in a top management position.

As all this was going on—and in San Francisco's defense, it was a scenario little different from those occurring in many major American cities—Ms. Young not only continued her work at modernizing her department, but also found time to institute an Alternative Work Plan program, including telecommuting, to which we will return in Chapter 6 in our discussion of the distributed workforce.

ATTRACTION AND RETENTION OF LABOR

Not only is an ocean of business experience in danger of evaporating as the workforce ages, but changing attitudes in the workforce have also made it harder to retain talent once it is acquired. In this particular business nightmare, companies pay the costs of recruitment and training over and over again, without the payoff that comes from employees settling into their jobs and becoming more and more engaged and productive over the years.

One study we were involved in several years ago showed pretty conclusively that the costs of finding, recruiting, hiring, supporting, and assimilating knowledge workers were so great that unless an organization retains a knowledge worker for at least four years it will not recoup its initial costs. In other words, anyone who leaves the company within four years of being hired has cost you more than the value of what they produced.

The evidence of this growing problem is everywhere, but we'd like to substantiate it by referring to some data from Jones Lang LaSalle's Leading Edge Seminar surveys, to which we referred in Chapter 1. Figure 4-1 shows the result of fifty corporate real estate directors' responses to the question, "Is your company worried about the war for talent?"

It's interesting to note that Jones Lang LaSalle found—at least anecdotally—that while corporate real estate departments are more focused on cost reduction and flexibility, executive leaders tend to back workplace strategies (WS) programs as a result of the talent gap.

Figure 4-1

Is your company worried about the war for "talent?"

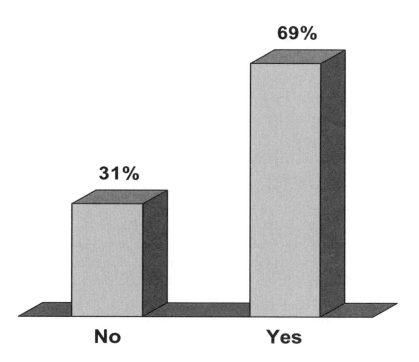

So, as the evidence mounts that human talent will be harder and harder to attract in the future, one of the great paradoxes of the future of work remains that since costs—both fixed and variable, present and prospective—must be reduced in order to increase corporate agility, the traditional lures used to attract human talent—pay, perquisites, and benefits—are no longer as freely available as they were in the past. This is happening, once again, while the pool of prospective knowledge workers continues to evaporate. Therefore, in addition to traditional compensation, forward-thinking corporate managers must begin to consider paying the knowledge worker of the future in a different coin. Before they can do that, however, they need to know what the new workforce wants.

Spherion Corporation, a leading recruiting, staffing, and workforce solutions provider—and a former *Future of Work* corporate member—conducts an ongoing multiyear study on changing attitudes in the workforce. Commissioned by Spherion and conducted on their behalf by Harris Interactive®, The Emerging Workforce® Study was first conducted in 1997, was followed-up in 1999, 2003, and 2005 and is now updated monthly.

Using a nationally representative sample of the U.S. workforce designed to uncover employee values and workplace expectations, the study provides invaluable insight into attracting, motivating, and retaining talent. In particular, the study paints a sobering picture of the future for those companies who have not prepared themselves for the coming shortage of qualified, engaged employees.

The Emerging Workforce® Study

Data from the Emerging Workforce® Study reveal that unlike traditional workers, the emergent worker believes that one's career is one's own responsibility, that promotion within the company should be based on merit rather than tenure, and that loyalty to a company can be an obstacle, rather than a means, to advancement. One finding, in particular, stands clear of all the others: *40 percent of U.S. workers say they are interested in seeking new job opportunities within the coming year.*

In addition, 20 percent report having actually made a job change in the past 12 months. Should even one half of those employees who say they are interested in seeking new job opportunities actually seek new employment, and should half of that group actually move to another job, then to your annual budget you can add the cost of replacing and training 20 percent of your workforce, to say nothing of the unquantifiable but certain disruption in your day-to-day operations.

Although estimates of the cost of recruiting and training a new employee vary, Spherion calculates that companies spend, on average, more than $55,000 to replace every knowledge worker who walks out the door. It's also worth bearing in mind that as the pool of sufficiently talented employees grows smaller and smaller, every time you have to look for someone new, it's going to be harder to find the right person for the job, it's going to cost your company more money, and it's going to take more of your HR department's time—in other words, escalating costs with dwindling returns.

In tracking changing employee attitudes, the Spherion study focuses on the trends for traditional and emerging workers, as well as a third group they refer to as *migrating*. This last category, made up of workers with a combination of traditional and emergent characteristics, describes approximately half of the workforce, and as a percentage has remained relatively stable since the study began in 1997. The trends in the traditional and emergent sectors of the workforce, however, have moved in opposite directions from the time they began to be tracked. In 1997, only 20 percent of workers were considered emergent, while 34 percent were considered traditional. By 2003, the numbers were nearly reversed, with 31 percent of the workforce emergent, and only 21 percent traditional. In other words:

- Traditional workers, far from rejecting the mores of the emergent workforce, are rapidly adopting them.

- There is no correlation between gender, age, or geographical region and the emergent workforce.

These findings have far-reaching implications for those who in years to come may have to draw from that section of the workforce nearing retirement in order to meet their workforce goals.

The Spherion study also reveals increased employee confidence in their ability to shape their own careers:

- Confidence in their employer's future does not necessarily reduce an employee's interest in seeking new job opportunities.

- Nearly seven out of ten U.S. workers say job change will be at their own initiative (and 78 percent believe it is unlikely that they will lose their job in the next twelve months)

- 85 percent of workers report growing confidence in their ability to earn a stable income within a conventional company.

- More than 59 percent report growing confidence in their ability to earn a stable income as a free agent.

Spherion's data also reveal the following sea changes in the emergent workforce's perceptions of the balance between work and life:

- 96 percent of respondents preferred employers that offer flexible work options.

- 86 percent listed the work/life balance among their career priorities.

- 73 percent say they would be willing to put their careers on hold for the good of their families.

More specifically, Spherion's studies identify the following workplace priorities of the emergent workforce to be future drivers of retention:

- 59 percent valued flex-time schedules.

- 48 percent said telecommuting was a factor.

- 32 percent included paid time off for community service as a workplace priority.

- 23 percent valued sabbaticals.

- 15 percent said on-site day care was important.

- 13 percent wanted job sharing.

In more general terms, Spherion finds the top drivers of retention for emergent workers to be culture and environment, compensation, training and development, relationship with supervisor, and growth and earning's potential.

It should be noted here that there are also other factors in the information economy that work against employee retention. One of them is the growing ability of the workforce to easily switch jobs from company to company within the same industry and/or geographic location. We recently spoke with the manager of a major wireless carrier's sales force and call center operation, who was experiencing just this problem.

> We did just about everything we could when we built out our new space to find good employees and keep them happy. We've got a pretty young labor pool, too, so we don't have a lot of generational conflict. We've got state of the art ergonomic furniture. The problem is we're located in a place that's well-known for its call centers, and so our reps—and those of our competitors—can easily switch jobs without changing industries, or having to move. That means there's really only one way to keep them around, and that's to offer them more money.

Emergent Employers

Not content to approach changes in the workforce solely from the supply side, Spherion divides employers into the same basic categories (i.e., traditional, emergent, and migrating) it does employees. Its continuing study reveals that *emergent employers*, or those who far exceed their peers in the use of HR best practices that are congruent with the needs and expectations of emergent workers, generally enjoy more financial success and stronger employee satisfaction than their traditional counterparts.

That said, it will surprise no one that most companies still fail to smell this particular brand of coffee (although that may be because their former employees are now enjoying their java, and the flexible work programs of their new employers, at the local coffee shop). Despite the data corroborating the emergent workforce's declining job loyalty, and the desire for a more reasonable balance between work and life, Spherion's study found that 81 percent of companies polled did not even have formal work/life balance programs. In addition:

- Only 24 percent of employers offer a formal flex-time program.
- Only 12 percent offer telecommuting.
- Only 10 percent offer paid time off for community service.
- Only 12 percent offer sabbaticals.
- Only 11 percent offer job sharing.

This is the case despite statistical evidence that 96 percent of workers agree that an employer is more attractive when it helps them meet family obligations through options like flex-time, job sharing, or telecommuting, and that employees who are offered and take advantage of work/life balance options report a 20 percent increase in their likelihood of staying at their employer for the next five years.[16]

Saratoga, a division of PricewaterhouseCooper, has compiled data corroborating the traditional company's lack of preparation for the coming talent shortage:

- Of companies surveyed, 57 percent did not have a formal retention strategy.
- Only 35 percent had specific retention or turnover goals.
- Over 44 percent indicated that their organizational structure had

changed over the last year, and 34 percent anticipate it will
change this year.

That last statistic, of course, is the most troublesome (i.e., nearly half the
companies polled experienced changes in organizational structure during the
last year, and yet had no formal programs to retain their employees).

Where no retention programs exist, higher rates of turnover can clearly
be expected, but even where they do exist, a lack of communication between
labor and management can make them ineffective. This is not management's
problem alone. According to the Emerging Workforce® Study, even though
workers considered growth and earnings potential as the most important factor in retaining them (after salary and benefits), the same workers rated training and development last on their list of eight retention drivers. This is further
evidence that the workforce has learned not to expect training and development, and that it has begun to accept training as one of its own responsibilities in this regard—in other words, look out for yourself because no one else
is going to.

What's more, despite some employers' efforts to offer ongoing learning
and skills enhancement, the labor force is often stubbornly unaware of their
existence. When assessing this disconnect, Spherion found the following:

- 92 percent of employers offered funds for seminars and trade
  shows, but only 28 percent of their workforce knew of such programs (a 64 percent gap in awareness).

- 91 percent of employers offered internal training programs, but
  only 46 percent of employees were aware of them (a 45 percent
  gap in awareness).

- 89 percent of employers offered external training sessions, but
  only 26 percent of employees knew about it (a 63 percent gap in
  awareness).

The same was true of tuition assistance (38 percent gap), online skills
training (38 percent gap), and online career development programs (23 percent gap). Perhaps most disheartening of all was the finding that of the minor-
ity of employees who are aware of such programs, nearly half, or 46 percent,
are dissatisfied with what is offered.

Another way to fill a company's talent needs may be through what Mc-

Kinsey & Company has called making a market in talent within a company. The consulting firm rightly points out that managers often treat their employees as their personal property, and as a result stifle employee job mobility within the company's own labor pool. In this way an ideal hire for another job within the company may be only a few doors down the corridor, but will have no idea there is an opportunity available, or, because of the fear of retaliation, no stomach to apply for it.

The Coming Generations

Rebecca Ryan, founder of Next Generation Consulting,[17] and an individual member of *Future of Work*, has built a successful business by offering companies an analysis of their strengths and weaknesses in attracting young talent (i.e., employees between the ages of twenty and forty). Using on- and off-the-job observation, in-depth one-on-one interviews, and focus groups made up of gen-X, gen-Y, and millennials, Next Generation Consulting goes beyond the numbers to the human factors that companies must understand in order to attract and retain the best young talent:

> Lots of consulting firms want to do your gap analysis. They want to tell you where you stink. Not us. We want to discover where you're already showing signs of greatness—and capitalize on it. A growing body of research shows that—dollar for dollar—helping clients capitalize on their strengths increases their ROI. Makes sense, doesn't it? It's like the heliotropic effect in nature: Plants grow toward the sun. Why not help yourself leverage the assets that appeal to the next generation?

Engaging the next generation, according to Ms. Ryan, is important not only because of demographics, but also because of psychographics:

> The next generation is different because they think and feel differently than their parents do about a variety of life/work issues. For starters, they have a "live first, work second" mentality.[18] After college, they pick a place to live, and then find a job. They're also doing what they can to push back adulthood; in the U.S., the average age of a first marriage is 27 for men and 25 for women. At work, they prefer life–work balance perks like flex time, compressed workweek, and sabbaticals over fat paychecks and mahogany workspaces.

This approach is built partly on the understanding that developed countries have already shifted from goods-based economies to knowledge-based economies, and that in the near future knowledge workers, rather than products, will drive growth.

MEANINGFUL WORK

A business is rightly judged by its product and service—but must also face scrutiny and judgment as to its humanity.
—D.J. DePree, founder, Herman Miller

From the beginning, Herman Miller's founder made it clear to all those who worked for him—and to anyone else who would listen—that the quality of his employees' lives was as important a part of his company as the machinery that produced its furniture. Eighty years later, that spirit survives in Herman Miller's intentional Employee Experience.

Built on its founder's belief that *people are what companies are made of*, and that demographic and cultural shifts are changing the face of the modern workforce, Herman Miller began to build its Employee Experience program in 2004 to ensure that the company remained one of the future's employers of choice.

In order to coordinate the program with the company's evolving business strategies, its designers first assembled a cross-functional core team composed of upper-level managers from HR, IT, and CRE, all of whom reported to a chief administration officer. The team then defined key ideas and integrated these ideas into the following simplified but clearly defined themes:

- *Meaning.* Most people want more from work than just a paycheck, they want meaning; they want work that allows them to indulge their curiosity, to explore new solutions, and to find unexpected answers.

- *Choice.* Intelligent, qualified employees don't like being told what to do. They want options—in compensation, benefits, workstyles, and work environments—and the ability to choose among those options according to the needs of their jobs, and their own tastes.

- *Opportunity.* Provided so that employees can propel the company forward, opportunity is necessary for employees to satisfy their need for growth. It should be available according to each employee's skills; customized development must fit each employee's goals within the company.

- *Engagement.* When meaning, choice, and opportunity combine to give employees the feeling that they, too, are owners of the company, employees will be engaged. They will feel that they have the power to make meaningful changes and also bear the responsibilities of ownership, both on the job and in the community.

- *Leadership.* Leadership makes meaning, choice, opportunity, and engagement possible; makes employees feel trusted and encouraged; and makes them eager to do their jobs well and to support those from whom they have received trust and encouragement.

Working from these basic principles, the team then came up with specific programs for HR, IT, and CRE to be implemented over the three-year period from 2005 to 2007.

Human Resources

- *Inclusiveness.* Develop I & D (inclusiveness and diversity) initiatives.

- *Work anyplace, anytime, anywhere.* Research distance employment and employee direct access.

- *Learning.* Install e-learning library; identify learning environment strategy; implement mentoring capability; implement design series WTLS (work team leader series) ; pilot end-to-end learning experiences for sales and leadership; implement core/elective leadership development (LD) offering for new and existing leaders.

- *Talent attraction.* Implement talent acquisition/management strategy; refine Recruitmax; pilot internal internships; align HMI employment brand; study aging workforce/talent management needs.

- *Community.* Coordinate community initiatives; promote HMI vision/mission/strategy.

Information Technology

■ *Worker effectiveness.* Use latest commercial tools/systems to reduce mundane tasks; refresh hardware to minimize down time; add system access points (kiosks, PCs, etc.).

■ *Work anyplace, anytime, anywhere.* Implement wireless network connection to promote freedom of movement; design applications with mobile considerations.

■ *Learning.* Provide on-demand personalized learning opportunities.

■ *Engagement.* Create portal to corporate measurements an owner expects.

Real Estate

■ *Inclusiveness.* Define work styles.

■ *Wellness.* Define Wellness Center guidelines; provide healthier food options for café and vending machines.

■ *Worker effectiveness.* Define work styles and space types; replace substandard size/quality workstations; provide one-point electronic learning entry for all development offerings.

■ *Work anyplace, anytime, anywhere.* Redefine telework program (home and in facility).

■ *Learning.* Provide career centers; training centers.

■ *Engagement.* Define and roll out housekeeping etiquette.

■ *Services.* Provide building concierge; café's, break areas.

■ *Community.* Provide community spaces to promote communication, celebrate successes, award people.

This list, from 2005 in the timetable, is already something of a relic at Herman Miller. Many of those programs whose descriptions began with *develop* or *define* are now actively being implemented, and we will return to them later in this book.

Before moving on, however, we'd like to point out what any careful reader will already have noticed—many of the programs making up the employee experience (i.e., work anyplace, worker effectiveness, learning, etc.) involve, once again, all three of our trio of HR, IT, and CRE functions. Of special interest are the requirements being placed on managers of human resources. Not only are there fewer people to choose from, and with more questionable competencies, but now there are also multiple generations to manage, each with a different set of expectations, a different psychology, and different motivators. This factor is going to bear heavily on corporate leadership's efforts to manage everyone, everywhere, anytime.

In short, it comes down to this: If you can manage to find qualified employees, and then succeed in hiring them, you'll find the emergent worker is less interested in jobs that lie at the end of a long commute, jobs that must be performed in dark, creativity-stifling, warehouselike spaces, or jobs that do not offer flexibility, meaning, and opportunity. Therefore, as the relative supply of creative labor shrinks, the pressure to achieve agility by tolerating differing workstyles, by redesigning and relocating the workplace, and by instituting alternative work programs will grow. We will return to this issue in Chapter 7, but for now let's continue to the last of the three major challenges—institutionalizing innovation.

CHAPTER 5

Innovation and Survival

Institutionalizing innovation is the last of the three major challenges facing businesses in the twenty-first century. Although innovation cannot be quantified as easily as reducing costs or attracting and retaining human talent, its absence is notable in businesses that fail to keep pace with industry leaders. To innovate means to make new, and most companies that fail, fail not only to develop new products and services, but also to develop new processes to promote agility.

What was missing from U.S. automakers' business plans, if not innovation? While Japanese, Korean, and European car makers saw that market forces favored smaller, more fuel-efficient vehicles, General Motors, Ford, and Chrysler continued to manufacture automobiles whose fuel ratings came ever closer to being measured in gallons per mile.

Russ Eckel, founder of Nommos Consulting, and an individual *Future of Work* member, put the question this way in his July 2006 article in *Future of Work Agenda*: "Who Let Detroit Burn?"

> On January 23 of 2006, William Ford, CEO of Ford Motor Company,
> held a nationally televised press conference announcing yet another round

of plant closings and layoffs totaling nearly 30,000 jobs. Few people in or out of the auto industry believe that these jobs will ever return. Despite some innovative work done fifteen years ago at a Ford Engine Plant in Cleveland—work that should have sparked a renaissance of the U.S. auto industry—Motown has failed to learn some key lessons.

In 1980 I began working as a consultant/trainer supporting an industry-led initiative to activate a newly formed fire brigade of union leaders and managers interested in collaborating to fight the complex and highly combustible mixture of rising energy prices, rising imports, and recession. Our work began at Cleveland Engine Plant No. 2, and was refreshing because the union and the company successfully worked together to create their own lean manufacturing model, the Cleveland Production System. The Cleveland plant was in danger of closing, but union leadership had the idea that it could work with management to create something new. Together, they went to Michigan to ask Ford to assign them the manufacture of the Duratec engine—already assigned to a plant in Europe. The executives in Dearborn, impressed by their zeal, agreed.

The Cleveland Production System, the most comprehensive example of lean manufacturing in the U.S. auto industry at that time, was the product of the efforts of hundreds of UAW members, Ford managers, and engineers, supported by a cadre of outside consultants. The system has a highly developed structure of self-managed teams, just-in-time production, and visual factory, and one of the most extensive employee development and training programs in the U.S. auto industry. It took more than two years to create the system, but the results more than justified the tremendous investment of both human and physical capital. The Duratec engine has been consistently rated one of the best engines in the world.

Why is this story not the story of the Ford Motor Company as a whole? If so much was learned about world-class manufacturing nearly thirty years ago, why is Detroit burning today?

Eckel blames leadership for failing to support innovation, and for continuing to consider manufacturing the poor stepchild of the business. His analysis doesn't spare union leadership, either:

> Not since the 1920s had any of these companies really competed on the basis of manufacturing excellence. The U.S. auto industry as a whole

completely misunderstood the competitive threat posed by Toyota and the other Japanese manufacturers in the 1970s and 1980s—manufacturers who understood that the customer is king.

The failure of leadership also extends to the United Auto Workers. Scores of local and international UAW leaders rose to prominence by opposing innovations like manufacturing teamwork, which they labeled *management by stress*. At the highest levels of the union, a decision was made to take a laissez-faire attitude toward local innovations in manufacturing practices.

Institutionalizing innovation, however, means changing more than the minds of management or union leadership. It is rooted, we believe, in the relationship between innovation and other factors:

- Technology
- Company culture
- The workplace of the future
- The workforce of the future

The lines between these areas of inquiry, just like those between HR, IT, and CRE, are no longer drawn as clearly as they once were, and in discussing them individually, we'll once again see their tendency to overlap, and the importance therefore of a companywide strategic approach to institutionalizing innovation.

TECHNOLOGY AND INNOVATION

The most telling case study of technological innovation in the *Future of Work* community came—not surprisingly—from IBM. The story of IBM's On Demand Workplace is all the more powerful today given the following postmortem, printed fifteen years ago in the *New York Times*. It is now hard to believe that the article referred to a company that is once again synonymous with the leading edge of business technology:

> The IBM Era is over . . . what was once one of the world's more
> vaunted high-tech companies has been reduced to the role of a follower,
> frequently responding slowly and ineffectively to the major technological
> forces reshaping the industry.

The *New York Times* was not alone in that assessment. *Fortune* magazine ran an article lumping IBM together with Sears Roebuck and General Motors as the dinosaurs of the Information Age. (Sears, though still in business, has since been swallowed by Kmart, formerly one of its fiercest rivals, while General Motors has become the national poster child for hidebound business giants on the verge of collapse.) What kept IBM from toppling over the edge?

According to the company itself, the decision to undertake a major financial, competitive, and cultural transformation focused on the simplification and integration of global processes necessary to first stabilize the company, and then prepare it for the future. Company leadership accurately foresaw that the success of a cultural and technological revolution of this magnitude depended on the creation of a single, centralized mechanism for communicating key strategies and messages, through which employees around the world could more quickly and efficiently access the company's staggering array of assets. The result—IBM's On Demand Workplace (ODW).

The intent was to build a collaborative, personalized online workplace that delivered relevant content and tools to employees no matter where or when they were working. To do so, the program had to link thousands of previously disparate resources into a single portal, through which employees could access the information and services necessary to do their jobs.

The central feature of the new program was the development of a core intranet site—which quickly became known as *W3*—that served as the company's voice of authority and its central repository of information. Although such an approach seems obvious in retrospect, the dot-com boom did not necessarily lead to centralization. In fact, in IBM's case the technological opportunity for individual or departmental infrastructure had resulted in a proliferation of company voices. At the time the On Demand Workplace was designed, there were more than 8,000 distinct company intranets, 29 million Web pages, and 5,600 domain names. Technological innovation had effectively isolated the company from itself.

"IBM has been a leader in pushing the capabilities of corporate intranets for almost ten years now," says David Yaun, vice president, corporate communications. "But we wanted a way to connect employees with customized information and resources quickly, based on their individual job roles, interests, and projects—and specific needs that shift dramatically over the course of the day."

With more than 320,000 employees, and tens of thousands of customers, the company had to produce a program capable of coordinating a nearly incalculable variety of jobs, products, services, and customers, and what's more, had to be integrated globally. The ODW's primary goals were as follows:

■   Cost savings

■   Employee satisfaction

■   Operational efficiency

■   Alignment of IT investments

Some cost savings were linked to specific ODW programs—that is, eLearning, Standard Software Installer, Asset Management Tool, Global Web Architecture, eCollaboration, Web conferencing, surveys, online travel services, and corporate communications—while others were enabled by the ODW—such as real estate savings made possible through a more mobile workforce, procurement and human resource savings achieved through online employee self-service, and greatly improved customer relationship management as a result of the ODW's many collaborative features.

By 2003, the ODW programs had reduced IBM's annual costs by $683 million. Of that figure, the company's On Demand eLearning program was alone responsible for annual savings of $284 million. By 2003, more than 60 percent of the company's employees had participated in online learning, and nearly 50 percent had received online training. The savings equation here is not hard to write; add the total cost of instructors, instructional materials, the space needed for classrooms, and student time and travel to those classrooms; then subtract the costs of building the online school.

Your online teachers, of course, will never have a sick day, nor will they ever retire with inflation-adjusted pensions and health care. Janitors will never stack chairs and mop floors, and classroom light bulbs will never need to be replaced. Then consider the issue of scheduling; real-world classes require employees to gather in specific locations at specific times—most often during working hours—and during mass instruction there is no way for individual students to speed through material they already understand, or to more carefully consider material they do not.

The IBM Standard Software Installer allows employees anytime, anywhere access to the software they need to do their jobs, using centralized servers and staff for software distribution. Here, too, the savings are easy to calculate. In 2003 alone, employees installed approximately 6 million software programs online, without using disks or printed manuals.

The Virtual Help Desk, although responsible for a comparatively small $6 million in savings a year, demonstrates the savings power of the On Demand Workplace for frequently repeated administrative requests. Although only 30 percent of help requests could be satisfied online—a number that is certain to rise as the system is refined—the cost breakdowns show a huge potential for long-term savings. Before, desk-side support cost the company $80 per incident, and agent calls cost the company $15. For those able to help themselves online, the cost is only $3.

IBM's Asset Management Tool, or e-AMT, allows employees to manage assets via the Web—again, from anywhere, at anytime—and allows the company to track and control inventory electronically. The result: a 90 percent reduction in costs for inventory administration, to say nothing of greater operational efficiency. The company's Global Web Architecture, or GWA, offers standards and guidelines for W3, Web architecture and infrastructure, Web hosting and processes. It reduced hosting fees by 60 percent, deployment time by 77 percent, and deployment costs by 68 percent. The On-Line Expense System now processes approximately 2 million forms per year, with the cost per form reduced from $15 to $2. Those savings aside—which total $26 million annually—the system allowed the company to reduce its support staff for expense report management by 82 percent. The company's eCollaboration program is used to arrange more than 10,000 Web conferences a month, totaling more than 141,000 person hours, and averaging nearly seven attendees per conference. As well, the program's online surveys have greatly increased response rates, and reduced administrative and analysis costs. On-line Travel in North America is now used to book 32 percent of all tickets, saving the company $1 million per month, and further savings are forecast with the deployment of Online Travel in Europe and Australia. The system also promotes compliance with company travel regulations, and results in lower fares. Finally, using the On Demand Workplace, the company's department of corporate communications was able to consolidate media tracking, increase analytics, and lower the costs of communicating with both employees and customers.

In addition to these direct savings, the On Demand Workplace enables additional annual savings of $1.3 billion. By allowing its employees to work anywhere, anytime, the On Demand Workplace produces annual real estate savings of more than $450 million. In addition, the company estimates that by enabling mobile work, its employees avoid 29 million hours of commuting time each year. In fact, cost savings and employee time savings are closely linked, and whenever the ODW reduces commutes, or the time it takes to find someone, to download an application, or to order office supplies, both the employee and the company profit.

IBM's Buy on Demand services, through volume discounts and centralization, yield savings of $450 million per year. Employees can view company catalogs online and order everything from furniture, to business cards, to hardware, software, office supplies, and services without ever leaving their desks—or in the case of the mobile workforce, without even coming to the office. They can also schedule maintenance and request repair services online, once again increasing operational efficiency while reducing costs.

Using HR employee self-service, 88 percent of employees now enroll online for benefits, and employee satisfaction with the program is greater than 90 percent. As well, the system has allowed the company to save nearly $250 million through HR staffing reductions, reducing the ratio of HR staff to employees from 1 to 59, to 1 to 113. Online customer relationship management (CRM) enabled by W3 is estimated to save the company $164 million through increased employee effectiveness and productivity, and a corresponding reduction in sales administration costs.

As it has improved cost savings and operational efficiency the ODW has greatly improved employee satisfaction, helping to make IBM an employer of choice, and providing yet one more example of the way in which the solution to one business challenge can assist in the solution of another. By supporting a wide variety of workstyles, the ODW offers employees the means to balance work and life according to individual tastes and needs, while its innovative eLearning programs offer an array of opportunities for personal growth and company advancement.

The ODW has also resulted in increased employee satisfaction by providing a reliable source of information about the company's assets, strategies, rules, and goals. In addition, its *Blue Pages* feature increases collaboration by offering an easy-to-use company directory to search for specific individuals, or for all employees with a certain skill set or type of experience.

Finally, the ODW makes it possible to quickly align the company's continuing IT investments with both its global processes and its internal opportunities. When, for example, IBM acquired PWC Consulting, W3 access and company e-mail was immediately made available to all its new employees, as was online access to health, pension, and savings applications. But the most telling sign of the program's success? Every day, nearly 80 percent of IBM employees access the On Demand Workplace.

We think there's a much deeper and more profound innovation buried within the On Demand Workplace that not even IBM's senior executives might have fully grasped. By creating the On Demand Workplace, IBM has essentially told its employees that they are in charge. IBM, like every global organization, essentially depends on its thousands of widely dispersed employees to take initiative, to make the *right* decisions, and to make things happen on their own, every hour of every day.

The On Demand Workplace is a perfect manifestation of the concept of an employee-centric work environment. No more command and control, no more us telling you what to do. Senior management's role at IBM has become one of setting direction, articulating goals, and then provisioning employees with the resources needed to get the job done.

And that is a management innovation second to none. It enables IBM employees to respond immediately and intelligently to challenges and opportunities all over the globe, as they occur, without having to move suggestions up the chain of command, and then wait for approval to come down. IBM has put decision making and information resources where they belong—in the hands of its front-line workers.

COMPANY CULTURE AND INNOVATION

In the previous chapter, we wrote of Herman Miller's legacy of concern for its workforce, and its commitment to remaining an employer of choice through its intentional employee experience. The company's history of innovation, however, is equally compelling, and just like the story of its labor relations, can be traced back to the company's beginnings.

Founded as a manufacturer of high-quality, traditional, residential furniture, the company made its first foray into uncharted business territory only four years after D.J. DePree took control of the company that he had rechristened with his father-in-law's name. In 1927, DePree founded the Herman Miller Clock Company and began to manufacture traditionally designed clocks as a complement to the company's furniture. Two years later, the stock market crashed.

Struggling to find a way to keep his factory's doors open during the Depression, DePree met with Gilbert Rohde, a designer from New York. Rohde offered simple advice: Throw out the catalog of intricately carved period furniture and begin manufacturing furniture based on the needs and tastes of modern, middle-class Americans. Three years later, employing Rohde's designs, the company presented its first line of modern residential furniture. (Herman Miller's decision to outsource its furniture design, a practice it has continued to the present day, was an early, innovative example of the variable-cost labor force we discussed in Chapters 3 and 4.)

The strategy paid off almost immediately—by the 1940s the company was an acknowledged leader in modern residential furniture design and manufacture, with showrooms in Chicago and Los Angeles, and manufacturing facilities in Michigan. Not content, however, to remain in its residential niche, in 1942 the company entered the office-furniture market with Rohde's Executive Office Group, a modular system that clearly pointed the company toward its systems furniture of the future. That path, however, came to a premature end with Rohde's death in 1944. Once again DePree had to chart a new course.

The five years that followed made the company's first two decades appear tranquil by comparison. As the Second World War came to an end, DePree hired George Nelson as the company's first design director after seeing photographs of his Storagewall design in *Life* magazine. Within a year, Nelson brought Charles and Ray Eames to Herman Miller. Their molded plywood and tubular steel designs, evolved from earlier work by Marcel Breuer, Ludwig Mies Van der Rohe, Le Corbusier, and Alvar Aalto, vaulted Herman Miller to the forefront of international furniture design. Nelson, however, was just warming up.

In 1948, Herman Miller published a bound, hardcover product catalog—written and designed by Nelson—that expressed both the company's business principles and its design aesthetic, and then took the extraordinary step of offering the catalog for sale, rather than simply giving it to prospective customers. Nor did Nelson limit the company's furniture to the Eameses' designs; later that same year, Herman Miller introduced Isamu Noguchi's now iconic glass-topped coffee table.

Today, knowing the company, its products, and designers as well as we do, it seems as if Herman Miller's future was in some way foreordained. Nothing could be further from the truth. DePree took a traditional furniture manufacturer—one of thousands just like it—and not only succeeded in shepherding it through the Great Depression and World War II, but—by dint of constant, unrelenting innovation—made it both an international trend setter in design and a world leader in manufacturing. As the troops came home and the United States retooled its war machine for domestic economic growth, DePree was poised for yet another round of rapid growth and innovation.

Like a drum roll of innovation, the company introduced the world's first molded fiberglass chairs (designed by Charles and Ray Eames), produced the Eames elliptical table, launched Nelson's bubble lamps, coconut chairs, and pedestal tables, introduced the Eameses' Hang-It-All, their compact sofa, and their stacking/ganging chairs, and began its association with noted colorist and textile designer Alexander Girard (who would lead the newly formed Herman Miller Textile Division). As if those innovations were insufficient, they were followed by the now world-famous Eames lounge chair and ottoman, introduced on *The Home Show*, Nelson's marshmallow sofa, the Eameses' aluminum group chairs, and Nelson's Comprehensive Storage System, which used vertical storage space to minimize the system's intrusion on the floor plan.

As we noted earlier, Herman Miller was also one of the first companies in the nation to adopt a Scanlon Plan, or *gainsharing* program, to engage its workforce by rewarding gains in productivity, and to reaffirm the company's belief in and respect for its employees. Finally, in 1958, the company brought Robert Propst aboard as part of Herman Miller's research team. Within a few short years, he, along with George Nelson, would forever change the face of the modern office interior.

Innovation, even more than its landmark designs, had become Herman Miller's signature, and the company's pace did not slow in the 1960s. In addition to another rapid-fire round of design innovations, the company's organizational structure underwent a series of fundamental changes. To begin, the Herman Miller Furniture Company incorporated, becoming Herman Miller, Inc., or HMI. The Herman Miller Research Division, soon to become the Herman Miller Research Corporation, opened in Ann Arbor, Michigan, as a wholly owned subsidiary. Its first president? Inventor and teacher Robert Propst. Finally, in 1962, after nearly forty years of leadership, D.J. DePree handed the company reins to his son, Hugh DePree.

In the midst of the company's continuing barrage of design innovations—including the Eames walnut stools, Nelson's sling sofa, and the Panton chair, a single-form, 100 percent plastic chair—Propst and Nelson began work on the Action Office 1, a group of freestanding units that four years later would evolve into the Action Office System, the world's first open-plan, modular system of panels and attached components. As we will note in Chapter 7, more than any design innovation that preceded it, the Action Office changed not just office interiors, but also the lives of those who worked in them.

Although Herman Miller's design innovations have continued to the present day—most notably in the field of ergonomics, which led to the Equa, Ergon, Mirra, Ambi, and Aeron chairs—from the 1970s forward the company began to make organizational changes that were in some ways even more innovative than its furniture.

One of the first efforts of this sort was the Facility Management Institute (FMI), which opened in 1979 in Ann Arbor, Michigan. Born of the understanding that as office buildings grew in size and number, responsibilities had become fragmented between architects, designers, human resources personnel, and maintenance staff, the FMI was an attempt to foster both a new and necessary discipline, as well as the creation of a new job, the facilities manager. This innovation was partly the result of the company's belief that its products were not being fully utilized in the field, and its understanding that office buildings were complex communities that needed to be governed, just as cities were.

By the 1980s the FMI had reached its initial goals—including the establishment of a professional association, the International Facilities Management Association—and Herman Miller's leadership understood that in order for the organization to grow, and for the facilities management profession to be recognized in its own right, it was time for the company to step back. Therefore, in 1985 the FMI in Ann Arbor was closed, and the IFMA was moved to Dallas, Texas. During this period the company also instituted a new stock-ownership plan to ensure that every Herman Miller employee was also a stock owner.

During the 1980s, Herman Miller also continued its efforts to create an ecologically sustainable business model, burning waste to generate power—both electrical and steam—for its million-square-foot main site manufacturing facilities. This initiative was followed in 1989 by the creation of the

Environmental Quality Action Team (EQAT) to coordinate environmental programs across all of the company's facilities. In 1991, the company launched its Supplier Diversity Program to increase opportunities for minority-owned and women-owned businesses. In 1993, the company began to use sustainable sources of native woods—mostly cherry and walnut—in place of the rapidly dwindling global stocks of rosewood, which had been used for its Eames lounge chair and ottoman. Finally, in the same year, HMI became a founding member of the U.S. Green Building Council, the only office furniture manufacturer on the association's initial roster.

INNOVATION AND THE WORKPLACE

Having described the way innovation has been institutionalized in two companies from radically different industries, we will now turn to the means by which all companies can encourage innovation—through the configuration of their workplace and the management of their workforce. In discussing this topic we cannot help but once again turn to Herman Miller for some of the most important contributions to this field.

HMI's first president of research, Robert Propst, was an early pioneer in the study of how the workplace affects creativity and productivity. The title alone of his 1968 publication, *The Office—A Facility Based on Change*, demonstrates that nearly three decades ago Propst had begun to consider many of the issues that still bedevil businesses today. It can perhaps be said that Propst, an artist by training, considered office space as a type of performance art, where human movement, creativity, and productivity all left their brushstrokes on the canvas.

Taking the position that radical, rapid change was a constant in the modern business world, and that like all organic beings businesses must grow or die, Propst recognized that interior design had the power both to constrain creative work and to encourage it. Influenced by the work of MIT Social Psychologist Douglas McGregor, Propst wrote of the emerging contrast in management modes between old line or reductive and new or developmental concepts. McGregor had labeled these two approaches Theory X and Theory Y, where, in Propst's words:

> Theory X considers management as a process of ordering and forbid-
> ding as a means to ensure performance. It says that people, in general, avoid

responsibility and therefore must be directed and told. In essence, the bosses set the objectives, exercise control. Ultimate knowledge lies at the top. Independence is discouraged and mistakes call for penalties.

The Developmental Theory Y assumes that it is natural for people to seek responsibility and that they enjoy it. Performers at any level need challenge and encouragement to gain top performance. Unique knowledge and skill lies at all levels in a healthy organization. The individual can participate in goal setting and will thus behave like a manager at any level.[1]

Continuing his studies, Propst took into account the human mind and its ability to process information, the power of visual recall, the effect of order—and disorder—on creative work, the multiple responsibilities of the modern office worker, the nature and structure of conversation, and the relationship between health and vitality. Of the modern office environment he wrote:

> The lack of even mild postural variation in offices accentuates the problem of maintaining reasonable body tone. We work long hours in a condition of physical imbalance and suffer continuous attrition.
>
> Man's physical machine has evolved to do many things well but no single thing continuously. In office facilities, a false assessment of comfort as a total maintenance concern coupled with a tendency to group all services around a single seated work station creates a direction that needs altering.[2]

Propst also considered the contradiction between the individual's need for privacy and the organization's need for involvement, office planning that treated human beings as elements of geometry, and the battle of communication devices for the office worker's attention. Taken together, these inquiries motivated Propst to design an office furniture system capable of continual change, tolerant of varying types of human movement, and one that served both management's need for order and the individual's right to be different. Again, the most difficult thing about reading Propst today is that you must constantly remind yourself that his observations were made almost forty years ago.

We will return to Robert Propst in Chapter 8, where we'll discuss the workplace of the future, but in the meantime we'd like to include one last entry in our history of innovators in the *Future of Work* Community—that of Johnson Controls.

Johnson Controls

Founded in 1883 by Warren S. Johnson, a professor at the State Normal School in Whitewater, Wisconsin, and the holder of the first patent for an electric room thermostat, the company quickly branched out into the manufacture, installation, and maintenance of temperature regulation systems for buildings. As the decades passed, and buildings grew larger and larger, the company proved itself an able innovator, staying ahead of its competitors by continually reexamining and responding to its customers' needs.

The company's Pneumatic Control Center is a good example. By the middle of the twentieth century buildings were occupied by multiple tenants—each of whom had their own needs and preferences for heating and cooling—and contained hundreds of thermostats, valves, dampers, and other temperature controls, all of them requiring daily maintenance. To address the problem, Johnson Controls created the Pneumatic Control Center, which enabled a single operator to operate all of a facility's temperature-control devices from one location.

As the computer age dawned, the company built the industry's first minicomputer—the JC80—dedicated to building temperature control. This was followed by the JC85, which through the use of digital technology made temperature control even faster and more precise. Today, in the company's words, its Metasys® Facilities Management System is reducing energy costs and improving indoor comfort in thousands of buildings around the world.

The company also pioneered open communications protocols, which allowed devices from various manufacturers to share data directly for the first time.

In addition to its core building controls business, over the years the company also became a leading supplier of temperature controls for automobiles. In the 1970s and the 1980s Johnson Controls further broadened its base by becoming a supplier of automobile interiors—seats, headliners, door panels, and so on—and finally, of automotive batteries. Today the company has more than 120,000 employees in more than 500 locations worldwide, with a customer base that includes BMW, SBC, GlaxoSmithKline, JCPenney, and consists of more than 7,000 school districts, more than 2,000 hospitals, and tens of thousands of commercial and governmental locations.

Comparisons with those companies now losing money in Detroit are hard to avoid, especially because innovation in the automobile industry, at least from the time of the Second World War, seems to have been about as welcome as Japanese cars in the UAW's parking lot. Market conditions were changing, as the oil embargo in 1973 well demonstrated, but no one saw it coming—that is, no one in America. More than thirty years later, after yet another decade of producing gas-guzzling vehicles, Detroit finally seems to have gotten the message, but it may be too late. What has Johnson Controls been doing in the meantime? Innovating, by branching out into battery manufacturing for electric cars.

We've already discussed Johnson Control's commitment to sustainability in Chapter 3, but we'd like to include a few more examples that we find near the intersection of innovation and environmental responsibility. First on that list is Johnson Control's latest version of its Solutions Navigator planning tool, the Sustainability Navigator.

The Sustainability Navigator is a game board–inspired planning tool that offers cross-functional teams a structured, interactive process for quickly assessing sustainability-related needs, as well as for developing best practices. The tool can be used to design and construct a green building, to improve the efficiency of an entire portfolio of facilities, or even to develop an enterprisewide sustainability strategic plan. "The Navigator provides an interactive approach to sustainability strategic planning for an entire organization," said Clay Nesler, Johnson Controls Innovation Services vice president.

What we really like is the process, because it's the process of this innovation, just like IBM's eLearning, that makes the Sustainability Navigator a tool for Collaborative Strategic Management. Think about it. It allows all key stakeholders—HR, CRE, and IT—to quickly assess and prioritize common organizational needs, and most importantly, to develop specific means for improvement. The Sustainability Navigator is just one of a series of Johnson Controls tools developed to support strategic planning for a variety of specific corporate functions, including facilities management and design, security, healthcare technology, manufacturing, and now sustainability.

But once again, what really appeals to us is that it facilitates collaborative management. The Sustainability Navigator tool itself is interactive IT in action, supporting on-the-job training (HR), and saving facilities costs (CRE), and all that while building consensus and accountability within the individual teams and across the organization as a whole.

What are the advantages of the sort of institutionalized innovation epitomized by Johnson Control's history of experimentation and diversification, of its culture of leading its industry rather than following its competitors, and of its early and prescient support of sustainability? How about a history of unbroken growth over the past century, to say nothing of consistent financial performance—Johnson Controls has been paying dividends year after year, all the way back to 1887.

UNDER CONSTRUCTION

The Work Design Collaborative's most recent work on the intersection of innovation and the workplace, a joint study with the Interactive Institute in Stockholm, Sweden, was christened *under construction* to remind its readers that the workplace is never truly finished. This fact, far from frustrating facilities managers and workers, should help in the creation of a more realistic concept of the workplace as a system that can and should change in response to the constantly shifting business environment around it. After all, if the nature of work is constantly changing, and if the style of every worker is not only different but variable, then how can the space in which that work is performed remain static? What's more, how can the company and its workforce achieve agility if the workplace is frozen in place?

To begin, we asked ourselves one simple question: Why do we go to work? We can all agree, it seems, on one answer—we go to work to be paid—even though we ask for a wide variety of payment—that is, money, prestige, or even the simple satisfaction of creating something from nothing. We go to work to be compensated, therefore, but also to fulfill our personal goals, and to seek advancement, whether personal or professional.

We also often go to work for social interaction, or work at home to avoid it. This line, too, has begun to blur in an age where one can easily communicate with one's colleagues using a variety of tools, including videoconferencing that allows you to study the face as well as hear the voice of the person with whom you're speaking.

For our study, we brought together two carefully selected networks of professionals for in-depth conversation and exploration—one based in San Francisco, in the United States, and the other in Stockholm, in Sweden. Each consisted of five to eight persons from differing professions, and each met in both in real and virtual space. To start the discussions we authored three papers intended both to provoke and focus thought:

1. *Workspace Design and Organizational Creativity*

2. *Nine Challenges to Creativity at Work*

3. *Information Technology and Media at Work*

Having established the basic structure of our intercontinental work-groups, and having framed our inquiries with the general topics listed, we then asked each group to explore the following issues:

- What piece of technology at your office do you like the most?

- Where in your office do you feel the most creative?

- Take a photo of an area in your office that was designed or intended for one purpose but used for another.

- List any literature about office design, creativity, and technology that you want to recommend.

- What is our tolerance for novel approaches, designs, and ways of working to achieve creativity?

The answers to the first question, not surprisingly, varied depending on each individual's personal tastes and preferred styles of work. Therefore, some said flexible furniture, while others favored specific personal computers, headsets, wireless Internet capabilities, or even pens. All, however, agreed that technology has forever changed the way we work, and expanded the potential for creative work.

Overall, technological advances have resulted not only in the reduction of space necessary to work—a laptop, after all, requires but a fraction of the space of a mainframe computer—but have also blurred the lines between home and the office. Fifteen years ago it would have been impossible to access your files, contact numbers, and so on, when at home. Now one's ability to access information is almost without physical limits. When the business community, however, crosses international lines and time zones, as ours did, the following conditions become critical:

- Seamless, reliable service across both small and large distances

- A balance between customization and the standardization necessary to support communication

Not surprisingly, no two persons had exactly the same feelings about where they were able to do their most creative work. (Actually, this is only partially true. The most common answer was that creativity emerged most often in nature, while at the same time it was generally acknowledged that such situations are rarely available to most workers.) All agreed, however, that creative spaces do not just happen—they are a product of a conscious and continuous design process that has a beginning, but no end.

This was demonstrated in the frequency with which spaces designed for one purpose were used for another. All participants reported that the creative, collaborative experience often occurred in spaces too small for the occasion. The energy created, however, by people gathering together, somehow made the space superfluous.

This, in turn, was yet another proof that successful, creative space could not be made so much as assembled, and that different groups of individuals had to be free to assemble, disassemble, reassemble, and reconfigure their workspace as the moment required.

INNOVATION AND THE WORKFORCE

The intertwined relationships between innovation and technology, company culture, the workplace, and the workforce often seem impossible to separate. Company culture, for instance, clearly affects the workforce's attitude. Len Pilon, of Herman Miller, noted that the café placed in the center of one floor in their Herman Miller MarketPlace facility remained largely unused until he was able to convince senior management to stop there for a cup of coffee and a little informal conversation. Once the other employees saw that their bosses considered it okay to take a moment's break for a cup of coffee, they too began to use the facility. In that way, one more opportunity for casual collaboration was created, while the open floor design made it impossible to disguise overuse.

The early days at H-P were somewhat similar. During World War II, with Bill Hewlett overseas, Dave Packard's leadership style, dubbed *management by walking around*, was instrumental in forming the open corporate culture that made innovation a central feature of the company.

What did the workforce learn? That personal involvement and listening skills were valued behaviors, and that management was not patrolling the floors in order to be certain that everyone was hunched over their desks, but out of the honest desire to exchange ideas. What's more, by engaging their employees, and using their first names, they let everyone know that they trusted them to meet their objectives, and weren't concerned about getting identical efforts from every minute the employees were on the job. This, in turn, led to a design style that encouraged openness, so that such movement and communication could freely occur.

PLANTING THE SEEDS OF INNOVATION

What is a chair? It is one of the great philosophical questions of the ages. The most common answer is something you sit on, but this is true of a couch, and a couch is not a chair. Neither does something you sit on with four legs answer the question, as Herman Miller's innovative designs over the years have shown. It cannot be defined as something with legs, a seat, and a back, because history has shown us that giant bean bags can be considered chairs, as can inflatable plastic envelopes. Nonetheless, we all know a chair when we see one.

Creative space, it seems, is equally recognizable. Walk into a dim, hushed, compartmentalized space, and you feel creativity in retreat. Walk into an open, busy, naturally lighted interior, and you feel your energy level rise, and you get the sense that you are once again in a community. Sometimes, it seems that all that's necessary is that first look, and then the way is clear.

For Jones Lang LaSalle, that's just what happened in the Aon Center. Of the six major groups that form the company, only the Strategic Consulting (SCON) team designed its new space to support a flexible, untethered workforce. As the other groups began to move into their new spaces, they couldn't help but compare them to what they saw in SCON's corner. The big change, though, came as they began to experience new needs for space, and found that they had to find a way to make do with what they had. When that happened, the seed that was SCON's workplace strategy began to grow on every floor in Chicago—and the talk now is of planting the idea across all of Jones Lang LaSalle's American locations.

That's the thing about innovation. In today's high-velocity, information economy, when an idea works the word spreads quickly. A great deal, in fact, had happened at Jones Lang LaSalle in the six months since the Workplace

Workshop Program had taken place. Before the restack in the Aon Center was complete, the Strategic Consulting team members were being asked to do the following:

- Provide an overview of Jones Lang LaSalle's pilot WS program
- Create greater awareness of WS tools and practices within the company
- Present the business case for WS changes across the Americas portfolio
- Obtain sponsorship for the next steps in the company's WS program

They were happy to comply. Since its inception in 2004, the group had successfully introduced WS programs for a wide range of clients—including BearingPoint and Motorola, in addition to those we've already named—and in a number of geographic regions. It didn't hurt that continuing data confirmed that the company's own workforce was becoming more mobile—in fact, the typical Jones Lang LaSalle employee is now away from his or her desk for more than 50 percent of the day. The IT infrastructure was in place as well, including Blackberry, wireless Internet, login phones, follow-me phones, wireless headsets, and wireless Internet cards. But more important than all of these, the pilot program had demonstrated that there was money to be saved—a lot of money. The old layout provided space for 90 desks per floor, while the WS pilot, rolled out across an entire floor, would result in an additional 60 desks, or workstations, for a total of 150. What's more, by increasing hoteling and teleworking programs, and by having teleworkers use shared desks when they came to the office, even greater densities could be achieved, and even greater savings realized.

Additional savings could be found in the company's offices across America. With 3,800 employees in the region, converting even 15 percent of the workforce to a joint hoteling and telecommuting program would allow the company to reduce its CRE footprint by more than 85,000 square feet— for an annual savings of $2,565,000. And better still, additional headcount growth could be absorbed through higher hoteling/teleworking participation rates, allowing Jones Lang LaSalle to grow, but without growing its real estate costs. That's corporate agility.

CHAPTER 6

The Virtual Workforce

THE HISTORY OF WORK

Having reviewed some of the means by which members of the *Future of Work* community are reducing their fixed operating costs, confronting the coming human talent gap, and attempting to institutionalize innovation, we want to step back from strategic concerns for a moment, take a closer look at the workforce of the future, and discuss its impact on corporate agility.

To begin, we believe that taking a quick look at the economic history of the nineteenth and twentieth centuries will give us a better perspective on what lies ahead. The following passage, taken from Microsoft's Encarta Encyclopedia, presents an accurate historical background for the economic upheavals now being experienced around the world.

> Many factors fueled industrial growth in the late nineteenth century: abundant resources, new technology, cheap energy, fast transport, and the availability of capital and labor. Mines, forests, and livestock in the west provided raw materials for major industries, as did iron in Ohio and oil in Pennsylvania. Railroad expansion enabled businesses to move raw materials

to factories and to send products to urban markets. A steady stream of immigrants arrived to work in America's mines and factories.

Technological advances transformed production. The new machine-tool industry, which turned out drilling, cutting, and milling machines, sped up manufacturing. A trail of inventions, including the telephone, typewriter, linotype, phonograph, electric light, cash register, air brake, refrigerator car, and automobile, led to new industries. Finally, business leaders learned how to operate and coordinate many different economic activities across broad geographic areas. Businesses were thus able to become larger, and the modern corporation became an important form of business organization[1]

The point here is that innovation led not only to improved processes of production, but also to the development of the office system—that is, separate working environments for laborers and managers. This division persisted even when the labor in question began to wear white collars, and management was right down the hall, and it has important implications for the workforce of the future.

Individual *Future of Work* member Dave McCarty, of the Chicago Design Network, has studied the evolution of work in an attempt to understand corporate community building in the mobile workforce, and the role that workplace design will play in its development. Following the evolution of the concept of work from the farm to the factory, McCarty sees the traditional office environment as a natural consequence of the changes that preceded it.

Before the Industrial Revolution, everyone was a skills-based free agent. Farmers, artisans, and craftsmen all had multiple talents, and when they couldn't do a job themselves, they bartered their skills or traded excess production to get what they needed. While most had trades, there was no real distinction drawn between working and doing what one had to do to live.

That changed when machines entered the picture. Machines were able to greatly increase capacity, but machines needed human guidance to function. So a trade-off occurred: In order to aid machines in increasing output, craftsmen began to focus on single skill sets, and to buy the things they no longer had the time to make or grow themselves. Henry Ford was one of the first to fully understand this conceptual shift, incorporating the idea of man-as-machine into his assembly line. The startling increase in output achieved using this paradigm led to its adoption across all types of work, and soon stenographers, accountants, salespeople, researchers, and even managers became interchangeable parts in the corporate machine. Tasks were reduced to their simplest level, making them easy to define and monitor, and made workers as interchangeable as the machines they used.

In other words, the Industrial-Age corporation, with its emphasis on routines, formal lines of authority, and the elimination of variability, grew up during the Industrial Revolution, when everyone was fascinated with machines and their capacity for high-volume production. In a very real sense the industrial corporate model was inspired by, and modeled after, the machine.

Unfortunately, what got lost in that translation was an appreciation for human creativity and innovation. It was people, after all, who invented and designed the machines, but with rare exceptions, thereafter those same people came to be seen as machine-tenders, relegated to single-task activities that fed the assembly line.

In such a system, McCarty notes, the space allocated to workers followed standards established on factory floors, even when the work being done was creative or administrative. Under this system, space, natural light, and fresh air were apportioned according to need, and decisions on where and under what conditions the workforce was to work were not much different than those made regarding where machines were to be positioned on the factory floor. With the exception of a few forward-thinking leaders such as D. J. DePree of Herman Miller, the distinction between man and machine grew smaller and smaller—again, even for those workers whose jobs were not directly concerned with manufacturing.

This was not the fault of management alone. Collective labor quickly adapted the new model to its own ends, insisting that jobs be divided and codified, with rules and responsibilities written in stone. The end result was that men and women, just like machines being turned on and off, began to punch in and punch out, and thus *work* was formally, mechanically separated from *life*. Under this system, as McCarty notes, space, light, and air soon began to serve another purpose—the designation of status:

> This system finally changed once the global workforce developed the skills to operate industrial machinery, and European and American companies began to move their machines to parts of the world where labor was

less expensive. The strange thing is that at more or less the same time the migration of production occurred, the appearance of the personal computer began to free the office worker from the drudgery of mundane, repetitive tasks, opening the door to the sort of innovation and invention that characterized the beginning of the industrial revolution—before the man-as-machine paradigm took hold. So in the space of a very few years a large percentage of factory workers became as obsolete as old machine tools, and office workers became valued as free-thinking individuals again.

No longer identical pegs forced into the same holes, office workers began to adopt whatever workstyles were most productive for them, and that is where office design reentered the picture. All of a sudden people were working everywhere, and doing different kinds of work—that is, teamwork, multitasking, or deeply focused individual work—over the course of the day. In the man-as-machine model, you had to be "at work" to do your job, but in the 1980s work strayed back across long-established boundaries—something like studying does at college—and life and work became harder to separate again.

Good office design now not only has to take these various workstyles into consideration, it's also expected to be the visual representation of a company's corporate culture—that is, people walking off the elevator should immediately sense the company's respect for the individual, should see physical evidence of the company's support of various workstyles, and all together the company's focus on innovation and invention.

In this way, morale and, therefore, productivity are boosted because the physical space serves as a daily demonstration, to employees and customers alike, that management thinks the worker is more important than the facility—again, a complete reversal of the mindset that governed the Industrial Revolution. This shift in values leads to a number of functional changes. Information storage, much of it now able to be accessed electronically, has to surrender the prime office space it once enjoyed. At the same time, the expanded role of IT, within the workplace and outside it, has to be acknowledged and supported. But the designer's most important task involves a change in thinking that is, in a certain sense, a return to the days before the industrial revolution—the time of small communities. As McCarty puts it:

> Even though the focus is now on supporting the individual, the true
> job of both the designer and the manager is community building. With the

workforce spread far and wide, and turnover much higher than it used to be, the designer has to use new office space to create a sense of belonging. That occurs only when both public and private spaces are provided, so that when employees are in the office together they can benefit from the varied environments necessary for them to do their jobs. Quiet, high-focus zones have to exist for individual work, small group spaces have to be available for two- to six-person meetings, larger conference rooms should be provided for ten- to twenty-person meetings, but the really important thing is to leave as much space as possible for spontaneous, unregulated meetings between random members of the workforce, because it's in those kinds of situations that new ideas are born, and a sense of community is achieved.

This sort of community, of course, cannot be achieved solely on the basis of design. Management must lead in the creation and maintenance of such a culture, and IT must not only react to but also anticipate frequent changes in the distribution of the workforce. Sasha Lacey of Accenture sees the problem not so much in terms of budget, but of coordination between CRE and IT. Sound familiar?

>I think the issue at Accenture is alignment between the corporate real estate and CIO strategies. For example, the initial focus of Accenture's New Workplace was real estate cost savings. A part of those savings was then used to fund laptop deployment for all employees. Previously, analysts and consultants had had to rely on desktop computers, or whatever else the client provided. Now, we're happy to say, few employees of Accenture can even remember that haphazard program.

>Fast forward to today. Our CIO is now looking at a pilot program using Softphones (similar to Skype) and VoIP as just one small part of a Network Transition Project to provide and promote increased workforce flexibility and anytime/anywhere communication. Further into the future IT predicts that there will be a large percentage of PDA users that will no longer even require laptops; their tool of choice will be a palmtop computer. Security will be biometric, and accessibility will be ubiquitous.

To return to our earlier discussion, while the twentieth century produced the automobile, the airplane, the telephone, the typewriter, the light bulb, the television, the motion picture, and manned space flight, the twenty-first century has arrived with its own dizzying array of innovations and inventions. Personal computers, a vast variety of applications, vastly improved cellular communication, and the Internet have ushered in a new age of easily accessed information, and in so doing have made collaboration possible from virtually anywhere on the globe. And while the world's economy is still measured by the aggregate value of products, services, commodities, and property, nearly every factor in the equation of production and sales has changed.

In at least one respect, however—that is, the growing scarcity of natural resources—the economy of the twenty-first century closely parallels that which preceded it. Just as oil, timber, fish, and potable water first propelled the old economy, and were then exhausted by it, the primary natural resource in the new economy—human talent—is disappearing even as we write.

In studying the workforce of the future, we will once again encounter the traditional difficulty in separating it from the workplace of the future, so great is the effect of one on the other. In the past, labor was brought to the workplace, whether the factory floor or the office building, and inserted into an existing, unquestioned framework. Then, the work defined the workforce; now the situation is changing. The workforce of the future, by virtue of its skills, attitudes, ambitions, and scruples, is now in the process of recreating—or at the very least contributing to the alteration of—the workplace of the future.

Consider technology. Continuing advances in communications and data processing technologies have lowered many traditional barriers to employment—that is, proximity, health, availability, language, and appearance—and in so doing can be said to be one of the few forces in the modern business world actually leading to an expansion of the labor pool. Before the IT revolution—the last blast of which, of course, we have yet to hear—the ability to work was dependent upon proximity or mobility. In order to work, one either had to be where the work was, or be able to get to the work.

That has all changed now.

THE DISTRIBUTED WORKFORCE

We've been studying and writing about distributed work and its impact for years, and while there are many more remote and distributed workers today than there were even a few years ago, we continue to be puzzled by the slow adoption rate, especially when the business case is so strong, and there are so many well-documented economic benefits.

Therefore we're going to begin by discussing the sources of resistance to change, and follow that up with what we think has to be done to promote a style of work that is not only logical, but inevitable. By this we do not mean that distributed work is right for every company, or for all jobs—or, put another way, we don't believe it's right for all parts of a business, and it's not right for *any* corporation all the time. H-P is a good example. Even as H-P's mobile workforce program is picking up steam, its IT staff is being pulled back into a central location in an effort to refocus the group's efforts. Just the same, many IT engineers, while not part of the distributed workforce, are still considered mobile workers by H-P.

There are at least six solid reasons to establish distributed work programs, and each, in its own way, contributes to corporate agility:

1. Reducing basic workforce support costs

2. Increasing workforce productivity

3. Attracting and retaining talent

4. Reducing the business risk of disruption from terrorism or natural disasters, or defending business continuity

5. Reducing traffic congestion, air pollution, and more generally, the impact of business on the environment

6. Moving work to where the workforce wants to live

Let's consider each of these factors briefly. Our own research, as well as the experiences of nearly every corporate and individual member of the *Future of Work* community, confirms that alternative workplace programs can reduce annual workforce support costs by as much as 40 percent, with most of those savings coming from real estate and facilities management (i.e., real estate costs, facilities operations costs, energy costs, cleaning costs, etc.).

It's important to remember that in the cases of many organizations— H-P and Sun Microsystems come immediately to mind—it was not necessary to launch a formal program, since employees were already taking advantage of advances in IT to work at home, while traveling, or while on clients' sites. In those cases, the question was how to react to all the empty offices. The answer, more often than not, was to reduce the corporate real estate footprint, and reconfigure the retained space with shared workplaces, or touchdown facilities that different employees used over the course of the day, the week, or the month.

However, there are other, subtler workforce cost-saving opportunities that go well beyond real estate and facilities. In many additional areas— including IT, HR, administrative support, and basic supervisory management—distributed workers operate more independently and need less support than do their traditional, office-based counterparts. In order to survive in the field, distributed workers *have* to learn to work on their own, and to solve their support problems quickly and inexpensively.

That said, technology costs often increase as the workforce is distributed and makes greater use of laptops, cell phones, and PDAs; these additional investments in technology are small, however, relative to the real estate and facilities cost savings. Sun Microsystems actually reduced its distributed workforce's IT costs by utilizing its Sun Ray ultra-thin client, and its "The Network is the Computer" approach to IT support. Finally, remote telecommunications and Internet access costs, once quite expensive, have continued to decline as service has increased.

In the next chapter we'll discuss the measurement of the knowledge worker's productivity, in both traditional and alternative workplaces. Although productivity measurement is a difficult and complex subject, our own research and consulting work with individual organizations has convinced us that distributed workers are *more* productive than their office-bound colleagues. We have conducted numerous studies of the productivity differential at both the individual and the group level, and they have consistently shown productivity gains of approximately 15 percent for distributed workers.[2]

For those of you who work both in and out of the office, that is easy to believe. Just think of the time distributed workers save by avoiding a daily commute, to say nothing of the fatigue and stress that go along with it. How about having to sit through the typical, interminable, staff meetings, seemingly unrelated to any immediate objectives? How about the two-martini lunches with clients, and the numerous coffee breaks necessary to overcome the fatigue of the commute? Although it's true that the water-cooler effect aids spontaneous collaboration among peers, there is no denying the distractions, interruptions, and plain disturbances that come from one's neighbors in traditional office settings.

In fact, we've heard numerous stories of people sneaking out of their corporate offices to work at home, or in a local coffee shop, when they have a serious report to write or a complicated analysis to complete. Interestingly enough, some people report working much more productively in a public place, surrounded by strangers producing white noise, than in a familiar workspace where it's virtually impossible not to overhear conversations in the hallway or from the next cubicle over because they involve familiar topics and voices.

What's more, having tracked the time that distributed workers spend on the job, we find that on average they give back to the company more than 50 percent of the time they save by not commuting. Moreover, they typically achieve their agreed-upon results in fewer hours—and the work is usually of higher quality, too (as reported both by themselves and by their supervisors). Once again, in our minds the one unanswered question regarding distributed work is why all companies that can aren't encouraging it. Between cost savings and increased productivity, distributed work is a win-win for the company and the individual worker.

The distributed workforce's value where HR is concerned is equally unassailable. Our original research on evolving working styles—begun over five years ago—was driven by our conviction that knowledge workers today want, and will soon demand, more control over where and when they work. Distributed work—or getting things done from wherever they happen, or want, to be—gives them exactly that kind of control.

That those knowledge workers—the group Richard Florida has dubbed the Creative Class[3]—are in the driver's seat is no longer in doubt, given the severe workforce shortage that will occur over the next decade, driven largely by the impending retirement of millions of baby boomers and the decline in birth rates in the generations that followed them. Combine that human talent shortage with the increasing importance of knowledge and innovation to competitive advantage, and you've got a recipe for a sellers' market when it comes to labor.

The value of the distributed workforce in reducing business risk—or defending continuity—is pretty obvious, too. Although many do not know it, one of the primary design objectives of the first Internet was the creation of a redundant communications network with no mission-critical center, so that if some portion of the system was down due to hardware or software crashes, natural disasters, or military attack, the rest of the net would pick up the slack by rerouting messages and data. In much the same way, a distributed business model is far less susceptible to disruption, whether from technological failure, extreme weather, terrorism, an earthquake, or an old-fashioned power outage. With the workforce spread over a wide area, and not tethered to one central facility, or even geographical region, business continuity is assured in the face of pretty much everything but a cataclysmic event.

This is as true, if not more so, for the public sector as it is for the private. Since her arrival in 1998, *Future of Work* corporate member Gloria Young, clerk and chief legislative administrator of the city of San Francisco Board of Supervisors, has led a behind-the-scenes revolution in the way she manages her staff, and in the way her department operates. In a time when both private- and public-sector organizations are reawakening to the need to plan for business continuity, the city and county of San Francisco are well ahead of the game with a pilot project focused on telecommuting and distributed work for members of both the Board of Supervisors and its management staff.

Ms. Young established the pilot project in late 2004/early 2005, with significant support from Sun Microsystems and SBC Communications. The telecommuting project, however, could not proceed before the organization itself was put in order. In Ms. Young's words:

> You must first optimize your business processes and procedures before implementing a distributed work program. If your systems and procedures are messed up before you distribute the work, they'll be a disaster when they are spread out all over the area. And above all, focus on managing by outcomes and results, not activities.

In the case of the San Francisco Board of Supervisors, optimizing business processes and procedures was no small task. When Ms. Young first reported for work in 1998, she discovered that 30 percent of the staff that reported to her were due to retire by 2006. In addition, most of these potential retirees were single points of failure, meaning they had no backups, and that virtually no one else knew precisely what they did from day to day. There were no personal computers on their desks; IT awareness was almost zero. Neither was there any documentation of the work processes—things got done only because the workers had years of experience on the job, and did the assignments by rote. Thus, while able to do their jobs, they had virtually no big-picture understanding, and no ability to innovate, or even to respond to out-of-the-ordinary problems.

More important, the heightened awareness of vulnerability in San Francisco after the 9/11 attacks on New York and Washington, combined with the Bay Area's history of earthquakes, had finally sensitized City Hall to the need for disaster recovery plans and the critical importance of keeping the city going in the event of disaster.

One of the obvious consequences of this need was the necessity for the Board of Supervisors (BOS) to continue to operate in an emergency even if individual supervisors were unable to get to City Hall. The mayor can declare an emergency, but the board must approve any action shortly thereafter. By charter, the BOS could only pass that kind of motion when a quorum was physically present in the meeting chamber. The logic—at least of the day— was that the supervisors had to be able to *see* original copies of any documents they were reviewing and approving.

Of course more than the supervisors themselves are needed to keep San Francisco operating. In a city where only 45 percent of the workforce lives within the city limits, there was also the serious risk that in the event of a disaster key employees might be unable to reach their assigned work locations.

Again, in this particular case a reduction in the CRE footprint was not the goal. Rather, a telecommuting program designed to address deficiencies in continuity and disaster preparation provided the additional goal of allowing Ms. Young to increase the size of her staff without requesting additional office space. By the fall of 2005 the concept had already proven its viability, and she is now focused on seeing the program expanded across the organization.

Minimizing the environmental impact of business is but another obvious benefit of a distributed workforce. The arithmetic here is simple: If every company in a major metropolitan area encouraged—or better yet, required— its entire organization to work from home, or in a neighborhood satellite facility, just one day a week, its transportation-related energy consumption— whether gasoline for their automobiles, or electricity for mass transit—would drop by 20 percent. Just think what we could do for energy independence in the United States if we could shift to distributed work models, to say nothing of the environmental benefits.

H-P, for instance, estimates that its telework program—and the program is still expanding—saves approximately 2 million round trip commutes every year in the United States and Canada, eliminating approximately 57 million miles of automobile travel, and reducing greenhouse gas emissions by more than 24,000 tons.

Finally, given that human talent is about to become as hard to find as a balanced federal budget, and that the millennials are choosing where to *live* before worrying about where they'll *work*, a distributed workforce program allows companies to throw a much broader recruitment net. (See *In Our Humble Opinion: Reality Bites*, *Future of Work Agenda*, July 2006; *Attracting the Young, College-Educated to Cities*, CEOs for Cities, June 2006). It may be, therefore, that the only way to convince an ever-smaller group of potential hires to work for you is by hiring location-independent employees who have chosen to live in smaller communities far removed from your corporate facilities. As we've said over and over, it's a whole lot less expensive today to send the work to the worker than it is to require the worker to come to the work.

Together, the individual benefits of a distributed workforce—reducing basic workforce support costs, increasing workforce productivity, attracting and retaining talent, reducing the business risk of disruption from terrorism or natural disasters, reducing the negative impact of business on the environment, and moving work to the workforce—combine to create a far more agile corporation. To begin, your fixed costs of real estate and facilities are greatly reduced, freeing up assets that can be put to work where your company needs them most. Your business can also grow or shrink more rapidly, and with far less expense, than it could when finding or disposing of office space constrained your real estate options.

With a distributed workforce your company is also far more likely to discover local business opportunities, get someone to a client site anywhere in the world more quickly, and be more successful at tapping into local pockets of unique talent. (It's no accident that western Michigan and the Carolinas are centers of furniture design, that New York City is awash with financial experts, that Silicon Valley is the software Mecca of the Western World, and that Los Angeles is overrepresented in all fields of entertainment.)

So the case for distributed work isn't just compelling—it's overwhelming. It reminds us of something Alvin and Heidi Toffler said way back in the 1970s in *Future Shock*, which, poorly paraphrased, went more or less like this: One of the most unproductive things we do in the entire economy is move millions of bodies into central business districts every morning and then back home again every evening.

In the Industrial Age, given the technologies of the time, there was no choice. Factory workers had to be in the factory to work, and were only somewhat more mobile than machines. Not only that, but the various operations on the assembly line had to operate in sync; activities were tightly interconnected, and they were highly dependent on one another. That is still true, of course—but now it's true in China and India, as well as in Europe and the Americas.

Although some knowledge work still needs to be done in real time—problem-solving customer service, for example—and some must still be done in face-to-face settings, much of it can now be done asynchronously, and remotely as well. Meanwhile, collaborative technologies are getting better and better at simulating face-to-face interaction, and although there is still no substitute for being there, technologies like H-P's Halo® videoconferencing systems are beginning to offer viable alternatives to the corporate dollars formerly spent on air travel. Add to the equation the current geopolitical climate, with security concerns leading to costly airport delays, and visa policies restricting the kind of international travel that was common in the last century, and it's hard to believe that technological collaboration, along with a steadily more distributed workforce, will not continue to expand.

Not only is the business case for distributed work easy to make, but there are social benefits as well. Let's start by questioning the wisdom of an economic model in which housing costs have become so high—especially where employees are forced to live near the metropolitan areas in which they work—that both parents must often work in order to pay the mortgage. What's more, with the workforce shrinking, and women graduating from college at a much higher rate than men, companies have to figure out a way to allow women to work and have families, or the global workforce will grow smaller still. Distributed work can be one of the answers.

The list goes on. Think about the annual expense of buying a wardrobe suitable for the office, and the weekly expense—both financial and environmental—of cleaning that clothing. Then consider health. Pasteur himself never cultivated bacteria as effectively as the average elementary school does, and given that children generally bring their illnesses home more often than they do their coats, both their mothers and their fathers have a pretty good chance of joining the party. With a distributed workforce, however, there is far less chance of employee X infecting an entire office.

Calculate your company's annual health-related absences, and then imagine this enormous drain on economic productivity greatly reduced through the introduction of flexible work rules allowing employees to work from home when ill. This solution, once again, is possible only when IT support is already in place. Even if a knowledge worker with a cold can't manage to put a full day in from home, he or she, if provided with the necessary technology, will certainly be able to get more done than the worker not so equipped—and that worker's productivity will not be offset by the likelihood that by coming to work, the illness will spread through the office.

Finally, if we're talking about colds or influenzas it's one thing. It's another thing entirely if an account manager just back from Hong Kong happens to bring home the avian flu.

RESISTANCE TO THE DISTRIBUTED WORKFORCE

So how is it, despite compelling economic and social justifications for distributing the workforce, that the business world not only hasn't embraced the concept, but is still actively resisting it? It's not a pretty picture, but that resistance is something we have to understand if we ever expect to move beyond the ideas and business plans gathering dust on the bookshelves of CEO's. (We've also been tracking the emergence of distributed work programs among public sector organizations, and while the issues there are somewhat different, the results are similar, and we'll return to the topic later in this chapter.)

The stubborn refusal of most businesses to distribute their workforces is truly more frustrating than puzzling, since organizational inertia and resistance to change are old friends to anyone surveying the business world. In this case, however, the economics are so compelling that we think there ought to be shareholder revolts at every corporate annual meeting. Indeed, it may take that kind of pressure to convince senior executives to exercise the kind of leadership they're being paid for. Apparently the only way we're going to convince leadership to get off their duffs is to understand what's behind their resistance to change, and then knock off their *yeah, but* excuses one at a time.

Neither is management the only culprit. Distributed work *does* mean working differently, and some employee fears are actually quite rational. Distributed work does require new skills, new attitudes, and new management systems, but the benefits so far outweigh the problems that most employees come around pretty quickly once they've experienced the change.

In the interest of better understanding the resistance to distributed work on the part of both labor and management, we've identified eight reasons that distributed work isn't the next big thing in business—again, despite the clear evidence in its favor. Not all are irrational or emotional barriers that can simply be overwhelmed with aggressive leadership:

1.   Inherent human inertia against externally imposed change

2.   Organizational inertia

3.   Management habits and Industrial-Age thinking

4.   Fear on the part of middle managers

5.   Fear on the part of front-line workers

6.   Uncertainty about communication and relationships in a distributed environment

7.   The CEO Edifice Complex that leads to visible corporate facilities

8.   Plain old complexity—distributed work is truly a big change

Inherent Human Resistance to Externally Imposed Change

Resistance to change is normal, and basically rational. When someone is told they're going to be thrust into a new situation—especially with little or no preparation, or the opportunity to think about why the change might actually be good for them—all kinds of fears and questions come bubbling up: What will it be like? Will I be able to be effective? What if I don't like it? What if my boss expects me to be more productive, but I don't have the skills she expects? Why can't we just do it the way we've been doing it—which requires very little effort on my part? Neither is this natural human distaste for change new; it was noted by Jefferson more than 230 years ago in the Declaration of Independence:

> . . . . and accordingly all experience hath shown, that mankind are
> more disposed to suffer, while evils are sufferable, than to right themselves
> by abolishing the forms to which they are accustomed.

That said, not everyone naturally resists change. While most organizations we've worked with have had their share of those who stubbornly supported the status quo—even if the shadow of disaster has already darkened their office windows—most have also had a large group actively seeking change and improvement. This ratio, between those who resist change and those who seek it, may be as effective an indicator of corporate agility as we'll ever find. In our opinion, though, the issue for most of those resisting change is not change per se, but *imposed* change.

Our view is that people resist *being changed*, because the loss of personal control leads to the quite sensible fear of a future in which they will no longer have the ability to actively manage their own successes—or failures. Imposed change, in other words, involves the loss of responsibility.

For those accustomed to coming into an office every day, distributed work places the burden of self-motivation and self-reliance on those whose productivity, to some extent, was associated with their visible presence in the workplace. Distributed work is clearly more work-focused than traditional, desk-based work, despite the comforting message, sent nonstop by every corporate facility, that simply by walking through the doors you're working, because you're *at* work. Most of us have grown so accustomed to those messages that we don't realize how much pressure they impose.

Just think about a typical office. Most of what you see—if you can see out of your cubicle at all, is others at work, and the boss walking down the hall every now and then to confirm that work is indeed being done. As well, you are surrounded by all the physical reminders that you are in the workplace: a lobby with secure doors and a receptionist; ID badges around everyone's neck; cubicles and conference rooms; institutional furniture; bland paintings on bland walls; imposing walls of filing cabinets; fluorescent lights recessed into the ceiling; tinted window glass, dark carpeting, a hush that cautions against conversation, and a big clock, high on the wall, balefully reminding all who work there that their time, while they are there, is no longer theirs.

Despite the spirit-crushing environment, it is home to those who spend their weekly forty hours there, and being denied the comfort of its familiarity, and expected to work in a different physical setting, whether it be a hotel lounge, an airport waiting area, a coffee shop, or even the spare bedroom at home, is a nearly overwhelming shock. It takes time to learn new behaviors in surroundings, familiar or not, that in the past were never associated with work.

Organizational Inertia

Most—though admittedly not all—organizational cultures are strongly biased toward stability and predictability, believing that together those behaviors will lead to efficiency. That, as Dave McCarty pointed out in his survey of the Industrial and Information Ages, was the prevailing belief when most large organizations were founded, and therefore was the philosophy that was preserved and rewarded as they grew.

But even though blind loyalty to stability—at least in today's information economy—will almost certainly lead to calcification and the loss of agility, it's also the reality that permeates almost every large enterprise these days. When nearly all the cultural and the physical signals point toward stability, and away from change, blind adherence—if not faith—in stability is what you'll get. Distributed work, accurately viewed as a very big change, is exactly what organizations have trained to fend off, to fight, and to prevent.

Management Habits and Industrial-Age Thinking

Industrial-Age managers, and even Information-Age managers who grew up in the Industrial Age (and that's just about every one of us) have been taught that *management by walking around* is essential. Part of it is supervisory, and founded on the belief that no one will work who isn't watched. That is what Dave Packard was thinking when he coined the phrase: It's important to interact with your staff on a regular basis, and not just about work-related activities. Walking the halls, stopping to share a cup of coffee or tea, observing pictures of kids and recreational events—that's what good management is all about. Organizational effectiveness is, after all, about people, motivation, and inspiration. And we all believe basically that face-to-face human interaction is the best way to understand and solve problems, build relationships, and guide behavior.

Distributed work flies in the face of that conventional wisdom. One of the underlying—and usually unstated—assumptions about distributed work is that with today's IT capabilities we can communicate and interact with others no matter where they, or we, are. So, once again, moving to a distributed work environment where people are out more than they are in, where you rely on conference calls and emails for communication, requires an enormous change in management style.

It may come naturally to some—and of course, there are managers who have been working that way for years—but for many who are used to life in traditional corporate facilities, it is a very difficult transition. When, for instance, someone reaches out to a distributed worker that person continues to expect an immediate answer—at least in North American business culture— just as if the person were standing there in the same room. This may not be such a good thing—we all know the stress that a few hundred e-mails a day can create, and the difficulty one has doing one's job if each of them must be answered when they arrive.

Middle Management Fear

The difficulty of that transition leads to the next source of resistance—the fear factor. Middle managers in particular, who remain accountable for organizational performance no matter what new program is being implemented, fear distributed work because it removes opportunities for direct observation and interaction with their subordinates, it requires new behaviors and new skills, and it creates the understandable concern that they may not be as successful in the new world. They fear not only obsolescence, but also irrelevance.

One thing we've learned over the years is that for individuals to operate successfully as remote or mobile workers, they must become much more independent and self-reliant. That means everything from starting to work in the morning—even if no one is watching—to learning how to install your own software and do your own debugging when the computer or the modem crashes. (Sun Microsystems solves this problem through its *the Network is the Computer* program, while IBM developed a user-friendly tool for its Workplace On Demand.)

It's only natural to assume that such self-reliant, distributed workers actually require less formal management, at least in the way in which management has been traditionally approached, and therefore fewer managers. In fact, our research shows that distributed work organizations *can* operate with far fewer front-line managers—or in a certain sense, with less control. And that, of course, is what it's really all about. It's all but impossible, it seems, for both frontline managers and senior executives to imagine how they can control—or even guide, or assist—employees they don't see regularly.

Another part of the fear of losing control involves management's maintaining its employees' sense of being part of the organization. Managers rightly fear that their employees' understanding of what the company is all about will be more difficult with a widely dispersed workforce, despite the availability of a variety of Internet-based tools that enable managers to communicate with their direct reports, whether down the hall, in another building on the campus, or across the country.

Finally, there is another logical and wholly understandable management fear—the loss or theft of critical information, either because of a hole in network security or the certainty that, sooner or later, one of the company's distributed workers will leave a laptop crammed with proprietary software and databases in the back of a cab.

Given continuing advances in technology, network security is nowhere as serious a threat as some managers seem to think it is, but it is a serious issue, nonetheless, and one that requires the continual re-education of middle management. It doesn't help that there seems to be a news story every other week about some remote worker who has had a laptop full of data stolen from a car, an airline club, or a hotel room. That is a very real risk, no matter how careful the company is with backup, awareness building, and password-protection schemes. All it really means, however, is that all change brings new risks—not that they can't be reduced to acceptable levels.

We'd like to conclude this topic—doing what we can to remain apolitical—by saying that in the past few years we have all seen examples of the ways in which fear can be used to protect the status quo; we can only hope that forward-thinking business leaders will not allow this to occur in their organizations.

Workforce Fear

The mirror image of management's fears of distributed work is the anxiety experienced by front-line workers who suddenly find themselves spending a lot of time away from the corporate womb. Not only are there new skills to master, but there are no longer any of the familiar work environment cues, no co-workers to provide assistance, no social stimulation, and no work-related norms of behavior. More than all these, however, there is the fear that no one will see what they are doing.

If such fears are well founded, then it's a bad sign for both the employee and the business. If self-respect and recognition are so closely tied to one's act, rather than the performance of the task itself, then management needs to reconsider its process of review, and the company's employees need to reexamine their work habits.

Perhaps the biggest fear of individual distributed workers is that the organization, and in particular the managers to whom they report, will forget about those who aren't in the office every day actively demonstrating how willing they are to suffer the daily commute along with everyone else, how diligently they are hunched down at their desks, and in general, how committed they are to doing their job. The problem with this view of work is that not a single one of those activities—and we include being hunched over a desk—necessarily contributes to any verifiable results. Riding the train—especially without a Blackberry, laptop, or a wireless card—does not bring a project any closer to completion, and neither does being hunched over your desk, if there's an open newspaper on it.

New Forms of Communication and New Media

In spite of the advances in information technology that now enable anytime/anyplace work, there is plenty of evidence that McLuhan's oft-quoted book title—*The Medium Is the Message*—is especially true in the case of the distributed workforce. In other words, if all of your contact with your colleagues, your clients, and your customers is electronic, you are sending a clear message that human interaction has nothing to do with our work. We, personally, do not want to send this message, nor do we endorse it for others.

Despite our belief in the inevitability of the distributed workforce, we also believe that certain kinds of communication and problem solving require face-to-face interaction, and same-time, same-place work. Why? Because when we rely solely on electronic media for communication in a distributed work environment—as virtually all remote and mobile workers do most of the time—there is a substantive difference in how our messages are received, understood, and accepted.

Like it or not, a telephone call is less rich than a face-to-face exchange, and an e-mail conveys far less information than a phone call. These differences have a significant impact not only on day-to-day communication, but more importantly, on the formation and evolution of the relationships that create the *context* for communication and problem solving. That's why we always insist on scheduling face-to-face meetings at key points in the progress of a distributed team project. You've got to sit down and break bread together every once in a while, and you can't do it when you are separated by miles, or you're in different time zones.

In our experience, most people who move into distributed work environments understand that the medium is the message intuitively, and understandably it makes them uncomfortable and uneasy. It's not what we're used to.

The CEO Edifice Complex

Like it or not, senior executives—most of whom are recognizably human—see value and take pleasure in seeing the company name on a big, gleaming office complex. There is something very visceral about this need to make an architectural statement about the company's—and therefore the CEO's—success. We are not the first to feel this way. Why were the Great Pyramids built, and the Roman Forum home to a new temple every time power passed from one Emperor's hands to another? More than just desiring a physical demonstration of the organization's power and importance, most business leaders take pleasure in seeing the workforce streaming in every morning, filling up all those empty spaces, and departing for home having put in a hard day's work.

Returning again to Dave McCarty's point that structure and the work rules of the office were (mistakenly) founded on the principles that ruled the factory floor, this makes sense in an industrial environment, but it did not and does not in a modern corporation. The problem is that the senior executives are comforted by such displays. Moreover, the physical manifestation of the company is important to customers, investors, and industry analysts, and the palpable presence of the buildings and the hum of the workforce make the company seem substantial and successful. In other words, it's a lot harder to show off the distributed workforce.

Complexity

As we've said several times already, moving to a distributed work environment involves a *variety* of changes, and in many dimensions. Even when it's done right, it's a big job, and the complexity and cost of such a transition often causes it to be done poorly. This, coupled with the well-understood fact that many of the attempts of some companies to implement distributed workforces have floundered or failed outright—although rarely because they attempted to change their workplace strategies—leads a majority of senior executives to be justifiably cautious and just a bit conservative about the whole idea.

But while caution is commendable, we believe the opportunity cost of failing to take advantage of the benefits of distributed work is inexcusable. The economic benefits are enormous; the advantages of becoming a preferred employer in a time where the global workforce is shrinking faster than the glaciers of the arctic couldn't be more clear; and the increased ability to attract and retain talent obviously outweighs the risks and difficulties. The distributed workforce, like the future, is already here—it just isn't evenly distributed.

Demographics

As we noted earlier, the historic change from land-working craftsman to clock-punching laborer gave rise not only to the commute, or the daily journey to where the work was, but also to vast population migrations, both interregional and transcontinental. Think of the great post-war migration from the American South to the industrial centers of the Midwest, and the great European migration to the Americas in the nineteenth and twentieth centuries. In the recorded history of the world, neither politics, nor war, nor religion, ever caused so many to move so far.

Today, the situation is fundamentally different; globally speaking, work is plentiful. The problem is that a great part of the global workforce lives far from where the jobs are. Nor do they have the requisite technology, or the technological skills, to gain access to the work. For those members of the modern workforce who do, however, it is becoming easier—and in some cases even preferable, from the employer's point of view—for the traditional equation to be reversed, and for the work to be sent to the workforce.

Think for just a moment how different the history of the twentieth century would have been had the IT revolution preceded the great European migration. To some extent, we can guess at the results by observing the scenario now being played out in India and China, where population growth, advances in education, the IT revolution, and politics have all combined to make immigration less necessary, and less desirable.

The political and economic consequences of this reversal in migratory trends are now being felt in all sectors of the labor market. As we noted in Chapter 4, the post-9/11 restrictions on immigration, combined with the growing ability of developing nations to offer career prospects previously available only in Europe or the United States, have further aggravated demographic trends in the workforce.

Furthermore, one cannot ignore the effects of illegal immigration—primarily from Mexico—that persists in America, especially since it consists of a workforce with skill sets more suited to the old economy than the new. These circumstances will change as children of Mexican heritage born in the United States are integrated into North American culture, just as the children of European immigrants were in the nineteenth century. It is unclear, however, whether the recent wave of Islamic immigrants in Europe will be as successfully assimilated.

Together, what do these factors portend for the workforce of the future? In three words: fewer white males.

Diversity

Diversity, whether you like it or not, is coming to the workforce, and soon the faces one sees in the corporations of the future are going to be predominantly female, Latina, African-American, Indian, and Asian. With the gender and color of the labor pool changing, employers who wish to continue to attract the best-qualified candidates have little choice but to accept, or better yet to embrace, diversity. Beyond the practical necessity of filling job openings, diversity makes sense for any company selling products or services in the global marketplace.

The old model, based on the superiority of certain cultures and economic systems, is giving way to a new model—the recognition that economic systems cannot trump culture, and that companies must adapt their business practices, and in some cases their products, to the traditions and the politics of the markets in which they wish to do business.

In addition to these more practical, operational considerations, diversity in the workforce has traditionally had a profound effect on innovation. Think, for instance, of Meucci, Lindbergh, and Chavez. Although Alexander Graham Bell patented the telephone in 1976, Antonio Meucci, working on his own, had produced a functioning model nearly twenty years earlier. Had Meucci been able to secure funding and to successfully navigate the tortured straits of patent law, it is almost certainly true that Bell's name would not today be synonymous with the telephone. Lindbergh's exploits are well known, of course, but it is worth remembering that he was the son of a Swedish immigrant (who, incidentally, became a lawyer, and subsequently a U.S. Congressman). Cesar Chavez was also the son of an immigrant, and after experiencing the effects of discrimination first hand, became a labor organizer and a cofounder of the National United Farm Workers, securing economic rights for farm workers that his own father had been unable to enjoy. In short, innovation is far less likely to occur when everyone in the organization—or the country—comes from the same place, has the same educational background, and thinks, works, and looks the same way.

Although the social and economic benefits of diversity may be obvious to some employers, others will be moved to change their workforces out of legal necessity. We would prefer to think that enlightenment, rather than fear, drives the policy of industry thought leaders, but change is coming no matter what the cause.

Littler Mendelson, a law firm specializing in employment law, has built a nationwide practice defending employers from the onslaught of governmental regulation, an aggressive plaintiffs' bar, and a resurgent labor movement. In its 2004–2005 white paper, "Strategic Initiatives for the Changing Workforce," Littler Mendelson has much to say about the legal implications of diversity programs:

> A diverse workforce means more and more workers have, and will continue to have, different beliefs, traditions, needs and desires than in the past. Understanding and reconciling these differences, while simultaneously promoting diversity, is a daunting task for employers that must be addressed to minimize exposure to liability for workplace discrimination. The solution of choice today is a diversity program.[4]

While sensitive to the legal implications of maintaining a homogenous workforce in today's multicultural society, Littler does not promote diversity solely as a legal defense, saying, rather, that it is simply good business:

> While many employers undertake such initiatives out of commitment without government encouragement (and sometimes resent such encouragement as unnecessary), others are at least partially motivated by the legal benefits of compliance. To the extent there is a serious recognition of the vital importance of having a workforce that looks like and reflects the values of the community and consumers, employers will be seeking skilled workers who are also diverse.[5]

ASSESSMENT

As companies reduce their CRE footprints and encourage more of their employees to work from home, in client's spaces, or in third places (to be discussed in more detail in Chapters 7 and 8), management must develop assessment techniques to determine which members of the workforce are capable of—or suited to—working outside traditional, supervised environments. Clearly, not everyone is right for distributed work, and even those who are will need some sort of reorientation. What's more, managers who do well in traditional managerial situations, with those working under them always in sight, may not be as successful in managing a more distributed workforce.

Of the available psychological assessment tools, Myers-Briggs is perhaps the best known. Based on four personality traits, each with two primary preferences, the Myers-Briggs model divides people into sixteen types. The four broad preferences are:

1. Energy (Extroverted or Introverted)
2. Information processing (Sensing or INtuition)
3. Decision making (Thinking or Feeling)
4. Organization (Judging or Perceiving)

Thus, if you are an extrovert who processes information intuitively, makes decisions by first thinking, and organizes things according to perceptions, your Myers-Briggs personality type is ENTP. Little training is necessary to predict that someone of this type would probably succeed in a job that involved daily contact with others—says sales, or public relations—but might not be right for an accountant or a software programmer whose work required hours spent in front of a computer monitor. While such Myers-Briggs analyses can be helpful in making broad, initial judgments, it is also true that with only sixteen variations, persons with different personalities and abilities can—and often do—end up in the same general occupational category.

For this reason, *Future of Work* Senior Fellow Robin Pratt, President of Enhanced Performance Services, prefers the TAIS® scale—or The Attentional and Interpersonal Style scale—as a means of assessing specific psychological tendencies. Developed by Robert M. Nideffer, PhD, the TAIS scale is used in selection and screening programs for major corporations, sports organizations (Dr. Nideffer was the psychologist for the U.S. Olympic track and field teams in 1984 and 1988 and for elite), military groups.

As its acronym reveals, the TAIS (rhymes with ace) scale measures both attentional and interpersonal styles. The 144-question survey, which can be taken online, measures three attentional processes, and predicts behaviors based on high or low scores:

1. Awareness (external attention/distractibility)

2. Analytical (internal attention/ distractibility)

3. Action (focused attention/reduced flexibility)

A high score on the awareness scale indicates an ability to see the big picture, and the power to read subtle, nonverbal signals. A high score in external distractibility, however, results when one is too aware of what's going on, and is unable to recede and focus on the task at hand.

A high score on the analytical section of the inventory indicates strong abilities for planning, strategy, and for learning from mistakes. Taken too far, though, analysis can lead to paralysis—through over-thinking an issue. This tendency is indicated by a high score in internal distractibility.

A high score on the action scale predicts a focused, detail-oriented work-style, and the ability to accurately predict the time necessary to complete a task. At its extreme, this approach can lead to perfectionism, and tunnel vision, and results in a high score on the reduced-flexibility scale.

The fourteen interpersonal processes in the TAIS inventory, some of which are self-explanatory, are listed as follows:

1. *Information processing.* High scorers like multitasking; low scorers prefer to do one job at a time.

2. *Rules and risk.* High scores indicate a greater preference for risk, and disregard for norms, while a low score is associated with those who follow the rules.

3. *Control of others.* High scores are associated with those who need to be in command, low scores indicate disinterest in, or fear of, leadership.

4. *Self-confidence.* High scores indicate optimism, self-worth, and self-confidence.

5. *Physical competitiveness:* High scorers enjoy physical competition.

6. *Decision-making style.* A high score indicates caution and a low tolerance for making mistakes; a low score predicts quick decision making, and a lack of patience for the indecision of others.

7. *Extroversion:* High scores indicate a social involvement and preference for leadership.

8. *Introversion:* High scores indicate a need for personal space and privacy.

9. *Expression of ideas.* A high score indicates a willingness to express one's thoughts and ideas, while a low score indicates a tendency to keep things to oneself.

10. *Expression of criticism.* High scores indicate a willingness to confront issues, set limits, and express anger, and low scores predict a shying away from confrontation.

11. *Expression of support.* A high score indicates a supportive approach, and a low one the absence of need, or taste, for affection.

12. *Self-critical.* A high score here could indicate a depressive personality, while a low score here is aligned with a high score in self-confidence.

13. *Focus over time.* A high score indicates the ability to undertake long-term projects, and a low score shows the need for immediate results.

14. *Performance under pressure:* High scores indicate someone ready, willing, and able to perform when everything rides on the outcome.

Once again, there is no ideal score on the TAIS inventory; attentional and interpersonal characteristics that suit one profession may be counterproductive in another. Air traffic controllers, for example, need the ability to sustain an almost obsessive concentration for hours, while high-powered salesmen need to be able to read—and react to—subtle signals from their prospects in the space of a few seconds. And just as Navy SEALS air-dropped into a research lab would quickly need, as Pratt puts it, an "action fix," legal researchers accustomed to working in quiet isolation would become overwhelmed on an exchange trading floor.

Since the TAIS inventory is based entirely on respondents' views of themselves, it cannot be used alone, but instead should be combined with interviews and, if possible, observation of the candidate in the atmosphere in which he or she will work. One of the possible uses, therefore, of assessment systems like the TAIS inventory is building more complementary management teams.

As the labor pool continues to shrink, however, such ideal team-building may no longer be possible. In such a case, upper-level managers can use the assessments to tailor their management styles to each group's individual needs in order to reduce internal pressure. Alternatively, the assessments can be used to encourage both employees and managers to face their shortcomings and take steps to change behaviors that reduce their job performance. Pratt finishes by saying that communication is a critical component of any assessment; managers need to let employees know what they expect, as well as what their employees can expect of them.

Spherion Corporation's Emerging Workforce® Study, as we noted in Chapter 3, tracks not only employee attitudes, but company behaviors as well. Kip Havel, Spherion's director of public relations and corporate marketing, has this to say about the increased use of employee screening:

> The Study also found that an increasing number of employers are turning to prescreening tools, to screen potential candidates in or out, and assessment programs to help streamline the process and identify best-fit talent. In fact, 60 percent of companies have increased their use of assessments in the past five years, and about half (51 percent) increased their use of prescreening programs in the same time period.[6]

The screening tools used included:

- Background checks
- Prescreening programs

- Skills testing
- Behavior interviewing
- Drug tests
- Behavioral assessments
- Credit checks

As noted earlier, those employers Spherion classifies as *emergent* are much more likely than their traditional counterparts to prescreen employees—65 percent to 46 percent—using behavioral assessments, skills testing, and behavioral interviewing. As a result, perhaps, emergent employers tend to interview fewer people on average for open positions than traditional employers.

PRODUCTIVITY

For those whose jobs involve creative work, productivity is often difficult to measure; for the distributed workforce, it seems harder still. Let's begin, though, by discussing some basic techniques for assessing the performance of knowledge workers.

Dr. Jacques Fitz-Enz, founder of the Saratoga Institute—now a part of PricewaterhouseCoopers—and a long-time friend of the *Future of Work*, divides human resource productivity measurement into three types: input measures, output measures, and outcome measures.

Input measures track investments in human resources, including remuneration, recruitment and staffing (decisions on the most profitable mix of professional, sales, and manufacturing employees), and training.

Output measures describe results attributable to human resources, and are therefore calculated using employees as variables. These can be considered in two ways. First, they can be measured in relation to actual goods or services produced (i.e., units produced per employee, clients serviced per employee, etc.). Second, they can be measured in relation to key areas of financial performance (i.e., profit per employee, revenue per employee, etc.).

Outcome measures, which are often confused with output measures, attempt to measure the effects of managerial decisions on the living, breathing employees themselves, rather than on the company's productivity, or finances. The resignation rate (or the number of employees who voluntarily leave the organization) is perhaps the most telling of the primary outcome measures, and describes employee response to both internal conditions (i.e., dissatisfaction with working conditions) and external factors (e.g., higher pay or more attractive living conditions elsewhere).

It is, of course, the relationship among these three basic measurement groups that reveals the health of a business. Low output and outcome measures, for example, are often directly attributable to decisions that lower company input. This can occur when companies seek to cut costs without understanding the impact such reductions will have on outputs (i.e., productivity and revenue) and outcomes (i.e., employee and/or customer dissatisfaction). Looked at from the other direction, outcome measures, like resignation rates, have a direct impact on costs (e.g., increased costs related to recruitment and training, or accounts that depart with former employees).

Standard input measures can include:

- Remuneration per employee

- Benefits per employee

- Real estate costs per employee

- Training and education costs per employee

- IT costs per employee

- HR costs per employee

Some of these measurements, when used to compare costs between fixed and distributed workforces, will yield some rather obvious differentials—greatly reduced real estate costs for the distributed workforce, and in most cases, higher IT costs. Training and education costs, however, as IBM's On Demand Workplace has ably demonstrated, can be equalized through the use of company intranets. HR costs per employee should include, of course, the cost of attracting employees, but might also take into account absence and resignation costs affecting disruption of day-to-day operations, and customer relations. Finally, total costs per employee—remuneration, benefits, real estate, training, IT, and HR—must also take into account post-employment costs such as changes in unemployment insurance premiums, legal action, and continuing benefits.

Standard output measures include:

- Average revenue per employee
- Average profit per employee
- Return on human investment ratio

A few caveats are in order here. Although average revenue per employee is easy enough to calculate, it will yield little information on the value of a more distributed workforce, unless the job descriptions of *tethered* and *untethered* can be differentiated. Average profit per employee, clearly the most direct and reliable measure of a company's total productivity, cannot be used to pinpoint the company's profit centers, because the data used to calculate the ratio are gathered across the entire enterprise.

This difficulty can, to some extent, be overcome with group-by-group assessments (excluding, of course, those departments devoted to support functions, whose costs must be apportioned across all groups). Those individual group numbers could then be compared to the mean or median scores in order to arrive at productivity/group assessments.

A similar but slightly different measurement is the return on human investment ratio, calculated by dividing profit by total costs per employee (including remuneration). If this ratio were, say, three to one, then every dollar spent on an employee would yield three dollars in profit. Here, dividing the workforce between those assigned to specific spaces, and those working in a distributed environment, we would expect to see a clear difference in profitability.

The two most standard outcome measures are as already noted:

- Absence rate
- Resignation rate

We want to make the point again that just as the numbers from input measures affect those from outcome measures—that is, low industry-specific pay leading to increased turnover—results from the outcome measures will trigger changes in many of the other rates—HR costs per employee, recruitment costs per new hire, customer satisfaction, and so on. Therefore, where the issue of productivity is concerned, whether in the office or on the road, the collaborative strategic management of CRE, HR, and IT can no longer be argued.

Now, having spent some time with the people, let's turn to the place.

CHAPTER 7

Offices Without Walls

THE WORKPLACE OF THE FUTURE

Turning now to the workplace of the future, we want to begin by making the point, just as we did in the previous chapter, that our discussion of this topic will stray back and forth across the line that separates the *place* where the work is done from *those who do the work*. That said, it is the nature of the work itself—whether in sales, client services, workforce support, or facilities management—that ultimately dictates both *where* the work should be done, and by *whom*. Or, in the words of Accenture's Corporate Real Estate Workplace team, "Work is not a place you go to, it's something you do."

That is certainly the case with CorasWorks, a software company founded in 2003, which has hundreds of customers spread across twenty-four major industries, in twenty countries, and whose software has more than 500,000 regular users. Yet CorasWorks has only two employees reporting to the office on a daily basis. It's a description that fits Agilent's Fieldscape program too, where super mobile employees rarely utilize company workspace, working instead out of their homes, in clients' facilities, or in *third places*. And it perfectly defines the Work Design Collaborative (WDC) live/work project in

161

Prescott, Arizona, a prototype home/office of the future that combines the workplace and the workforce of the future in a location about thirty seconds from the kitchen.

These examples, while somewhat extreme, are familiar to anyone responsible for corporate real estate planning, or involved in workplace strategies today. They demonstrate once again the way real estate, human resources, and information technology all come together in the future of work.

Keeping that thought in mind, we will begin this chapter with a case study of Accenture's Flexible Workplace program and the changes it made in its Atlanta offices and operations about three years ago. This case study, by the way, would have fit just as well in our chapter on reducing fixed operating costs, or, for that matter, in any discussion of collaborative strategic management. But we happen to think it's as good an example as we've seen of what the corporate workplace of the future is going to look like, resulting from the consolidation of CRE, outsourced labor forces working on client sites, a mobile workforce, and of course, the IT that enables all of this to happen.

At the peak of its operations in the late 1990s, Accenture had 186,000 square feet leased in the Atlanta market. With the national and regional economies booming, and the company's revenues climbing, management seriously considered the construction of a sixty-story, 225,000-square-foot flagship building in downtown Atlanta. Caution prevailed, however, and not only did Accenture make do with the corporate real estate it then had under lease, but by the time of the dot-com bust, the company had also succeeded in reducing the company's holdings to approximately 143,000 square feet.

Despite the reduction in square feet under lease, Accenture had more than 600 workstations spread out over three locations, Accenture had spent approximately $8,750 per workstation, each one of which required about 240 square feet of real estate. The company also had a large percentage of its workforce—in fact, more than half of the area employees—reporting to a single client's site every day as part of their business process outsourcing, or BPO work.

This part of Accenture's business involves taking over a single aspect of a company's operations—financial, transactions, IT, educational, etc.—called a *one-to-one BPO*—or providing the same sort of services to a number of clients—or a *one-to-many BPO*. In the former case, the employees typically remain in the client's space, even though they become employees of Accenture.

In the latter case, Accenture houses its operations at one of its own locations, and then contracts services to a variety of clients in various locations.

The changes in Accenture's Atlanta operations (see Figure 7-1), made in keeping with the workplace strategy principles we reviewed in Chapter 3, could hardly have been more complete—especially if you keep in mind that the company had very nearly committed to building its own headquarters just six years before, in 1998, before it undertook the following initiative, in 2004.

The plan focused on accommodating Accenture's wish to keep its real estate commitments flexible, so that the firm could expand or contract its CRE footprint as market conditions changed. The most important measure of the success of that program was the utilization rate. Before the changes began, in 2004, it stood at 62 percent. Now, only two and a half years later, it has climbed to 93 percent—higher than the company's optimistic goal of 85 percent.

Take a good look at those numbers, because this is an exceptionally rare example of a company actually losing agility by *exceeding* its workplace strategy goals—that is, by increasing workplace density beyond its own goals— and then having to add additional satellite space to maintain flexibility. If only every company were so successful at utilizing its space. Once again, the point is to keep the space filled so that you're not paying for real estate you don't need, but with a utilization rate as high as Accenture's in Atlanta, you almost expect to see a desk or two between parked cars.

At the heart of Accenture's Atlanta model was the office *hub,* which could

Figure 7-1

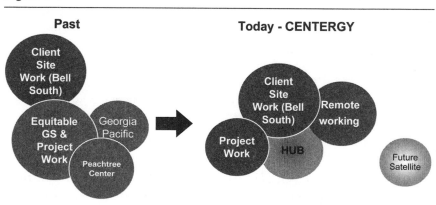

be scaled up or down far more quickly than a traditional, inflexible lease, and also offered the use of satellite sites should they become necessary. This, in fact, is just what the company is doing as we write, given its over-the-top utilization rate.

In order to select the location of its first satellite site in Atlanta, the company undertook a zip code analysis of the residences of all employees expected to work in the new location. That data, along with real estate rate analysis in the metropolitan area, will make it possible for management to select a site that is not only less costly than its downtown space, but also much closer to the homes of those employees who will work there (thus cutting down on the time they'll need to commute, reducing air pollution and energy use, and increasing employee satisfaction). It may have begun to seem a little repetitive, but this comprehensive approach to change is just what we mean by collaborative strategic management.

The company's real estate solutions were also differentiated according to the various needs of its workforce—that is, on-site dedicated client space, remote space, hub and satellite space, and project workspace. As well, all project space—that is, space leased to serve a specific client, has the same lease length as the client's service contract. Finally, overall strategy takes into account not only the physical plant—the real estate where some of the work is being done—but also the work that is being done out of the office. In other words, Accenture has matched flexible workstyles with flexible support systems. It put laptops—paid for with the savings realized from its real estate consolidation—in the hands of nearly every one of its employees.

The overall result? A dramatic, quantifiable reduction in fixed operating costs, and an almost incalculable increase in corporate agility. From concept to completion, in the space of a single year (2004), Accenture's Flexible Workplace program in Atlanta was responsible for several accomplishments:

- Annual fixed costs were reduced by nearly 60 percent.
- Total workstations were cut from 605 to 435.
- The space per workstation went from 235 square feet to 185 square feet.
- Cost per workstation fell nearly 50 percent.

These regional numbers are backed up by global data. In the past three years—from 2003 to 2006—Accenture has posted the following results:

■ Net operating costs reductions were more than 26 percent.

■ Average space utilization increased from 68 percent to 81 percent.

■ There was an 18 percent improvement in efficiency of facilities and services staff.

■ Total cash recovery was more than $350 million (due to portfolio restructuring).

To conclude, Accenture's workplace strategy is about flexibility and performance, and as Figure 7-2 demonstrates, the company understands that both require comprehensive solutions, beginning with the individual, leading to the team, and concluding with the corporation.

Before moving on to another case study, we'd like to turn for just a moment to a portion of the data from one of Jones Lang LaSalle's Leading Edge surveys, which reveals the effect that corporate cost-cutting will have on the workplace of the future. Beginning in 2003, and then again in 2005, Jones Lang LaSalle asked a group of 50 corporate real estate directors what cost-reduction strategies they thought offered the most potential for their companies. As Figure 7-3 demonstrates, eliminating surplus space and real

Figure 7-2

	Corporation	Team	Individual
Flexibility	• Respond to changes in organization quickly • Reduce space inventory, "just in case" becomes "just in time"	• Ability to get new team members up to speed quickly • Less disruption from moves, space changes	• Work where needed to get the job done • Easier response to personal life challenges, work life/ personal life balance
Performance	• Smaller real estate portfolio • More flexibility reduces costs associated with change • Increased employee productivity	• Closer to clients and team members • Hire and retain best performers • Better tools for remote collaboration	• More productive time between sites and between activities

Figure 7-3

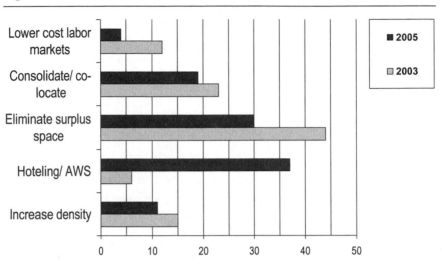

estate portfolio consolidation, while still important, are no longer the primary focus of cost reduction efforts. In the two years between the first and second surveys, Alternative Workplace Strategies—again, now most commonly referred to simply as workplace strategies (WS)—were expected to produce the most significant savings. Sound familiar?

Those results were born out by the directors' response to the next question: To what extent have you planned or implemented a workplace strategy program? The results (shown in Figure 7-4) were somewhat surprising, both

Figure 7-4

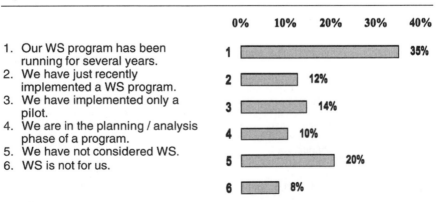

because of the percentage of companies that had already begun WS programs (35 percent), and because of the percentage that had made no attempt whatsoever (20 percent), or had no intention of implementing a workplace strategy program (8 percent).

The final question we'll cite from the survey, regarding the use of wireless technology, supported the earlier results in a revealing manner (see Figure 7-5). As you can see, the number of companies who reported an extensive use of wireless technology was nearly equal to the number who had already implemented some form of WS. Although there is no way, given the survey's format, to know if those groups are one and the same, it's a good guess, given that wireless technology is a key driver in workplace strategies.

As interesting as the results of the survey are, they only confirm what virtually everyone in corporate real estate has known for some time—things are changing, and they're never again going to be the way they were. Although for some the office of the future may still require a daily commute, a ride in an elevator, a walk down a long corridor, and eight hours at the same desk, for most white-collar workers those days are long over.

True, the workplace of the future may be down the hall, but that hall may, more and more often, lead to the den, instead of to a desk on the twenty-third floor of a downtown skyscraper. Or it may be in a local coffee shop, an airport lounge, or in the offices of a company by whom the worker is not employed. Therefore, while a certain design vocabulary—flexible furniture systems, the treatment of natural light as a resource, and large, small, formal, and informal meeting spaces—is now being spoken when modern business interiors are discussed, successful workplace solutions, as we already noted, still must begin with an understanding of the work being done in them.

Figure 7-5

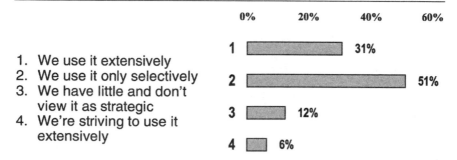

In today's world, that understanding sometimes means dispensing entirely with the workplace, and simply supporting the workforce wherever the work takes them. Or, in the words of CoreNet Global, a leading organization of corporate real estate leaders, the role of the infrastructure executive is now to "support work wherever and whenever it takes place."[1]

Johnson Controls

Johnson Controls (JCI), first introduced in our discussion of institutionalized innovation in Chapter 5, is no stranger to this concept. Innovation at Johnson Controls, in fact, was not limited to tangible products. In the latter part of the last century, the company expanded its range of facilities services, offering clients internal mail distribution, janitorial services, reprographics, meeting and conference room logistics, and porters. More recently, as the workforce has become more mobile and distributed, the company's clients began to face the same difficulties in providing support services that plagued IBM, H-P, Jones Lang LaSalle, and Herman Miller. How do you serve the needs of the mobile workforce when they no longer report to a facility, or, in the words of JCI's Tom Baker, global program manager, "How do you provide facilities services without the facilities?"

> The needs are still the same—mail, shipping and receiving, reprographics, new communications and IT challenges—but the methods and the delivery vehicles are much more challenging. What typically happens is that mobile professionals have to meet their needs by using solutions that are not easy, cost-effective, or productive. Rather than lose those folks as a component of our client's population, we had to think outside our paradigm of the *facility* as the definer of service needs and build programs using national suppliers of enabling products, services and technology to meet the job needs of the mobile professional. And these programs had to be replicable, consistent and cost-effective for the company, but easy to use for the individual.

Once again, the changing nature of the work redefines the concept of the workplace. Baker goes on to say that when mobile workers are onsite, there is little difference in the way they and *fixed workers* are provided with support services. When mobile workers touch down in any company space, they just have to find a copier, printer, a fax machine, or make their way to shipping/ receiving or IT for the services they need. Outside the office, providing the same sort of workforce support not only becomes much more difficult, but also more costly.

JCI now offers a Mobile Services program that breaks that paradigm. The scope covers any services needed by mobile workers—reprographics, presentations, package shipping/receiving, mobile communications, meeting logistics, catering, and so on—in a program that leverages JCI's relationships with national suppliers to reduce spending, and utilizes a concierge system focused on the needs of mobile workers.

JCI's Mobile Services program can be engaged via a Web site or an 800 number, and provides not only a one-stop solution for the mobile worker, but also a means of controlling costs for the client company. Although many companies have tools and services for the mobile worker, they're often hard to find or difficult to understand. JCI's Mobile Services program is easy to use and offers the human touch—through the program concierge—should the person seeking services want or need it.

Baker credits the program with benefits well beyond the cost savings.

> These enablers can also help to increase the adoption and retention rate of mobile workers. And that increases the rate at which the company can expand shared space, or even get rid of dedicated space within facilities. Agilent Technologies was able to increase their mobile workforce from approximately 40 percent of their total field sales and support population to 80 percent in 18 months.
>
> From our company's perspective, this program works for us because JCI now has an innovative offering that transcends most companies' traditional limitations, and that provides us with a competitive differentiator. Our clients are always looking for leading edge, innovative solutions and this program delivers. It also allows JCI to capitalize on a growing population of mobile workers that could have been lost to someone other than a provider of FM services.

Given this Nth example of growing workforce mobility, let's take a quick look at some Bureau of Labor Statistics data from its most recent American Time Use Survey. We think that this study has much to tell us about the live/ work balance, and therefore might be very helpful in optimizing workplace strategies of the future. The numbers also have some rather grave implications for employers of the future, given declining college graduation rates, and the difference in the average hours per day spent working by those with a bachelor's degree—7.1—and those put in by workers without a high school diploma—3.7.[2] The same data show employed men working about an hour more a day than employed women—7.9 hours for men, as opposed to 7.1 for women.

With men entering college in ever lower numbers, and graduating far less frequently than women, this statistic should make employers of the future pause and consider the options they need to offer women to make work attractive to them—especially when they begin to raise families. On a related topic—and working women will not be surprised to hear this—the study also found that on average women did 50 percent more work around the house than men did—employed or not.[3]

That said, it's important to keep in mind that sleep is still the single longest activity in everyone's day, and with other personal care activities added—bathing, dressing, and so on—it takes up almost nine and a half hours of every day.[4] Add another hour and a half for eating, a half an hour for preparation and clean up, and nearly three hours of television, and you can begin to see some of the benefits of flexible work schedules, and the advantages of telecommuting. Given the daily workload the average person has at home, and the cost of renting real estate for a desk, shining light on it, and keeping the air warm or cool, depending on the season, might there not be some advantage to allowing your workforce to skip the two hours they lose to their daily commute?

Agilent Technologies and Fieldscape

We come now to founding *Future of Work* corporate member Agilent Technologies. In 2000, after H-P had broken the record for the largest initial public offering (IPO) in Silicon Valley history, Agilent was spun off from the parent company, just months before the dot-com bust. As an industry leader in communications, electronics, and life sciences, Agilent was hit hard by the market revaluation and the subsequent turn in the economy, and in the first years of the new millennium it watched its net revenue plummet.

By late 2003, the company had suffered eight straight quarters of financial loss, a near-death scenario similar to that experienced by IBM ten years earlier. In order to survive, management called for the immediate elimination of $48 million in the global run rate, with the bulk of those savings to come from the consolidation of locations and the shift to a mobile workforce, as well as an improved infrastructure and increased organizational effectiveness.

As costs were being cut and offices closed, however, the company realized that somehow it also had to sustain a sense of community and vitality in its workforce, without which it would face an even bleaker future. Therefore, it set out to identify and satisfy the evolving needs of its recently untethered workforce, and in so doing create its workplace of the future. To its credit, and in the true spirit of collaborative strategic management, Agilent realized that as bad as things were, the situation also provided a rare opportunity for innovation, given that change was no longer an option, but a necessity.

To begin its transition to the field office of the future, which the company dubbed the *Fieldscape program,* Agilent focused on the three Cs:

1. Consolidate office/site locations.

2. Create a new environment and services to meet the needs of its newly mobile workforce.

3. Configure remaining space to maximize collaboration.

At the program's inception in 2003, only about 20 percent of the company's workforce required off-site services; in the space of little more than two years, that number had grown to nearly 70 percent. In order to help it determine how best to support its rapidly changing workforce, the company divided its employees into three groups:

1. *Dedicated.* This group maintains a dedicated workspace within a site/office.

2. *Mobile.* Occasionally, these employees utilize temporary workspace within a site/office; their primary office is at home or at client facilities.

3. *Super mobile.* Very rarely do these employees utilize company workspace; their primary office is at home, client facilities, or an alternative e-suite.

In order to assist each group according to its needs, Agilent created an online tool it called The Mobile Pages, providing its mobile workforce with 24/7 access to the following:

- *Policies and guidelines.* It is important for mobile workers to have access to HR resources, remote work policy, safety and security, and spending guidelines.

- *Technology.* Consumer select, DSL installation, high-speed connection, Internet speed test, IT client backup, IT supported printers, LAN requirements, system requirements, and telephony allow the mobile force to be mobile.

- *Services.* Copy services, hot desks, mail and distribution, office supplies give mobile workers a sense that they are not handling everything themselves.

- *Information.* The latest information on best practices for employees, best practices for managers, international shipping, remote access cost matrix, reverse mobile process, and voice cost matrix keeps mobile employees at the top of their game.

- *Furniture, printers, phone.* Mobile employees are provided with furniture and other equipment, pre-move ergonomic worksheet, and safer ergonomic reference.

- *Support.* HR yellow pages, IT global services, IT help desk/ status board, and remote work contact (WPS) are available with the click of a mouse.

The Agilent Mobile Pages also provided assistance for setting up communications—both between mobile workers, and from the field to dedicated office space—gaining access to company news, and offered a step-by-step guide to setting up a home office. The site made it much easier for the workforce to make the change from dedicated workspace to the field, and helped maintain the company culture and a sense of belonging as the workforce was dispersed.

Meanwhile, the retained office space was going through its own changes, becoming a free address model with a variety of unique work and meeting spaces—that is, functional touchdown space, open flexible space, cubes with privacy, small group spaces, conference rooms, and so on. The majority of the workforce was now in the field, so their occasional presence in the office had to be leveraged to create the maximum sense of community and belonging, to encourage the exchange of ideas and collective information, and to recognize accomplishments. With offices spread around the world—from

Santa Clara, California, to Beijing, China—supporting manufacturing, research, and services, the company began a wave of renovation it labeled *design, test, and create.*

Using a portion of the savings from reductions in its global run rate, retained offices in the United States were converted into flexible, shared space to support the newly mobile workforce (with markets in Canada, Europe, and Asia to follow). By the end of 2006, 95 percent of Agilent's U.S. workforce, and 75 percent of Agilent's global workforce, had become mobile. With the cost per mobile employee 60 percent less than it is for dedicated employees, the savings have been significant, and are continuing. Combined with the divestiture of three of Agilent's businesses—which together represented nearly a third of the company's revenue—the company is now in a position to further solidify its return to profitability, and its prospects for the future.

That said, the company has not quit trying to make Fieldscape even more efficient, paying special attention to employee feedback. When asked to rank the greatest challenges to mobile workstyles, focus groups responded as follows:

- 23 percent—lack of personal networking
- 17 percent—isolation
- 10 percent—IT support (primarily computers)
- 10 percent—home distractions (spouse, children)
- 7 percent—slower access to information
- 7 percent—reduced access to corporate services
- 4 percent—procuring office supplies

Of equal interest are the focus group responses to being asked how they stay in touch:

- 31 percent—telephone calls
- 26 percent—e-mail/instant messaging
- 14 percent—events (lunch, etc.)
- 11 percent—travel to local office
- 9 percent—don't know
- 3 percent—voice mail

■ 3 percent—advanced Internet technology

■ 3 percent—Net meetings

As we already noted, to better serve its mobile workforce, Agilent contracts Concierge services from Johnson Controls. Designed as a virtual one-stop shop for mobile employees, the Web site services include the following:

■ Scheduling bridge lines or audio conferencing services

■ Reserving conference rooms

■ Reserving audio/visual equipment

■ Directions

■ Mobile office information (i.e., printers, local contacts, restaurants, etc.)

■ Shipping assistance (local FedEx, international shipping, etc.)

■ Office security access requests

■ Projector loaner program

By the end of 2006, Agilent had vacated more than 6 million square feet of space, eliminating $40 million from its global run rate. The Fieldscape program—including the Agilent Concierge—has been successfully implemented in the United States, so it is now being rolled out in Canada, Latin America, China, and Japan, with multiple projects scheduled for the company's European offices in 2007. What's more, the company's internal research shows that annual infrastructure support survey results (for 2005) improved 15 percent over those of the previous year.

CorasWorks

As we noted at the beginning of this chapter, some companies, such as software innovator CorasWorks, have approached the problem of excess corporate real estate from the opposite direction. Founded in 2003, the company began to lease space only after realizing that it spent more money renting conference rooms for customer training sessions than it would have to spend to lease a space of its own. Until that moment, which didn't occur until two and a half years into the company's existence, every single CorasWorks employee worked from home or on the road.

As good an example of a high-tech company founded after the dot-com bust as we've come across, CorasWorks' all-modular software architecture—built on the Microsoft SharePoint platform—makes it easy, according to the company, "to design, build, and manage an integrated workplace of collaborative business applications, without the time and expense of custom development."

The virtual company grew so quickly and successfully that there was little pressure to adopt the traditional forms of business. The earliest hires were already well known to the principals; subsequent additions to the workforce began with phone screens and were followed by face-to-face meetings in airports or hotels. The company uses its own software and an accounting program to run its entire business, and the company's real estate exists only to provide little-used touchdown space for the sales force and for basic administrative functions.

Of the company's revenues, 95 percent come from product sales and maintenance, while the remaining 5 percent are generated by paid training sessions. Concentrated wholly on delivering its core products, the company provides no paid professional services, relying instead on a managed services partner network it has developed, with more than seventy-five partners worldwide.

Its model, of course, will be of little use to a corporation with millions of square feet of real estate under lease, tens of thousands of employees, and the need to maintain a physical presence in long-occupied prestige markets. Nonetheless, it's clear to us that the future of work lies somewhere between, say, CorasWorks and General Motors, and that the scale is no longer tipping in Motown's favor.

WORKPLACE STRATEGY

In reviewing the ways in which a number of very different organizations have created new work environments, or adapted old ones to the requirements of today and tomorrow, several themes evolve. In every case where the transformation was reasonably successful, all three of the critical support functions—our triumvirate of HR, IT, and real estate—were actively and strategically involved in both the planning and the execution of the change. In addition, there was extensive end-user involvement.

It shouldn't be a radical concept, though it still apparently is, to involve the residents of a new workspace design in the design process, but it clearly makes a huge difference. Those who are consulted not only become invested in the outcomes, but the outcomes themselves are usually an order of magnitude better and more relevant to the needs of those who use the space.

Let's now summarize the key components of what these success stories all included by outlining the formal methodology we use when developing a workplace strategy. Now that companies have begun to understand that the workplace is more than just the space in which work is done, innovative options for workplace design and services have begun to appear.

In our view workplace strategy includes the active coordination of all resources required to enable work wherever and whenever it takes place. The workplace of the future will be highly agile, mobile, and distributed in time and space. How do you develop a comprehensive corporate strategy to deal with this changing environment? From a project management point of view, we believe five sequential steps must be undertaken to make this vision come alive:

1. Assess business requirements, capabilities, and audit processes.

2. Define a workplace strategy, complete with a vision of its business value and impact.

3. Make specific tactical and operational recommendations for change.

4. Implement a staged plan of action.

5. Evaluate outcomes and make additional changes as needed.

The last four steps of the process depend on the outcome of the assessment analysis. At this juncture we can outline in some detail what needs to occur during the assessment phase, and to a lesser degree, specify some of the activities that will take place during the development of operational recommendations.

Assessment

Five specific activities typically take place as part of the assessment phase. They are not necessarily sequential, and separate teams may be deployed to conduct them in parallel, thus speeding up the process. However, we strongly recommend that the first step be essentially complete before continuing with those that remain.

Stage One: Business Strategy Alignment

It is imperative that any workplace strategy be completely aligned with the core business mission and plan. We need to know (roughly within a five-year time frame):

- What the product development strategy is for both production and market channel
- What the workforce staffing plans are
- The financial management strategy for the business
- An overview analysis of the branding program
- How the technology deployment plan will support all of these initiatives

The optimal method of doing this review is a short series of executive roundtables where the external team brings information about state of the practice, and internal resources present briefings centered on these five key questions.

Stage Two: Initial Consultation and Strategy Workshop

Purpose. Specification of the business problem to be solved and the measurable results required. Development, testing, and agreement from upper management on a broad strategy should be pursued in this context.[5]

Factors Examined. Business drivers, competitive threats, strategy development and decision process, as well as the changing psychology of your consumers, employees and markets and linkages to an integrated strategic asset management program.

Result. Statement of the business problem and specification of the results desired. This is then used for an internal return on investment (ROI) analysis prior to proceeding with other steps. The goal is to come up with a set of recommended tactical programs that, when executed, will lead to the results required.

Stage Three: Organizational Readiness Assessment

There are six key structural factors that must be the foundation of any workplace strategy design. These are operational factors that indicate a firm's relative readiness, and willingness, to implement a significant change in workplace strategy. The factors we have identified as critical are: direction setting; planning; customer service; information technology; human resource capability; and facilities planning.

This assessment is conducted through a series of brief executive interviews and document reviews. The results are fed into an analytical process that yields reliable, quantifiable data. These findings can then be compared to national norms to indicate which areas require attention (and possibly significant remedial effort) prior to implementation of a new workplace strategy.

Purpose. The purpose at this stage is to develop a quantitative baseline measurement of organizational readiness and willingness to implement a comprehensive and integrated workplace strategies program.

Factors Examined. At this stage, factors pertaining to the Organizational Assessment System (direction setting; planning; customer service; information technology; human resource capability; and facilities planning) will be examined.

Result. A technical report details benchmarked areas that may or may not require preparatory work prior to program implementation. An overall assessment of the probability of success of such a program will result.

Stage Four: Workforce Requirements Assessment

A key part of strategy development is finding out exactly how people currently work, the tools they use, and what kinds of infrastructure support they need. You also need to determine what kinds of infrastructure would be needed to support an optimized, ideal work environment (as seen by both management and the individual workers themselves).

We generally perform the workforce requirements assessment through a standardized, online survey research process. We retain a normative database and recommend a minimal sample size of 250 people, strategically selected in the context of the priorities identified in the business strategy alignment process.

Purpose. To develop a quantitative baseline measurement of worker be-haviors, use of spaces, technology, and human resource support requirements. These are all examined both in today's configuration and in the most desired configuration.

Factors Examined. Worker task-related behavior, technology use, space use, work/life balance issues and use of third places—public or private spaces not owned by the company—are all examined.

Result. A technical report will be prepared detailing all factors, as will a comparative analysis with national norms.

Stage Five: Real Estate Portfolio Optimization

Real estate is perhaps the most underutilized strategic asset any company has today. Our research indicates that most current real estate portfolios are at best only operating at a 50 percent efficiency ratio. Before you begin develop-ing programs to shift the balance and utilization of real estate assets you need a complete inventory of all existing assets and how they are being utilized today. You need data that identify the amount of space, geographic dispersion, occupancy rates, and types of utilization, maturity, and quality of all your real estate assets.

Again, this information is fed into standard analytical processes to indi-cate where cost savings could be realized even before any restructuring, or rebalancing, of the portfolio occurs.

Purpose. The purpose at this stage is to develop a quantitative baseline measurement of real estate portfolio utilization.

Factors Examined. Current portfolio structure, types, locations, and costs of space. Utilization rates of these spaces are also examined.

Result. A strategy of place includes an analysis of the projected geo-graphic distribution of key talent pools and alternative plans for expansion into satellite areas. We often refer to these satellite facilities as Business Com-munity Centers®, discussed at the end of this chapter.

Stage Six: Return on Investment Scenario Construction

When the five preceding steps have been completed, we can then do a return on investment analysis quantifying the costs and benefits of strategic changes in human resource management (recruitment, turnover, and training), information technology (outsourcing end-user support, mobile technologies), and real estate management (reductions in space, outsourcing facilities management). Using our proprietary ROI Calculator, we can construct scenarios for different workplace strategies, with separate analyses for all variables, and in so doing estimate the effect different programs will have on the bottom line.

Purpose. To develop a quantitative baseline measurement and monetized cost/benefit analysis of up to four space-utilization scenarios of workspace design. This would include mixed use of headquarters space, home-based work programs, and mobile worker program options.

Factors Examined. Costs and benefits for real estate portfolio use; information technology infrastructure, and human resource management programs to support distributed/mobile work would be examined. Follow-up would include a comprehensive, reliable ROI analysis of various options identified in all previous work activities.

Result. A suite of alternative scenarios would be able to predict the bottom-line impact of different collaborative strategic management possibilities. Another possible result is the sensitivity analysis of CRE/IT and HR tactical plans.

Operational Recommendations

The first steps toward developing operational recommendations flow from the ROI analysis. At this point in the process we can identify one or two priority workplace strategy scenarios specifying which infrastructure functions will remain core to the business, which can be maintained in partnership with a few vendors and which should be considered for business process outsourcing.

The second step in developing these recommendations is to develop a plan for integrated infrastructure governance and management. Closely coupled with this activity is the specification of an audit system to be deployed in conjunction with any changes in workplace strategy. The other initial steps in this phase are the selection of business subunits for prototype testing and establishment of a concept Design Studio that enables the organization to test out new design concepts in a real-world setting.

Planning and Implementation

Although it is difficult to completely specify the exact actions that take place in the last phases of workplace strategy development and rollout, we do know there are a few core tasks that must be accomplished under any imaginable strategy. Certainly implementation, program development, and selection of a program management team are key. A corporate communications plan and a linked training and development plan for initial program participants are also important components. And although design work will remain to be done within the context of the particular business—that is, its culture, its specific business pressures, and market factors—this programmatic outline is sufficient to begin the workplace strategy development process.

We will expand this discussion of workplace strategy significantly in Chapter 9, where we will describe the methodology of collaborative strategic management in greater detail. First, however, we want to spend just a few moments considering what sort of impact these innovations in workplace design will have on local communities. When you stop to think about it, as workers learn to tackle their jobs from wherever they happen to be, changing their commuting patterns in the process, the neighborhoods and towns where they live, shop, and relax are bound to be affected as well. We'll turn to that issue now, in our review of alternative work spaces.

THE LIVE/WORK PROJECT

Continuing with the less-is-more theory for the workplace of the future, we turn now to our own prototype of the live/work residence. The Work Design Collaborative (WDC) live/work project began in 2000 as an exercise in incorporating all the design work we had done to date on what a combined residential/home office environment might actually look like. Our workforce research, as well as that of the *Future of Work* community, consistently shows that knowledge workers will be spending increasing amounts of time working from a home office.

Given that new reality, the retrofitted second bedroom, or the unused corner of the garage, is clearly no longer sufficient to meet employee needs. And while we don't expect corporate America to model itself after us, we might as well admit right here that all three authors of this book call their home offices home—that is, when they're not in the air or on the road chasing the future of work.

WDC's first attempt at the design and construction of a live/work space met with stiff opposition from planning and zoning officials in Northern California, where the mere suggestion of combining a business operation with a residence powerfully offended local sensibilities. Never mind the obvious benefits to productivity, or the environment—these bureaucrats were married to the old industrial model of people living in one place, and traveling to work in another. So, we voted with our feet and moved the project to Prescott, Arizona.

Live/Work Residence at Prescott, Arizona

The live/work project began in earnest in mid-2001. Borrowing on Ellen Grantham's years of experience in the construction industry, and Charlie's graduate degree in urban planning, we acted as our own architects, hiring a draftsman only to prepare (1) detailed plans for the building permit and (2) the necessary paperwork to placate the local review board—who, it turned out, were not-too-distant relations of their regulatory cousins to the north.

Despite having to endure questions like, "Why does the centerline of the house have to be aligned with the north–south meridian?" and "Why does the main door have to face southwest?" and "What do you mean by energy flows?" we persevered, and were finally granted permission to move on to the construction phase. We constructed the live/work residence by following these simple design rules:

- *Segregation of living and working areas.* All of the research we reviewed confirmed that a healthy balance between working and living in the same space starts with a visible—and audible—separation of those activities. That means no laptops on the kitchen table, no sneaking downstairs at 11:00 P.M. to surreptitiously check e-mail, and no eating dinner while trying to make sense of the bank statement. In Prescott, we chose the simple solution of living on one level and working on another. Although individual tastes should always be accommodated, we think it generally advisable to put workspace on an acoustically isolated separate level so that the drumbeat of foot traffic is not a continual distraction.

- *Contemporary, modern design.* This, admittedly, is a matter of taste, which in the Grantham family runs to Feng Shui and Frank Lloyd Wright. Our overall design motif is watered-down Scandinavian, with an overlay of Sonora desert. The house sits at 6,000 feet above sea level, all but embedded in a national forest (and one of only a few national spaces the GSA has not yet reengineered). No man-made barriers separate it from the environment—except, of course, the bulldozed space that protects it from the occasional brush fire.

- *No exotic materials, construction techniques, or building code variances.* This one took some engineering work. All HVAC, power, and communication lines had to be routed inside flooring and walls without interfering with normal traffic flow, allowing 26-foot spans with no vertical support. Standard cabinets, flooring materials, and fixtures all came off the (Home Depot) shelf, significantly reducing costs.

- *Energy efficiency.* The house was sited to provide maximum shade during the daytime, but with the sunrise striking all the major glass surfaces for passive solar heating. As well, the structure is built into the hillside to provide earth mass regulation, which moderates temperatures throughout the seasons and eliminates the need for energy-wasting air conditioning. To complete the effect, and confound the electric meter, the exterior walls are 16 inches thick, super-insulated, and topped off with reflective concrete tile roofing material.

- *Internet enabled.* The original design called for three-tiered redundant wiring in all rooms (i.e., cable, CAT5, and regular wired telephony with five paired backup lines, all routed through one network patch panel so everything could be connected to everything else). As luck would have it, wireless technology came into its own during the construction phase, and the house is now as completely wireless as its original IT design was clueless. As technology has continued to evolve, so has the house; it is now off the telephone grid, using satellite for television, high-speed cable for Internet access, and internal VoIP (Voice over Internet Protocol).

■ *Hospitable.* The invitation to comfort draws you into the workspace. Lighting, temperature control, fresh air, and a general openness to the environment all make it easy, even preferable, to go to work. This means larger-than-normal door openings, higher-than-usual ceilings, adjustable lighting, and in fact, adjustable everything, so that the work area accommodates different seasons, different moods, and ad hoc uses of the space. Why not have a teleconference on the deck? Why not take a conference call while taking in the sun?

■ *A work of art in every room.* This, much like the design aesthetic, is admittedly a matter of personal taste. Atmosphere is what makes a place both appealing and productive. In Prescott we divided the workspace into Southwestern, Chinese, Art Deco, and New Urban Chic, each with its own decoration, color, and views. It drove the builder nuts, but the workforce—of two— gets the benefit of walking through an eclectic collection of art as they move around the workspace.

Given that our live/work project is a continuously evolving experiment, it's fair to ask what we've learned so far. First, the economics are exceptionally attractive. Compared to the typical solution of retrofitting an existing space with new furniture, wiring, and file storage, we realized a 48 percent reduction in the cost of doing business. In other words, new construction is much more cost-effective than renovation. The final cost of our live/work experiment—way back in 2003—was $98/square foot for construction, and $125/ square foot total, including property and furnishings.

In the four years that have passed since construction was completed, real estate costs have almost doubled, which means that the appreciation in value has been ours, not some landlord's. And although the evidence is anecdotal, those who have participated in live/work experiments around the country concur that they are far more productive than the typical corporate environment.

As for the future of live/work environments, we believe they will become a standard approach to both new urban and suburban developments before this decade is over, and will be a feature not only of custom, upscale homes, but also of every mainstream residential development.

Forest City Covington

In support of that belief, we'd like to turn our attention for a moment to Mesa Del Sol, a city within a city currently taking shape in Albuquerque, New Mexico, under the direction of *Future of Work* corporate member Forest City Covington. This massive project, which calls for the construction of 38,000 residences—to be divided among six separate villages—will also boast community centers, employment centers, and commercial, industrial, and office space.

A unique example of cooperation between the public and private sectors, the project's partners include the City of Albuquerque, Bernalillo County, the University of New Mexico, the New Mexico State Land Office, and the State of New Mexico. Covering nearly 20 square miles on a mesa in southeast Albuquerque, the planned community is just minutes to the south of the city's airport and within easy reach of downtown. These last factors, in conjunction with the geographic desirability of the location—that is, year-round warm weather, clean air, and reduced urban congestion—will be especially important in attracting one important element of the evolving national workforce—the independent contractor, or what you might call the self-distributed worker.

Given that executives must look to reduce fixed operating costs in order to increase corporate agility, and that the labor pool is steadily shrinking, we expect that more and more work will be done by independent contractors working out of home offices, regardless of where their employers are located. We further believe that such independent contractors will be attracted to areas like Mesa del Sol, where developers are creating suburban environments that can be navigated without automobiles, and that are within easy reach of airports when the work cannot be done remotely and travel is necessary.

Clearly, plans of such magnitude and complexity depend on far more than the developer's ability to acquire land, obtain permits, and throw up houses, office buildings, and industrial space. Mark Lautman, director of economic cevelopment for Forest City Covington, has this to say about Mesa del Sol, and his company's approach to the future of work:

I've been coming at the future of work topic from the perspective of how it will change the practice of economic development. Mesa del Sol, Forest City Covington's planned community in Albuquerque, New Mexico, is intended to provide homes for approximately 100,000 residents. I'm responsible for recruiting employers to create an economic base of 50,000 new jobs for the community.

In 2008, a year after we break ground on the first residential subdivision, most of the developed countries in the world will enter an unprecedented period in human history—for the first time those generations entering the workforce will be smaller and less productive than the ones that came before them. From now on, instead of the workforce and the economy growing faster than the overall population, the reverse will occur. This condition will cause economic development to cease in many places.

Lautman's larger point is this: Economic growth in the past century was sustained because each generation was larger in number, and better educated, than the generation that came before it. Since this will no longer be the case, economic development, at least in the near future, is going to depend on winning the war for the dwindling number of knowledge workers in the talent pool, assisting the businesses that can succeed in attracting them, and in this way building sustainable economies capable of growing the local economy faster than the population.

This phenomenon, while outside the purview of the typical corporate executive, is nonetheless a truth that needs to be acknowledged, and where possible, made part of overall corporate strategy. In some cases, the goals of corporate managers will be nearly identical with those of the economic developers whose communities may one day provide part of their workforce.

Where Mesa del Sol is concerned, a large part of the process involves picking industrial niches that match New Mexico's geography, demographics, and meteorological conditions. If so, Lautman could hardly have done better than he did with Advent Solar, the first new company he brought to Mesa del Sol, or the "Plateau of the Sun." As we write, the nearly 90,000-square-foot home of Advent Solar's research, development, and manufacturing plant is nearly complete, and by early 2007 the company's first solar panels will begin to hit the rapidly expanding market for sources of alternative energy.

Although the company's 150 employees are just a drop in the development's projected labor bucket, the company is expected to draw other alternative energy companies to the solar cluster that Lautman's economic development team has in mind. In addition to manufacturing, Lautman sees the cluster as a showcase for the technology itself, and envisions use of the surrounding acreage for renewable energy demonstrations. The Advent Solar building itself will be LEEDS certified, and using its own panels to generate electricity will be a functioning example of the sustainable focus of the entire community.

In addition to the attraction of industry, Mesa del Sol also has a well-developed workforce crisis plan that involves identifying likely student populations to steer into strategic career paths, attracting mid-career-change candidates into specialized training programs, recruiting talent from outside the economy, and exploring innovative ways to keep aging workers employed. Part of that process, once again, involves building communities attractive to the self-distributed worker, and that means providing not only housing that can serve as both home and office, but appropriate business services as well. These will often be provided by *third places*.

THIRD PLACES

One of the most striking findings of our original *Future of Work* research program was the discovery of a demand for *third-place* work locations for mobile knowledge workers. We believe that within the next several years as many as 20 million people will be choosing to work one or more days a week in third-place facilities—that is, public or private spaces built specifically for the temporary, or semipermanent, business purposes of companies and individuals.

In fact, we wouldn't be surprised if that many people are already working one or more days a week in third places right now—they just don't know it. Think about your own work patterns; how often do you log on from a coffee shop, an airport hot spot, a hotel lobby, or some other location outside either your corporate office or your home office? And yet the concept of third places seems to be missing in most current discussions of workplace design.

Third place, a term first used by author Ray Oldenburg way back in 1989, meant a place you worked in that was neither a living area nor an office *per se*.[6] Today, third places typically mean smallish facilities—10,000 to

15,000 square feet—where business people gather for a variety of reasons, to perform a variety of different tasks. Think of a Starbucks on steroids.

Not intended to supplant traditional workplaces, third places, just as the phrase explains, are an alternative to the first place, the office, and the second place, your home. Of course, that order may well change over time. Our research, in fact, shows that workers of the future will most likely spend approximately 40 percent of their time in corporate facilities (either theirs or the client's), 30 percent in a home office, and the remaining 30 percent in a third place. Actually, they will most likely be working that last 30 percent in a variety of third places.

Indeed, portions of this book were written and edited in local coffee shops, hotel rooms, airplanes, and other places we can't even remember. With three authors living in three different states, these ideas were shaped and documented in more third places than we ever expected. Our personal experiences aside, however, we believe the use of such third workplaces will become very common over the next several years, for the following reasons:

- Organizations will continue to move away from fixed-cost structures to variable cost models in order to reduce capital requirements and risk, and to increase their agility, or responsiveness to changing environments.

- Remote and mobile workers do not have adequate alternate meeting places, office services, or technical support that are affordable and convenient.

- Home-based independent workers also need and want better technical support and services—after all, they're already paying for the real estate themselves, to say nothing of the fact that most home workspaces are limited in size and don't include appropriate meeting spaces.

- In order to meet all of their business needs today, workers typically have to go to a variety of different places (e.g., FedEx Kinko's, Staples, the UPS store, Starbucks, hotel conference rooms, etc.).

The point is that third places are locations where people might spend part of a day, or even two or three days a week, working. Within these evolving business environments there will be plenty of variety. Some will be urban third places, serving primarily local working residents. Some will be suburban, situated at the intersections of major transportation routes—both airports and interstates. And some will be in rural locations, functioning as outposts for major metropolitan areas, much as they did in the Old West.

Wherever they're found, such third places will most likely take on the characteristics of the communities in which they exist. In Berkeley they may be more like coffeehouses, while in Manhattan they may more closely resemble traditional office space.

BUSINESS COMMUNITY CENTERS

Our vision is that there will ultimately emerge a network of such places, locally owned and operated. In a sense, they'll be like individual ISPs—locally owned, but connected through the Internet. (And after all, just who owns that?) At any rate, they will be connected electronically and socially, and will be an operating company without leadership—something like the Open Source Network. The list of business models is as variable and as infinite as the global market itself. That said, we have already identified four primary segments, although we're sure that number will expand as we fine-tune our model.

In response to our own research and, more importantly, our sense that the distributed workforce has created a vacuum that must be filled, we developed a model for a specific type of third place we call the Business Community Center®, or BCC®. We expect the first few prototypes to be in operation by the end of 2007.

Business Community Centers will be membership-based organizations that provide workstations, communications equipment, document handling, meeting space, and other office amenities on a shared, as-needed basis. They are intended to serve both local businessmen and national business travelers, from one-man shops to *Fortune* 500 companies. Think of a health club, or even a country club; as a member, you don't own the facility or the equipment outright; you divide its cost and share its use with the other members. And while most members use the facility only occasionally, you may play eighteen holes every day if you like—though, of course, it will cost you.

If you are a small businessman, this shared-cost, shared-use approach gives you access to a far better facility than you could afford on your own, and if you work for a large company, the cost of membership and usage fees for the BCC will cost your corporation far, far less than traditional real estate. What's more, if your business moves, you simply find a new BCC to fit your changed needs.

While our model presumes that BCCs will provide a working environment primarily for residents of the local community and its environs—whether remote employees of larger organizations, self-employed professionals, or small business owners—they are also intended to serve as unofficial business development agencies, helping to make national business travelers, who'll stop in for the much the same reasons locals do, aware of opportunities in the region. Of course, the same sort of cross-fertilization will occur between local businesses, especially in more rural areas where contact with the larger business community is rare.

We also expect BCCs to be used by commuters in the event of transportation disruptions, or during personal emergencies—say the illness of a child—that would make it difficult to be an hour away in the office, rather than ten minutes away at the BCC. They will also be used either by people who choose not to go to a distant corporate facility one or several days a week, or who as small business owners, sole practitioners, and/or free agents need part-time access to a workplace infrastructure and community on a cost-effective basis.

The keys to the BCC model are location, the specific nature of the services provided—which may change location by location—and cost. In contrast to traditional office leases, BCC members would pay for space and services only when they need to use them (in addition to a base-level monthly fee required to maintain membership). This business model produces much lower costs for individual members, yet ensures high usage of the space, which in turn provides equity investors and lenders with profitable returns on their real estate and facilities investments.

BCCs will provide their members with a variety of technologically advanced amenities such as conference rooms, workstations, IT technical support, wireless broadband Internet connectivity, back-office administrative support, and informal café-type facilities—all in an ergonomically designed environment and complemented by on-site professional development and business development activities and assistance. The real *stealth feature* of this model is that many of those providers of specialized business development and support services would themselves be members of the very same Business Community Center.

It is our expectation that each local BCC would be locally owned and managed, with guidance and consultation (as well as some support services) being provided by a national management company formed to promote and guide the development of BCC franchises. Local BCC's would, in turn, be networked with each other so as to provide all national members with access to one other, and, through a focused virtual marketplace, enable individual BCCs to supply each other with customers. If, for example, a member of a western Michigan BCC needed to travel to upstate New York for business, he or she could simply set up shop at the nearest BCC.

We are currently in the process of forming a national management company to promote investment in and support for Business Community Centers around the country. Also, we are actively discussing the BCC concept with several different commercial property developers and local economic development groups with the goal of launching the first small network of BCCs in the near future. You could say we've decided it's time to stop talking about the future of work and begin building it. And speaking of building, let's continue on to Chapter 8, where we'll turn our attention to the well-designed workplace.

The Well-Designed Workplace

It is hard to understand now, especially for those who entered the workforce after 1980, that the workplace was not always discussed in terms of its flexibility, its comfort, or its ergonomics. With that in mind, we'd like to begin our section on workplace design by looking back almost forty years to where it all began, with Robert Propst's Action Office design for Herman Miller.

Even now, Propst seems current. To leaf through his 1968 book *The Office—A Facility Based on Change* is to encounter the first expression of virtually every important advance in workstation and workplace design. But rather than speak for him, we'd like to start this section by quoting his introduction, titled "The Office—A Search for Definition."

> We are a nation of office dwellers. For 34 million people in the United States, or approximately 40 percent of the working population, it is our place to work. We spend one third of our lives there.
>
> How much do we know about the office as a place for humans? What are its present aims? How well does it function?
>
> In one generation, the office has migrated from a place of little consequence in man's affairs to one of most serious effect. The office, as we have

come to know it, is an adolescent statement starved for appropriate definition and somewhat oblivious to the forces of change.

For most of us the office is a place where we go to suffer a variety of
environmental accidents. Some turn out to be advantageous, even to the
point of giving unfair leverage over others. Most of the time however, they
are bad accidents—wasters of effectiveness, vitality, health, and motivation.

But, it may be asked, hasn't the office developed by a long and sensitive
evolution into something highly appropriate for the human user, a sort of
knife and fork for processing business matters?

Such respectability is not deserved. Its history is short and fitful.[1]

One gets the feeling that Propst, although calling us a nation of office-
dwellers, wouldn't be surprised by the increasing mobility of the workforce,
nor that the design revolution he started would, through its flexibility, end in
helping facilities managers move workers out of the office. The section titles
and subtitles of the book alone reveal his obsession with change—for example,
"Grow or Die State of Organizations," "A Place for Transacting Abstrac-
tions," "Geometry vs. Humanism," "The Right to Be Different"—and his
belief in the constant state of radical change.[2]

Once he has set the stage with lengthy discussions of "Office Change
Makers," "The Human Performer," "The Office Conflicts, Change, and The
New Rules," he goes on to call planning the *key to expression*, and asserts the
importance of modeling and pre-gaming as a means of testing design. As part
of that discussion, a facility planner is shown—again, in 1968—in front of a
keyboard and a tube on which computer-generated workstation solutions are
displayed.

Equally as prescient was Propst's understanding that the efficient use of
space saved not just space but also money, and therefore, that it was as important to good design as human comfort or productivity. Just look at these early
drawings (see Figures 8-1 and 8-2).

In explaining this fundamental shift in design perspective, which over the
years has put incalculable amounts of wasted interior space back into use,
Propst makes the following rather obvious point, ignored up to that time by
most office designers: "Man is a vertically oriented machine. It stands to
reason that work function should organize to meet this characteristic."[3]

Figure 8-1

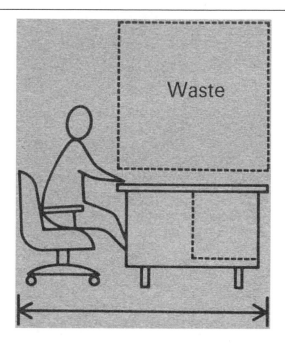

Although we could devote pages to this design visionary, in the interest of moving along we'll finish by including a few basic line drawings that illustrate the genesis of the office designs that now rule the corporate workplace. The first (see Figure 8-3) shows a solitary figure in open space. Propst uses it to show that human beings are uncomfortable in open space, without a back-up element. The second (see Figure 8-4) he explains by saying, "A back-up element provides us with a great psychological comfort. We now have a personal reference point."

Propst describes the third (see Figure 8-5) as follows: "If the back-up can give us some enclosure, we are even better off . . . now we have a way to express relative exposure and gain a greater degree of privacy." Finally, of the drawing he labels *best*, (Figure 8-6), he says: "Three sides with a slightly widened opening appears to the best enclosure of all as a generality. There is good definition of territory or domain . . . privacy is well-expressed and the ability to survey or participate is well maintained."

Although we will not include it here, Propst finishes this discussion by

Figure 8-2

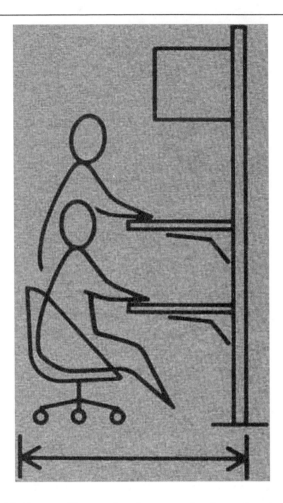

putting his stick figure office worker in a completely enclosed space, remarking that such an arrangement is bad for the wide awake and activity-oriented man. He is isolated, insulated, and remote. His ability to be part of an organizational family is diminished.[4] If you think about it, Jones Lang LaSalle, H-P, Accenture, and Agilent all had pretty much the same thing to say when changing the configuration of their office space to encourage greater collaboration.

We'd now like to move from workstation design to more general principles of office design, and to do so we'll call on John Campbell of Francis Cauffman Architects:

Figure 8-3

1   Bad

From an architect or interior designer's perspective we are at a point of tremendous design opportunity. The workplace paradigm of hierarchy and standardization, which led to the acres of Dilbertville, is being turned on its head by many factors.

The business drivers for today's companies have changed dramatically in the globally competitive environment, now operating 24/7/365. Companies are constantly looking for ways to innovate, to produce new ideas, enhance productivity, and reduce cycle times to market. Competition now also means attracting and retaining the best and the brightest in an age of changing demographics. Many of these changes have been fueled by the exponential growth in technology and the resulting ease of global communication. The growing mobility of workers, no longer tethered to their desk, has also made it commonplace to have teams based in multiple locations working on a single project.

Still, the primary purpose of a workplace is to support the organization's mission. When seen from this perspective, senior management can view the workplace as an asset that adds value to business performance, rather than simple real estate, or a drain on the bottom line. In the past,

Figure 8-4

the focus has first been on cost, but to see its true value the company needs to consider the impact of lifecycle costs, productivity, and ROI / shareholder value. It requires rethinking the cost and value of the workplace in a holistic view, providing efficient buildings that enable people to work more effectively—and express the culture and values of the company. This has significant implications in that it requires a change in company structure, from a hierarchy to a flatter, more nimble organization where employees feel vested in their work.

Campbell goes on to say that from the perspective of the architect/ interior designer, this means looking beyond traditional programming methods to develop a deeper understanding of the project's business drivers. This means that in addition to spatial considerations, the designer has to consider the following:

Figure 8-5

3 Better

- Product cycle times
- Creativity
- Transparency
- Adaptability
- Productivity
- Culture and values

According to Campbell, this means that each company will have a workplace tailored to its particular business needs, because what suits one company will most likely not suit another, even within the same industry. He also believes that since each set of employees is unquestionably unique, such office tailoring is critical to employee satisfaction, and therefore to retention.

Figure 8-6

The search for general principles of design for the modern workplace is by no means limited to the private sector. In fact, we think the General Services Administration has produced one of the finest, most comprehensive, and codified approaches to workplace design we've seen, exemplified by its program *Leading by Example: A Demonstration Toolkit for Creating a GSA World Class Workplace.* This is the result not only of the organization's leadership and staff, but also of the lessons learned from the vast number and varied characteristics of the projects the organization has undertaken over the years. In the words of GSA Acting Administrator David L. Bibb:

> The attached toolkit . . . illustrates how the principles and hallmarks that collectively represent the GSA brand may be applied in a variety of organizational settings. The toolkit will be of great help to GSA's World Class Workplace advocates and the agency's senior manager as they strive

to link workplaces with strategic outcomes. In particular, the toolkit's demonstration section, outlining key steps with sample workplace plans and physical elements, will prove invaluable to those just getting started in the planning process. Those further along will find related case studies and resources section of interest in choosing best practices.[5]

THE SEVEN HALLMARKS OF
THE PRODUCTIVE WORKPLACE

The GSA toolkit, not intended to endorse a standard solution, is meant to help the GSA design, construct, occupy, and maintain workplaces for its associates in a manner that is optimal for the nature of the organization's work, that fosters its business strategy, and that expresses the agency's mission, values, and culture. Its guidelines and processes are drawn from the Seven Hallmarks of the Productive Workplace first introduced in the GSA's Integrated Workplace. Its principle features are as follows.

Spatial Equity

Design the workplace to meet the functional needs of the users by accommodating the tasks to be undertaken without compromising individual access to privacy, daylight, outside views, and aesthetics. Specific requirements include the following:

- *Natural daylight.* Everyone should have access to natural daylight. This promotes good health and increases productivity.
- *Views.* The company should provide all employees with seated views to the exterior. This also promotes good health and productivity.
- *Fairness.* Space should be appropriate to the type of work conducted. Therefore, rank of hierarchy is neutral in space standards. This supports collaboration, mentoring, and knowledge sharing. In open-plan office areas, provide accommodation for individual acoustic and visual privacy.
- *Multiple work settings.* Offer multiple approaches and solutions. This stimulates creativity and supports flexibility, knowledge sharing, and mentoring.

Figure 8-7

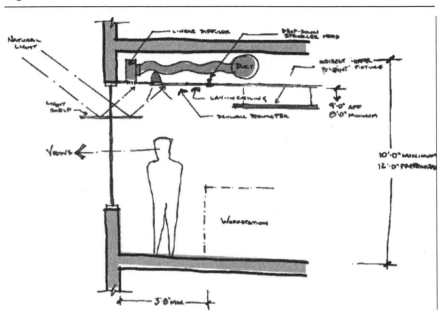

Healthfulness

Create workplaces with a clean, healthy building environment free of harmful contaminants and excessive noise, with access to clean air, light, and water. There are specific requirements:

- *Air.* Provide clean, fresh air. Monitor and maintain air-quality levels that meet or exceed those of EPA and DOE standards. Perform routine building maintenance with trained mechanics to maintain specified air-quality standards. A system that provides user control is ideal. Consider underfloor air supply. Use only construction materials and methods that will not contain or re-lease harmful contaminants that could adversely affect indoor air quality or require special treatment (such as abatement) during future modifications. See Figures 8-7 and 8-8.

- *Water.* Provide water that is drinkable, free of contaminants, and readily available

- *Ventilation.* Provide exhaust ventilation (and consider negative air pressure) per applicable codes and EPA and DOE standards for all noxious fumes and odors, including those from copy areas, food preparation or storage, toilet rooms, janitor's closets, battery/rectifier, UPS rooms, and diesel generator rooms. Try to group like spaces together wherever possible.

■ *Ergonomics.* Provide certified, ergonomically sound furniture, lighting, and equipment, including task chairs, variable-height work surfaces, computer monitor stands, adjustable keyboard trays, and adjustable, demountable task lights. Provide ergonomic consultation and training on office use and procedures for all new employees.

■ *Restrooms.* All restrooms should be clean, maintained, and sanitary; locate restrooms within 150 feet maximum travel distance from individual work areas.

■ *Amenities.* A coffee bar, fitness center, health center, and day care center all provide a greater level of healthfulness and community.

Flexibility

Choose workplace configuration components that can be easily adapted to organizational or work process changes, and can be readily restructured to accommodate key functional changes with a minimum of time, effort, and waste. Specific requirements include the following:

■ *Furniture strategy.* Use modular work stations appropriate to function and tasks allowing varied arrangements and providing maximum surface area in the space provided; avoid free-form work surfaces that do not function with other components and panel-hung elements that are not compatible with freestanding panels; explore the use of demountable wall systems instead of hard wall construction.

■ *Kit-of-parts workstation.* Use workstations that allow user adjustment and reconfiguration, including furniture, task lighting, power, data and communications connections, and air supply control.

■ *Fluid layouts.* Base workplace layouts on function, not building grid, encouraging creativity and a sense of community. Provide free-standing, modular furniture components for all offices and

Figure 8-8

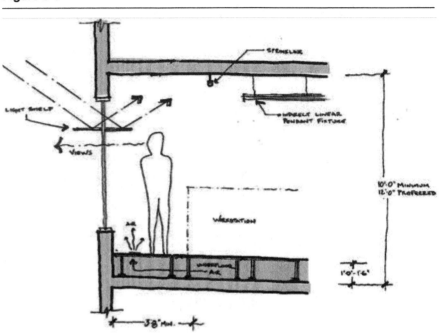

workstations; provide light work surfaces, and put file storage towers, bookcases, and all other heavy components on wheels so that when fully loaded one person can easily move them.

■ *Technology*. Provide power, data, and communications services through plug-and-play systems with integrated cable management.

■ *Telework*. Offer workplaces compatible with alternative work strategies (i.e., telework, shared workstations, touchdown space, hoteling, collaborative space, and community centers) and provide equipment and services necessary to support remote work at the same level as on-site work.

Comfort

Distribute workplace services, systems, and components that allow occupants to adjust thermal, lighting, acoustic, and furniture systems to meet personal and group comfort levels. Specific requirements include the following:

- *Thermal control.* Provide easily accessible individual user control of temperature and ventilation conditions at each workstation.

- *Lighting.* Provide individual user control of task and ambient lighting, including natural daylight.

- *Ergonomics.* Within the workstation, provide ergonomically sound furniture, lighting, computer desk surfaces, storage elements, and computer monitors that can be easily reconfigured by the user without tools or special expertise.

- *Multiple work settings.* Create a variety of work settings with varied types of seating to suit all types of work and individual needs.

- *Adequate space.* Provide supportive office space, work surfaces, and technology that support all job functions for all employees.

- *Security.* Create a secure work environment for all employees.

Technological Connectivity

Enable full communication and simultaneous access to data among distributed co-workers for both on-site workplaces (including individual workstations, team space, conference/multimedia space, hoteling space, etc.) and off-site workplaces (including telework or commuting center, home office, travel venues, etc.). Specific requirements include the following:

- *Coordination.* Collaborate with IT to ensure technology standards are flexible and appropriate to organizational goals

- *Plug and play.* Provide power, data, and communications services through plug-and-play systems that allow the occupant to easily make connections to any components anywhere within the workstation.

- *Data sharing.* Provide a unified, enterprisewide voice and data system that allows data sharing/access across the organization.

- *Telephone service.* Provide direct inward dialing (DID) with one phone number access to each person regardless of location that links both desk and mobile handsets.

- *Network access.* Provide universal network access and support for remote workers from any location.

- *Virtual meeting needs*. Provide for current and future virtual meeting needs, including the capability for video teleconferencing in all meeting rooms and at the workstation desktop.

- *Wireless*. Provide data, voice, and software systems that can accommodate wireless equipment or devices and larger collaborative groups.

Reliability

Support the workplace with efficient, state-of-the-art heating, ventilating, air conditioning (HVAC), lighting, power, security, and telecommunication systems and equipment that require little maintenance and are designed with battery and/or greater back-up capabilities to ensure minimal loss of service or downtime. Specific requirements include the following:

- *Clean air and ventilation*. Provide clean, continually refreshed air.

- *Lighting*. Provide both natural and artificial lighting.

- *HVAC*. Provide HVAC systems with effective ventilation and individual user control of temperature and airflow. Select systems that can be adapted to changing space configurations and uses without involving demolition and renovation work.

- *Instructions*. Provide training and written operating instructions to all occupants on the use of building systems and features, office equipment, and software.

- *Security*. Provide building systems security and access control.

- *Maintenance*. Develop and implement a comprehensive maintenance program to keep all building systems and equipment in good operating condition and to minimize breakdowns.

- *System confirmation*. Commission all systems, especially ventilation and lighting systems, after installation to ensure they are providing intended benefits.

Sense of Place

Endow the workplace with a unique character, appropriate GSA image, and business identity to enable a sense of pride, purpose, and dedication among both the individual and the workplace community. Specific requirements include the following:

- *Environmental graphics.* Provide well-designed signage and graphics to reinforce the identity of space and enhance the experience of both employees and visitors.

- *Connectivity.* Use signage, GSA logo, furniture, and lighting to ensure that employees and visitors know they are in a GSA space from the entrance to the workplace. Reinforce the GSA identity from location to location, but without a one-size-fits-all approach.

- *Brand, values, and beliefs.* Make sure the space clearly demonstrates the GSA brand, values, and beliefs without diminishing opportunities to express uniqueness.

- *Sense of ownership.* Provide clean, attractive, accessible, functional spaces that occupants can take pride in showing to customers, colleagues, family, and friends.

- *First impressions.* Provide amenities valued by the building's occupants; enhance way-finding, image, identity, sense of pride, ownership, and community.

- *Color scheme and finishes.* Use color strategically to create desirable moods and themes, to create a calm work environment that promotes and encourages interaction, and stimulates creativity and innovative solutions. Use accent colors and finishes to delineate function, onstage/offstage areas, and to draw attention to particular aspects of the space (i.e., identity wall or conference center).

- *Continued up-keep.* Space should be maintained to preserve original design quality, appearance, and intent; replacement elements should be consistent with the original design intent.

THE SEVEN HALLMARKS EXEMPLIFIED

The seven hallmarks of the productive workplace, far from being confined to the pages of a government manual, are today exemplified in GSA workplaces around the country. The following summaries—of completed projects in Auburn, Washington; Philadelphia, Pennsylvania; Denver, Colorado; and Oakland, California—demonstrate the versatility of the hallmarks, given the projects' differing requirements, and their varied solutions. More important, each project taught the GSA a different lesson about redesigning its workplaces. Each of them also utilized the *rapid engagement process* (see Figure 8-9), which promotes innovation early in the design process, when flexibility is high and costs are low.

The Senior Leadership Space in Auburn, Washington, created in 2000, was designed to encourage cross-service collaboration between senior executives from the GSA's three branches: the Public Buildings Service (PBS), the Federal Technology Service (FTS), and the Federal Supply Service (FSS). Doing away with traditional office space, it put senior managers from all three GSA branches side by side in cubicles located in a central, open environment surrounded by meeting space and conference rooms. The intent, much like Jones Lang LaSalle's No Barriers/No Boundaries program, was to increase spontaneous interaction, promote the free exchange of information, and encourage upper-level managers from all three branches to work together strategically, rather than narrowly focusing on day-to-day operations.

Figure 8-9

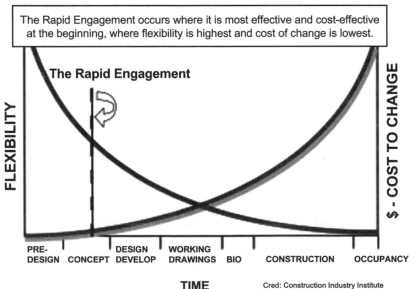

Initial feedback was not favorable. Those in the space resented the loss of privacy, which they felt led to more frequent interruptions, and unacceptably high noise levels. And while collaboration within each branch increased, the primary objective of the workplace design—increased cross-service collaboration—was infrequent, at best.

The GSA, though, aware of the difficulty a change of this magnitude was likely to face, did not abandon the project, trusting that over time the benefits of the design would become clear to those working in the building. Although four years passed before the workforce settled into the new environment, that patience was finally rewarded, and today no one wants to return to the isolation of a private office.

The Auburn project taught the GSA the value of patience, and the necessity of giving the workforce the time necessary to accept change. The Philadelphia project, with completely different parameters, taught the value of experimentation. The two primary factors affecting the redesign were the limitations of the existing space—the historic Wanamaker Building, in downtown Philadelphia—and the changing nature of work at the PBS.

In this case, as leadership searched for new space, it decided that rather than dictate the nature of the new work environment, it would set up a 12,000 square foot workplace laboratory, and rotate each of its departments through the experimental space. In three-month increments, each department studied its own workstyles, and then experimented with different design solutions.

Interestingly enough, some of those decisions—the need for a variety of meeting spaces, the benefits of cross-disciplinary, geographically-based teams, and the increased collaboration resulting from an open office environment—were similar to the design goals in Auburn. The difference, however, was that the workforce had more invested in the changes, having participated in the decision-making themselves, and having been given the opportunity to identify and address potential problems before the new buildout.

The lessons learned in the workplace laboratory were then incorporated into the new space, the 13,000-square-foot Strawbridge Building, originally a department store. Featuring the high ceilings and open interiors typically associated with retail space, the building allowed the design team to provide for the specific needs of each of the six separate workstyles identified by the Workplace Laboratory project, and yet preserve an overall sense of design continuity. In addition, the high ceilings allowed the use of a raised floor, permitting underfloor wire management and plug-and-play technology. Other innovations included the transformation of an existing auditorium into a Data Network Access (DNA) Center, including a library, informal meeting spaces, and centralized filing and support services.

Although the organizational goals of supporting project integration, encouraging face-to-face interaction, and promoting cross-functional learning were achieved by the new design, those results were not accompanied by increased occupant satisfaction. Although this could be due to the workforce's affection for its previous workplace, the Wanamaker Building, it may also be that just as in the case of the senior leadership space in Auburn, the workforce needs time to adjust to its new surroundings.

The PBS Rocky Mountain Regional Office in Denver, Colorado, presented yet another set of design challenges. A World War II–era munitions factory, the space was so vast that whole sections of the interior had little or no access to windows or daylight. Turned over to the PBS in the 1950s, in the years that followed the building was renovated in a haphazard fashion, without a master plan or a design focus. And although spectacular views of the Rocky Mountains were available to the west, the building's design limitations literally kept the workforce in the dark, in windowless workspaces buried deep within the former factory.

The planning stage began with a series of focus group meetings attended by managers, staff, and the GSA's workplace consulting team. Following is a short list of the design goals that resulted from those meetings:

- Showcase a design solution that supports business functions.

- Use the workplace to attract and retain talent.

- Create a quality work environment that reduces workplace stress.

- Facilitate interaction, communication, and collaboration.

- Establish a small-town look and feel.

- Maintain flexibility, efficiency, and adaptability.

- Demonstrate progressive leadership.

To these goals, similar to those of the other GSA projects we've discussed, the design team added one overriding objective—letting in the light. Toward that end, private offices were moved to the interior, workstations were fitted with glazed panels that allowed natural light to penetrate the building's interior, and large skylights were placed above common areas, including the building's entrance, the new café, and former warehouse space transformed into a social area dubbed the P.I.T. (People Interacting Together). Furnished by the staff themselves with the proceeds of various fundraising efforts, the space includes couches, televisions, a pool table, a workout facility, a locker room, and conference rooms. And though not intended for such use, it has also become a preferred site for informal business meetings, most likely because of the relaxed atmosphere, and the natural light from the skylight high above it.

In the case of the Denver project, all the initial feedback has been positive. In particular, respondents said that the new design fostered a stronger sense of community, and led to increased opportunities to develop friendships on the job. Hardly a surprising finding, given that just a few years earlier they had been working in a space originally designed to fuel the engines of war.

The last GSA project we'd like to review involved the transfer of certain Coast Guard operations—specifically those for whom security was not a top priority—from an island in the middle of San Francisco Bay to the Federal Building and Courthouse in nearby downtown Oakland. One of many governmental changes that followed the attacks of 9/11, the Coast Guard case not only required the GSA Workplace consulting team to design a space compatible with the missions and work patterns of the divisions being transferred to Oakland, but also to sustain the culture of the Coast Guard itself—something many in the organization feared would be left behind on the island they had once called home. And just as in every other workplace redesign we've discussed to this point—from Jones Lang LaSalle's restack in the AON Center to Herman Miller's MarketPlace—the consulting team sought to bring the disparate elements of the company into closer contact, in hopes of encouraging collaboration, and furthering the Coast Guard's mission.

In the GSA's own words:

> Using the full complement of workplace tools, the team made a comprehensive examination of workstyles, organizational relationships, workplace performance, and mission objectives. Discussions considered the barriers, constraints, and supports people experienced in everyday activities, as well as when they responded to more urgent, unanticipated activities. The team found that the Vessels division was under tremendous pressure to

balance the conflicting requirements of a budget largely allocated to routine maintenance of ships and a growing need to respond to emergency break-downs of an aging fleet. Furthermore, a cultural divide had grown between the groups responsible for maintenance and those for emergency response, and the workplace did not help these groups work together effectively. The groups were functioning largely independently in different buildings.[6]

In order to address this cultural divide, the GSA team called several town hall meetings to identify organizational goals, and the strategies used to support them. Those goals unaffected by the physical design of the workplace were separated out, and those that remained were organized into a framework that guided the design team's efforts.

Everyone involved in the process agreed that the town meetings resulted in a sense of ownership in the proposed changes, and assured those employees affected by the move that management was listening. This made the buildout itself much easier, both for the GSA, and its client.

In addition to the information gathered at the town hall meetings, the workplace team also asked the following questions:

- Who really needs to talk to whom, and about what?

- How can we create a culture that values communication?

- How can we bring newcomers up to speed more quickly?

- How do people spend their time individually and in groups?

- Are there more effective ways to work?

The answers to these questions yielded valuable insights into the way the new design could further the Coast Guard's mission. Employing the Balanced Scorecard method, the team then used the Coast Guard's core operational goals—i.e., reducing operations expenses, managing customer expectations, continuously improving key processes, promoting work/life balance, etc.—to formulate the new workplace strategy. To point to but a few of the many changes, groups that needed to work together were located in adjacent areas, and the ability of groups to meet informally was expanded. This led to improved informal learning, the generation of common knowledge, and improved ad hoc collaboration. The same workplace strategies also helped devise the metrics eventually used to measure the success of the reorganization. By all accounts, the GSA's workplace design for the Coast Guard's new operations space not only succeeded in mitigating initial worries about the move, it actually made use of the occasion to improve organizational efficiency and employee satisfaction—an example of collaborative strategic management at its best.

IA INTERIOR ARCHITECTS

Having reviewed the broad reach of the GSA's Workplace Consulting team, whose mandate has brought it face-to-face with every major workplace issue of the day, we'd now like to turn back to the private sector, and the work of IA Interior Architects (IA), an architectural firm that has been at the center of two of the major projects we've discussed to this point—the Jones Lang LaSalle restack in the Aon Center and the Herman Miller MarketPlace. With offices across the continental United States, as well as London and Shanghai, IA is, in its own words "the only global architecture firm to concentrate exclusively on interior architecture."

IA has transformed major public and private spaces from the inside out since 1984. Its client list includes Tivo, Sony, Bank of America, Merrill Lynch, PG&E, Del Monte, the Federal Reserve Bank of Chicago, the United Brotherhood of Carpenters, and Sheraton—as well as the two *Future of Work* community members already mentioned and the GSA. Concentrating on the connection between interior aesthetics and organizational success, IA's work is intended to promote brand image, improve efficiency and productivity, reduce churn, and increase employee satisfaction.

IA is an active proponent of sustainable design. Its solutions incorporate environmentally friendly materials, include protocols for demolition and disposal, and embrace, wherever possible, the use of natural light. In connection with its design services, IA also offers its clients workplace consulting focused on improved performance, adaptability, and cost savings.

Having covered the Aon Center and Herman Miller MarketPlace earlier in these pages, we'd like to take a brief look at two of the firm's recent projects—one for a major Internet retailer and the other for a national financial institution.

The first of these involved the redesign of 70,000 square feet of office space that had evolved into an overcrowded patchwork of offices, storage areas, and conference rooms with little regard for individual work patterns, traffic flow, or departmental functions. Jobs that required quiet concentration were exposed to constant noise, and due to the constantly changing needs of the business areas, designs for one purpose frequently ended up being used for another. The firm's assignment, given the chaos of the existing use, was as follows:

- Provide a master plan for the facility that allowed for rapid growth and constant, unpredictable change.

- Increase productivity and employee satisfaction.

- Create customizable workspaces to reduce the time and costs of the adaptation that was certain to occur.

- Incorporate environmentally sustainable solutions throughout the plan.

All of this had to occur, of course, in an exceptionally short time frame, while the space was in use, and as a precursor to the plan's rollout across the rest of the client's vast real estate holdings. Accordingly, IA immediately convened a series of staff interviews to identify individual and departmental needs, intending to meet the varying demands of the company's workforce with a single, adaptable, cost-effective and environmentally sustainable solution.

Its solution was a demountable wall and spine system, constructed of sustainable materials and allowing for the rapid reconfiguration and customization of the workspace, no matter its function. As well, the master plan incorporated the company's legacy panel system and its iconic door desk, a fixture of the company's culture from the day it opened for business. The wall panels were constructed of recycled steel on one side—which could be used as a dry erase board, and for magnetic applications like chart holders and task lamps—and wheatboard on the other, made from the natural byproducts of grain production, which lent warmth to the office interiors.

Although these elements were initially arrayed in response to the declared needs of the company's various divisions and the design team's traffic solutions, the system is flexible enough that facilities managers can reconfigure the floor plan in the space of a weekend. Walls can be moved to create more meeting areas, more heads-down workstations, or even to accommodate the company's seasonal staff fluctuations without resorting to additional leased space or costly demolition and construction. This reduces the burden on local landfills. Even more important, the design succeeded in increasing the efficient use of the workspace, increasing productivity and employee satisfaction without sacrificing the traditionally exuberant company culture.

The second project, unlike most of the designs we have reviewed up to this point, involved IA's work on the interiors of a skyscraper to be built in a major metropolitan area in the Northwest. In contrast to the GSA's renovation of its space in the Kluczinski Federal Building in Chicago, or H-P's retrofit of its Bracknell site outside London, the modifications IA requested in the floor plate—for the purposes of increasing headcount and improving traffic flow—were so cost-effective that they eventually led to changes to the building's shell itself. What's more, the alterations not only added the equivalent of nearly six additional floors of workspace, they also reduced construction costs, and thus delivered in truly spectacular fashion on IA's promise to design space from the inside out.

Although the sheer number and the differing interests of the developers, construction companies, architectural firms, and tenants involved in the project have made it impossible for us to name the building here, we can present a brief outline of the project's history in order to give you a sense of its complexity, and the radical impact of IA's contribution to the eventual architectural solution.

The building was constructed to house the headquarters of a major national financial institution whose revenues had soared as a result of the expansion of the real estate loan industry, as well as various mergers and acquisitions. It was meant to consolidate the bank's operations, which at the time were spread out across eleven different locations in the same city. The original plans, which resulted from a series of complicated and nuanced negotiations, called for the bank's new home to rise above an underground parking garage, with its ground floors, or pedestal, occupied by a major arts organization.

Despite the financial institution's economic health, the project depended on certain cost efficiencies, without which the project would not proceed. Because the layout of the lower floors, intended for a use entirely different than those above it, would impact not only the floor plate of the offices above it, but also the delivery of mechanical services, finding a solution that satisfied both prospective occupants was by no means guaranteed.

Moreover, not only did the two organizations have vastly different needs for security, exit scenarios, and parking, but over time the arts organization was expected to expand its presence to all twelve floors of the building's pedestal, thus requiring an interim solution to the use of the lower floors that would change over time, but without a specific timetable. As if that weren't enough, the office space above was to be configured according to IA's Village Plan, which called for an open office environment with flexible meeting spaces, and did away with most private offices, long a hallmark of banking tradition.

IA's job, therefore, was to collaborate with the architectural firm responsible for the design of the shell and core in taking maximum advantage of the site's buildable volume, while satisfying the differing needs of the financial institution and the arts organization. That the architectural team succeeded at all, given the constraints, is commendable—that it was able to do so while vastly increasing the building's headcount and reducing construction costs is hard to believe.

The trick lay in the reversal of the usual process of design—that is, the floor plate first and the interior design second. Given IA's familiarity with the bank's workstation standards, and their archetypical Village Plan, it quickly determined that the shell and core team's initial floor plate proposals—based on typical core-to-perimeter distances, bay sizes, and zoning restrictions—were incompatible with the most efficient interior solution. Therefore, it reversed the traditional design process, beginning with the optimal workstation layout, using the Village Plan, and then analyzing options that would support them.

In a stroke of luck—or genius—the team discovered that by reducing the perimeter column spacing to 20 feet rather than 30 feet, and shifting the core 4.5 feet to one side, not only would the bank's standard furniture fit the new floor plate, but the building would support an additional 600 workstations over its thirty-two floors of office space. What's more, the shell and core team discovered that not only would the capacity of the building be increased, but that the cost would be reduced because of the smaller size of the structural members needed to span the 20-foot space between the respaced perimeter columns. Finally, in what seemed like a case of snowballing serendipity, the new floor plate worked not only for the arts spaces in the pedestal, but also for traffic patterns in the garage below it.

Thus, through an innovative reversal of the design process, the collaborative spirit of the shell and core team and the construction company, and a little bit of luck experimenting with the perimeter column placement, IA arrived at a solution favorable to all, through a quintessential example of corporate agility. In our next chapter, we'll examine in greater depth our own methodology for such success—*collaborative strategic management*.

CHAPTER 9

Collaborative Strategic Management

Having been in the consulting business for many years, we feel we have a pretty good understanding of the varied natures and the diverse needs of businesses large and small around the world. We know, therefore, that it is unlikely that the experiences of the *Future of Work* community members whose stories fill this book will match those of all of our readers. As a result, we'd like to start the discussion of collaborative strategic management (CSM) by sharing with you the management approaches we've seen that don't work—which is why we've been inspired to develop a new, more collaborative approach—and then continue on to some general scenarios, one or all of which should more closely resemble your actual experiences.

Most of you have had some experience with systems thinking, which for our purposes is defined as the process of looking at an organization by considering the different characteristics of its parts and the way in which they interact, sometimes toward a common purpose, and sometimes not. In our opinion, the reason that most efforts at strategic systems integration fail, be they in the area of merger and acquisitions or collaborative strategic management, is that political and psychological motivations lead people to optimize their own areas of responsibility to the detriment of the entire enterprise.

As we've seen in previous chapters, it's relatively easy to align either IT, or HR, or CRE to work with the company's strategic goals. But even if one or all of those functions are humming along smoothly, the whole rarely if ever operates as well as it might. IT is often outsourced to a low-cost overseas supplier; HR may be managed by a third party whose motivation goes no further than reduced cost per transaction; CRE is often locked into exorbitant, long-term, inflexible leases. This all-too-typical reality—that optimizing the operations of individual divisions can cripple corporate agility—is the primary point we wish to make in this book.

A SYSTEMS APPROACH

We'd now like to lead you through a process, or a methodology if you will, that we believe will optimize corporate agility—that is, the ability to continuously adapt the *entire* organization to the rapidly changing external forces that we discussed in Chapters 3, 4, and 5. But first, let's step back and take a satellite-level view from above. Just what is it that causes a *suboptimum* process? Again, in our opinion the issues are primarily psychological.

Look at the title of this chapter for a moment. Our focus is on *collaboration,* not coordination or cooperation. (We struggled over this critical choice of words for some time, for reasons that we hope will soon become apparent.)

Perhaps the best way to begin is to look at the issue from one of the most important aspects of corporate behavior—the way decisions are made. We are suggesting that the rules by which decisions have been made in the past are no longer suitable to today's rapidly changing business world, and that changing those decision-making rules will lead to different, more appropriate decisions. Although this is true in the case of mandates that affect a group rather than a specific individual, it is especially true when more than one group is affected. In that case, it is very important that we distinguish between the terms *coordination, cooperation,* and *collaboration,* since they are all too often used interchangeably.

When multiple groups are involved, it is necessary to differentiate between three types of groups. Some groups simply coordinate clearly separated responsibilities—that is, two or three groups work on different parts of a report, the separate sections of which must be combined according to an agreed upon schedule. Other groups do cooperative work—that is, they divide single tasks into parts and complete them by working within and across group lines. It is necessary to differentiate both of these patterns from groups that function at a collaborative level—that is, they do not necessarily work on the same project, or even in the same place, but rather, work collaboratively toward some higher strategic goal. (The definition of cooperation, by the way, at least in the sense of computer supported cooperative work [CSCW], does not imply that there is no competition among cooperating work units.) Table 9-1 relates three types of decision making to the rules and characteristics of the communication style, and to the level of group function.

Groups sometimes decide that rewards—both explicit and implicit—will be distributed on an input/output basis. In that case, you receive as an output a reward that is directly proportional to your input. This situation is seen as an equity-decision type and is characterized by impersonal relationships, mostly task-oriented. In this scenario we would say the group is functioning at a *coordination* level that would be typical of functional units whose managers derive their status from the size of their budget, headcount, or contribution to profit.

Alternatively, groups may choose to treat everyone in the group the same. Then we would call their decision type *equality*. In this situation, group communications are built around strong social network relationships among workgroup members. We would call this group *cooperative*. As a matter of fact, a lot of organizational development work has been done in the past decade around the *quality movement* to shift workers from decisions based on principles of equity to ones of equality. This is also the dominant decision style for Asian and some European organizations.

Finally, you may see groups making reward distributions based on their determination of who is the neediest. These groups base their decisions on requirements that shift over time. Their communications are characterized as *intimate* and the group functions at a *collaborative* level. Most observers would

Table 9-1

Decision Rule	Decision Type	Communication Characteristic	Level of Group Functioning
Input/Output	Equity	Impersonal	Coordination
Everyone the same	Equality	Strong Ties	Cooperation
Neediest	Requirement	Intimacy	Collaboration

see these kinds of groups as high performing. This is how groups that are sustainable operate—and we mean sustainable over decades, not mere business cycles.

The style of communication must also match the task at hand. If group norms are being determined, then communication should include a significant socioemotional aspect. If decisions about who does what are paramount, then a more task-oriented style would be appropriate. If the style of communication (e.g., in type and context) does not match performance requirements, then communication becomes dysfunctional. Again, this kind of mismatch is often a major problem in strategic management. Consider, for a moment, the recent rage of private equity buyouts, restructuring and flipping businesses for a profit. Buyout decisions are made to maximize immediate profit/loss with little thought to long-term impacts.

In our scheme, we link the types of decision making to the characteristics of communication functions, thus providing a communication map. In ideal situations, following that map, we attempt to move communication from an impersonal level toward a level of intimacy, which means an *increasingly common understanding of values and respect for differences.* This occurs when groups move from simply coordinating their activities to acting in a truly collaborative fashion. In this sense, the structure of the communication network is the foundation upon which you can build task structures and therefore organizational effectiveness.

That, in short, is the shift in the psychology of strategic decision making that is required to move from silo-type thinking to truly collaborative strategic management. Decisions must be made from the perspective of the overall benefit to the organization, considering both task requirements and the social and psychological needs of executives, managers, and the workforce itself.

WHAT DOES COLLABORATIVE STRATEGIC MANAGEMENT LOOK LIKE?

Given our definition of collaboration as a group approach to decision making, we would now like to elaborate our concept of collaborative strategic management by describing four general scenarios, in the expectation that one or more of them will appear familiar.

Once we have shown you what collaborative strategic management looks like from the eyes of the CIO, CRE, and HR executives as individuals, we'll come back and demonstrate how to put the pieces together. Remember that these scenarios presume executives have moved their decision-making styles, and the ways in which their groups function, to a collaborative level in which they are working with their peers to develop cross-functional solutions that serve their businesses as a whole.

The first three scenarios focus on issues that are restricted—at least at first glance—to human resources (HR), commercial real estate management (CRE), or information technology (IT). Please keep in mind that these are but hypothetical examples of the sort of challenges that corporate managers face today, and as such are meant more to stimulate awareness of the issues involved than to be used as actual templates for organizational change.

Scenario One: Real Estate Management

You are responsible for real estate management in a large multinational firm. Business has been off for several quarters, and everyone is struggling. The CEO makes it public knowledge that the future of the company depends on keeping key talent from going to the competition. While you're still digesting this information, you are directed by the CFO to cut costs by closing 50 percent of your field operations offices, a move that will displace hundreds of employees. You fear that taking away these employees' offices will result in tremendous dissatisfaction, adversely affect morale in the sales force, and increase the risk that those very employees you've been directed to retain will jump ship. What do you do?

In this scenario, the CFO's directive that 50 percent of the field offices be closed is a precursor, presumably, to serious morale problems within the displaced sales force—and this after the CEO has warned that the key to the company's future lies in protecting its human resources! A corporate manager who practiced collaborative strategic management could begin by doing the following:

- Immediately assemble a task force of upper-level managers, including human resources, information technology, sales, and operations.

- Assign a high-potential manager the responsibility of project management and cross-discipline collaboration.

- Design a communications campaign aimed at the soon-to-be-displaced workers, focusing on the implementation of a distributed work program offering those in the field greater freedom and flexibility in choosing how and where they work.

- Stress management's commitment to providing whatever additional technology and training are needed in order to make the change.

- Organize and conduct face-to-face focus groups with all affected employees in order to identify their needs, desires, and constraints.

- Ask senior executives to explain the necessity for this change in operations and have them stress the importance of the members of the distributed workforce to the future of the company.

- Conduct an analysis of all locations subject to closure to determine which ones can be most expeditiously jettisoned, given lease requirements and local market conditions.

- Perform a geographic *cluster analysis* of the workplaces of all affected employees, and use this data to select the centralized, regional locations that will remain open.

- Immediately begin redesigning the remaining locations to improve their *touch down* and *hotel* functions.

- Design and institute a distributed work-training program, and appoint a project manager to monitor the progress of the transition, giving him or her the authority to solve any problems associated with the transition.

Although both management and the workforce will undoubtedly find such adjustments difficult at first, if properly designed and executed the process can actually increase corporate financial health, *and* boost morale. Once they have been convinced of the necessity for change, reassured of their importance to the company, and made aware of the personal benefits associated with more flexible work schedules and self-management, the sales force will soon realize that the changes, far from reducing their job satisfaction, will actually result in an improvement in the quality of their lives, to say nothing of increasing the fiscal health of the company that pays them.

The solution to this scenario, which at first seems to affect only real estate management, is a classic example of collaborative strategic management in action. The plan, coordinating as it does the management of CRE, HR, and IT, succeeds not only in cutting costs, but also in improving morale. Now let's switch hats for the next scenario, and take a look at one example of the sort of challenges faced by HR executives in the modern, global economy.

Scenario Two: Human Resources

You're a senior human resources director and are given responsibility for an important project with high visibility among the executive staff. You must develop a program to find, attract, and retain key talent in anticipation of an upswing in business. You've got two quarters to put a plan in place and begin implementation. However, the executive team has also decided to reduce the relocation budget for new hires, offer fewer stock incentive plans across the company, and alter the benefits plan, shifting more health insurance costs to the employees. What can you do to give your company a competitive recruiting advantage in a business environment with shrinking benefits?

This scenario, in which the HR director is asked to develop a program to find, attract, and retain key talent—in spite of planned reductions in the relocation, stock incentive, and benefits budgets—could be resolved using the same methodology we described in the first scenario.

Your first job is to rebrand the company as one sympathetic to the emergent workforce. This can be a delicate issue if top management, and the board, don't see the strategic necessity of such a change. Toward that end, you should form a task force of peers from corporate marketing, IT, and the CRE group, and hire an external marketing consultant who specializes in reaching emerging workers. Together you should seek to do the following:

- Develop catchy new recruitment slogans ("If you own an iPod, you'll like working with our team").

- Cast a wide geographic net in order to land the kind of talent that is already looking to relocate to an existing corporate location.

- Prepare a new contract for employment based on pay for performance, regular assignment rotation, a mentoring program, biannual sabbaticals, and time off for community service.

- Develop an *onboarding* process in order to bring the distributed workforce into regular physical contact with existing company talent.

- Ask IT to deploy a distance-insensitive collaboration program, using the Internet as a connectivity platform, but with no company proprietary standards.

- Contract with a nationwide Infrastructure Service Provider to support the new workforce.

- Develop a compensation program for managers that rewards them for retaining talent.

- Develop a training program for managers intended to increase their ability to manage talent they can't see.

Here, once again, potential liabilities have been turned into opportunities, both for the sought-after employees *and* the cost-conscious company managers. As in the real estate management scenario, savings in the relocation, stock incentives, and benefits budgets can be reallocated for IT needs and specialized training.

This brings us to our third scenario.

Scenario Three: Information Technology

You are the new chief information technology officer in a mid-sized company. The CEO announces that 40 percent of employees will begin a "work anywhere, anytime" program next month. The directors in charge of system security and business continuity say it can't be done—that is, not and still maintain the security of company databases and provide applications support. At the same time, the CFO directs you to reduce your operational support costs by 20 percent within twelve months. What do you do?

This scenario presents difficulties similar to the first two, but based on necessary innovations in IT. To reconcile the company's various needs, we believe management should do the following:

■ Immediately begin negotiations with a global provider of integrated applications support and telecommunications to provide support to the newly created "anytime, anywhere" workforce.

■ Along with the human resources staff, develop an outplacement package for your applications support staff (or, in other words, do not fire your displaced staff; make them employees of the companies with which you contract services).

■ Develop a training program for managers intended to increase their ability to manage talent they can't see.

Scenario Four: Crisis Affecting All Components

Our last scenario is an example of a hypothetical business crisis simultaneously affecting HR, CRE, and IT. In each of the scenarios just presented, a fix in one functional area produced side effects in the other two; in the following scenario, all have to be considered simultaneously.

> You are a successful chief executive officer with a great track record, and you've been hitting your numbers quarter after quarter. Then, one day, your board of directors calls you in and tells you that despite your results, some board members are concerned about your strategic planning process. They are convinced that a combination of globalization, unpredictable shifts in the market, and a growing worldwide human resource shortage is about to upset your currently stable business. They ask you, therefore, to develop a five-year strategic business plan based on three market assumptions:
>
> 1. 50 percent of your customers in the next three years will be new customers with whom you currently have no contact, in areas where you have no physical presence.
>
> 2. 75 percent of the products and services those new customers will want aren't currently in your product development pipeline.
>
> 3. 50 percent of your upper-level workforce is expected to leave your organization within the next twenty-four months.

How can you continue to manage your company successfully, while addressing the board's concerns for your company's future? And how do you tactfully present a business plan to the heads of the various divisions that will convince them that their departmentally focused behavior, while profitable in the past, has suddenly become inconsistent with the corporation's health outlook for the future?

Businesses around the world have faced similar scenarios in recent years, but today, without acknowledging the increasing interdependence of IT, HR, and CRE, lasting comprehensive solutions enabling corporate agility are all but impossible to devise. Whatever a company's motivation, financial health, or goals, change of this magnitude depends on two things: the collaborative strategic management of CRE, HR, and IT, and the explicit support of the executive team throughout the process of change. Therefore, our solution to the last scenario focuses both on the CEO and on his or her team:

- Set the tone with your executive team by letting them know that the company might soon face a *near-death experience* that can be avoided only through vigorous, far-reaching action.

- Accordingly, announce that you will shrink the executive workforce by 25 percent and ask for volunteers for outplacement (which, more than anything else you do, will get their attention, and warn those incapable of radical change that the time has come for them to go).

- Charge your CFO with increasing R&D funding by 20 percent (with the resources to come from reduced operational costs).

- Select key members of your team to develop a new business model that redefines your product development process by putting the company in closer touch with existing customers, better understanding their projected needs, and seeking new customer bases within the industry.

- Reach down into your organization and select managers to work on this team, making sure that it includes as broad a mixture as is possible of all business disciplines, demographics, and experiences.

- Charge these subteams with the development of plans to execute each of the core planning assumptions.

- Establish an organizational development-training program that reaches out to external educational resources in the areas of product design, strategic marketing, acquisitions, branding, and compensation.

■ Present this plan to your board within ninety days, introduce the new business model team, and seek the board's vocal and visible support. If they refuse, sell your company stock, move your retirement account out of the company-managed plan, and start looking for another job as quickly as you can—*before* the company is forced into bankruptcy.

THE WORKPLACE/WORKFORCE TRANSFORMATION PROGRAM

As we have said in the past, functional managers have attempted—or have been encouraged—to reach their goals independently, often even at the expense of other divisions within the company. Now, however, with the advent of truly global markets, the continuing revolution in information technology, the globally distributed workforce, and the growing, worldwide human talent gap, senior managers are beginning to understand that they may no longer be able to hit their own targets without the strategic cooperation of the company's other business units. In fact, it seems increasingly clear that those corporate entities unable to adapt their management practices to the growing interdependence of IT, HR, and CRE will soon find themselves marginalized by their more strategically coordinated competitors.

So, having set the stage by discussing hypothetical responses to changes in the global marketplace, we now turn to our methodology for transforming the workforce and the workplace of the future. No matter the company, the industry, or the scope of the plan for change, the first order of business is the creation of a task force made up of upper-level executives from the departments of real estate management, human resources, and information technology.

Without sufficient, well-advertised involvement from upper-level management, the momentum necessary to overcome a company's natural resistance to change cannot be achieved. What's more, no such plan can succeed without everyone in charge having a complete understanding of the company's core business plan, its financial strategies—both short and long term—

and its product development and marketing strategies. In addition, those heading the task force need an understanding of the market forces that drive the industry and an awareness of the competitive atmosphere, both local and global, within which the company operates.

The first step in the process is to get everyone operating off the same strategic goals and understanding what the decision rules are and what level of group functioning is required.

The first task is strategic alignment of goals. It is imperative that any workplace strategy be completely aligned with the core business mission and plan. We need to know (within a five-year time frame) these key elements:

- What the product development strategy is for both production and market channel

- What the workforce staffing plans are

- The financial management strategy

- An overview analysis of the branding program

- How the technology deployment plan will support all these

The optimal method of conducting this review is a short series of executive roundtables where the external team brings information on state-of-the-practice and internal resources present. Briefings center on key questions regarding such issues as business drivers, competitive threats, strategy development, and decision processes. The result of this first step is a *statement of the business problem* and specification of the results desired. This statement is then used for an internal return on investment (ROI) analysis prior to proceeding with the next steps. This process allows creation of a set of recommended tactical programs that, when executed, will lead to the results required.

At this point, the leadership team should assemble a task force to lead the job of defining a new workplace strategy. Once assembled, the task force will follow four simple, quantifiable, steps:

1. Assessment

2. Recommendation(s)

3. Implementation

4. Evaluation

Overall the process looks like Figure 9-1.

Figure 9-1

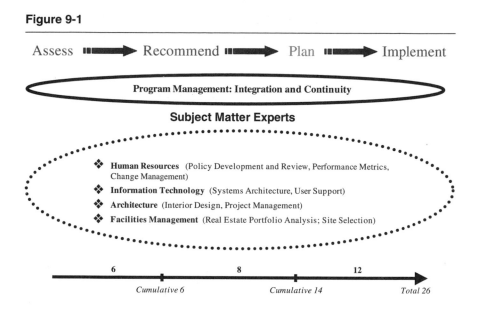

Assess ➤ Recommend ➤ Plan ➤ Implement

Program Management: Integration and Continuity

Subject Matter Experts

❖ **Human Resources** (Policy Development and Review, Performance Metrics, Change Management)
❖ **Information Technology** (Systems Architecture, User Support)
❖ **Architecture** (Interior Design, Project Management)
❖ **Facilities Management** (Real Estate Portfolio Analysis; Site Selection)

6 — 8 — 12

Cumulative 6   *Cumulative 14*   *Total 26*

Assessment

During assessment we are trying to do the following:

- Deconstruct departmental activities.

- Map work processes.

- Conduct task/activity analysis.

- Assess organizational readiness.

- Conduct workforce survey (needs, expectations).

- Develop alternate scenarios.

Specifically, assessment begins with a review of current costs, division by division, and requires verifiable figures for the following:

- Direct workforce costs (including the cost of benefits and pensions)

- Administrative support costs

- HR costs (including rate and cost of turnover)

- Facilities costs (including all maintenance, insurance, taxes, etc.)

- IT costs (including necessary software updates, scheduled hard-ware replacement, Web site maintenance, and intranet opera-tions)

The task force will also collect more general operational data for each critical area. In the case of real estate, for example, the task force will chart the company's total space under management, occupancy rates, utilization, and geographic dispersion. In the case of human resources, the task force will examine hiring rates, turnover rates, changing demographics within the workforce—gender, age, experience, education, and so on—as well as current trends in outsourcing for the industry. A review of the IT function will include an assessment of the company's current IT investments (both hardware and software), trends in employee usage of existing technologies, and, of course, emerging technologies.

The tool we use to consolidate these data is the ROI Calculator. The ROI Calculator is an economic analysis and decision support tool that enables an organization to compile data on the full costs of supporting knowledge work-ers, to build alternative scenarios of different workplaces and work arrange-ments, and to conduct return-on-investment analysis of the value of moving from the current baseline to one future scenario or another. The ROI Calcula-tor is a spreadsheet-based analytic tool that allows users to enter both current financial data and estimated future costs in a comprehensive chart of accounts structure. The tool then produces a pro forma income and expense statement for each completed scenario, as well as analysis of the economic changes over time as new work arrangements are introduced.

Next, having established the company's benchmark costs and sketched its general features, the task force will conclude its assessment by reviewing the results of a workforce survey, administered online to a representative sam-ple of the company's employees. The survey is used to determine the fol-lowing:

- The type of work people do
- Where people work, and for how many hours each week
- Characteristics of a workplace that people consider desirable
- Mix of work activities in a typical day (meetings, private work, etc.)
- Importance of various technologies and support services

- Social context in which work takes place

- Perspectives on personal productivity and the factors that enhance or detract from productivity

- Degree of satisfaction with the social, technical, and physical contexts in which people work

- Personal demographics

The results of the survey, like those of the cost analyses that precede it, will be used to develop a quantitative, baseline measurement of the company's requirements, capabilities, and characteristics.

Lastly we use another proprietary assessment tool to find out which organizational practices are working and which ones need improvement. Here, we use the Organizational Assessment System (OAS). The OAS is designed to provide decision makers with a reliable, quantifiable assessment of a work group's *potential* and *readiness* for successfully making a transition to a new way of working. No matter what the vision of the end state of an organizational change process is, we have to know six things:

1. How well is the direction of the workgroup articulated and communicated to the talent in the group?

2. How much human capital exists, and how is it developed?

3. How well does the group deliver on its value proposition to its customers?

4. How close are its information systems to state of the practice?

5. How well does its planning and improvement process operate?

6. What is the availability of and potential to provide, appropriate physical facilities to support emerging forms of work process.

The OAS also calculates a number of intellectual capital indices. It gives a reliable measure of the amount of customer, structural, and human intellectual capital that currently exists in the business. An appropriate balance of these three factors significantly enhances the agility of the company.

Administration of the OAS requires about two hours of a workgroup leader's time to participate in a structured interview with one of the project staff. An additional hour of telephone conversation may be required to obtain some data not immediately available to the group leader.

Our research shows that workgroups that score more than one standard deviation below national norms on three or more of the five core factors, in 95 percent of cases fail to make a successful transition to a new work state.

Recommendations

All of the task force's recommendations flow from an integration of the findings from the ROI analysis; the workforce survey, and the OAS. The key here is a comprehensive analysis of where suboptimization is occurring, where money can be saved, and where funds should be reinvested to reach a set of collaborative strategies. Although each case is different, the task force's recommendations will almost certainly include:

- A series of gradual reductions in total square footage under company management, taking into account each division's needs given the company's new workforce/workplace strategies

- A geographic realignment of the company's real estate assets, taking into account local real estate markets, supplier locations, customer bases, global competitors, and workplace preferences of the emergent workforce

The recommended changes in real estate management would be closely coordinated with new strategies and tactics for human resources and information technology. The task force would do the following:

- Propose reductions in the fixed workforce commensurate with the company's goals for lowered operational costs, in alignment with the reductions in real estate already recommended.

- Propose guidelines, incentives, and a timetable for increasing the percentage of distributed employees in its workforce.

- Establish targets for its outsourced and insourced workforce, and establish guidelines for communication between c-level management and human resources designed to increase the company's agility in the face of rapidly changing market conditions.

- Coordinate new hiring strategies with the proposed changes in real estate management and human resource development.

Finally, the task force will outline new responsibilities for the information technology function, given the increased distribution of the company's workplaces and workforce. Its recommendations, although once again dependent on individual circumstances, will typically include the following:

- A comprehensive plan to ensure the division's continued ability to connect the company's more distributed workforce with corporate headquarters while maintaining network security

- A new plan for hardware and software acquisitions

- A new plan for the division's maintenance staff, given the described changes

- Technology requirements for new hires, including skills and equipment

- Construction of an intranet matched to the division's changed responsibilities and the company's shifting characteristics

Implementation

Once recommendations have been made, the task force must carefully coordinate the implementation of its recommendations with upper management's timetable for change. During this critical stage, the focus turns to IT, without which the attempt to distribute the workforce will fail. Specifically, the task force must ensure that these steps have been taken:

- The IT function has been prepared well in advance of any changes in staffing and real estate.

- The company's internal communications (i.e., Web site, company intranet, e-mail, telephony, etc.) have been reconfigured *before* organizational change occurs.

- Coming changes in technology and the infrastructures they will require have been thoroughly considered before the company's systems are revamped.

Although a reduction in real estate is clearly the most cost-effective way to reduce fixed operational costs, the reconfiguration of the workforce and the shift to outsourced, project-based work, will have the longest running impact on the company's agility, and therefore on its profitability.

As the fixed workforce is reduced, however, the company's core employees will become even more important to its ability to reach its goals. Therefore, special care must be taken to ensure that the following areas are covered:

■ The human resources function is given clear directions for gradual reductions in personnel and the preferred redistribution of the remaining workforce (either to new company space, to "shared" space, or to home offices), and that progress toward hitting these numbers is continually monitored.

■ The workforce itself understands the changes being made, the need for them, the employees most likely to be affected, and the company's timetable.

■ Mechanisms for employee grievances are maintained, in order to reduce the loss of valued employees due to unintended consequences of the program.

■ Adequate retraining is provided for those whose jobs now require them to work in different environments and/or to use different tools.

Real estate presents the fewest difficulties in implementation—one need not invest in new technology, after all, nor consider the morale of abandoned space—but it does require the longest time frame. That time should be used to ensure that the new spaces recommended by the task force will better fit the company's changing needs. Therefore, implementation should include the following:

■ Oversight of a design team to ensure that new space conforms to the task force's recommendations, and that old space is modified to the extent possible

■ The process by which the search for new space will be made—in what locations and in what order—as well as a timetable for relinquishing, or selling, some of the company's existing space

■ Recognition that the company's long-term requirements have changed, and that the terms under which space is leased must change as well

The team also has to confront the inherent contradiction between outsourced facilities management and CRE, and make the former a more integral, strategic partner in the company's strategic decision making. Outsourced management, while unable to take a seat in the boardroom, must be kept up to date, and must be asked for input.

Another key part of this implementation activity is disposing of unneeded real estate assets. A significant part of the cost savings associated with collaborative strategic management comes from shedding that 30 to 50 percent of unnecessary real estate. The quicker you can get that fixed cost asset off your books, the sooner you realize bottom-line gains. Firms that represent tenants looking for good deals—and therefore bypassing traditional brokers—are already emerging in the market. The traditional broker is losing his or her place as a mediator, a development already underway in the automotive, airline, and banking industries with the advent of e-commerce. Our recommendation is to find an alternative resource to help you divest those assets you no longer need, once they have been identified by the CSM process.

Evaluation

Changes of this magnitude cannot proceed without difficulty, and therefore the task force must continue its work throughout the process of implementation, monitoring the plan's effectiveness, and amending it as necessary. In addition, as the plan becomes a reality, new assessments must be made, and those numbers must be compared to the benchmarks established at the beginning of the process (using the same ROI analysis used during the task force's recommendations).

The task force will also be required, in conjunction with upper-level management, to continually reexamine the company's core goals and strategies, in order to recommend adjustments in workforce/workplace strategy. CSM is a continuous process. Toward this end, management must consider these factors:

- Establishment of units within each division for prototype testing
- A linked training and development plan for initial program participants
- A mechanism by which customers and suppliers can respond to the changes
- Making permanent a new business model team that continuously looks for more effective, and more efficient, ways to organize your business.

WRAPPING IT ALL UP

Applying this methodology from end to end clearly entails a lot of work. Our suggested approach is to use as many internal resources as possible, guided by outside experts as required. We like to use a business model approach that is adapted from the film industry.

Think of the entire collaborative strategic management methodology as a *script*. The role of the external experts, such as the Work Design Collaborative, is to act as a producer that orchestrates the undertaking, while the director, cast, and crew (project manager and team members) generally come from within the company undertaking the transformation. The case studies and interviews reported elsewhere in this book can all be linked to various parts of this suggested approach.

We want to make one final point: The kind of process we've outlined here should really be done continuously. As soon as you implement one set of recommendations you need to start the process all over again. In business terms, you have to reinvent your business, using a CSM approach, every three years or so. In short, the only way to create agility is to continuously invent your future—over and over and over again.

CHAPTER 10

Achieving Corporate Agility

We began this book by suggesting that corporate agility will be *the* critical capability for organizational survival in the future. Further, we believe that achieving agility requires executives and managers to adopt fundamentally new ways of thinking. They have to shift away from the old linear, industrial model toward a more collaborative, systemic, and holistic view of the world and their role in it. In Chapter 9 we carried that notion further by suggesting there must be a significant shift in how decisions are made in agile corporations, as opposed to a more traditional organizing and governance style.

As we conclude this exploration of corporate agility and how to create it, we want to look ahead to see what's even further around the corner. Agility is a continuous process, so we can virtually guarantee that just as you master the techniques and ideas we've discussed here, the rules will change again.

We want to leave you, therefore, with a toolkit that will not only help you create agile organizations, but will ensure that you remain agile yourself. Thus, our concluding questions are, "What do you need to consider to be prepared for the next wave of change?" and, "How should you organize to remain perpetually agile?"

Why now, you may ask? What is so unique about the present that it requires such foresight, reinforced by so much hard work? The answer can be summed up in three words—the Information Age. Taken together, the two decades from 1985 to the present have brought us to a moment of unprecedented change. A failure to adapt to this change, which affects both our society and the global economy, will leave the dinosaur organizations of our day lumbering about vainly in search of food and water, while the more agile creatures of recent business evolution run circles around them.

In order to understand what we as managers need to be doing, let's look at two different but highly complementary perspectives on this issue. First, let's consider the sociological view.

WHY NOW? CHANGE IS MORE DRAMATIC THAN EVER

At first glance, this economic climate hardly seems like the time to begin planning and testing new models of corporate infrastructure. Many organizations are still recovering from massive layoffs, and in some cases—although mostly in manufacturing—are continuing to shed resources. As we write, therefore, corporate human resources are being challenged to deliver like never before, and at the same time being forced to transform the way they operate. Information technology, by contrast, is rapidly becoming a commodity, leading to the routine outsourcing of most IT services. Corporate real estate has its own problems, what with facilities vacancy rates varying widely around the world, and continuing financial pressures to consolidate space.

Under these circumstances, why should a prudent company allocate scarce management time and funding to integrate these diverse functional areas, even though in so doing it can make itself an employer of choice, enhancing the quality of its employees' work experience while reducing its fixed operating costs?

Well, the short answer to "Why now?" is that business cycles haven't gone away. But our experiences within those cycles has changed. By that we mean that as the economy moves beyond its current contraction into its next phase of expansion, forward-thinking leaders cannot afford to make strategic management decisions the same way they did during the last cycle.

Why do we think the next cycle will be so different? What's changing? Figure 10-1 highlights some trends that may help to explain our views on

Figure 10-1

Aspect of Time	Industrial Age	Internet Age
Direction	Linear	Cyclic
Scale	Quarters	Days
Sequencing	Serial	Parallel
Pace	Predictable norms	Situational
Salience	Past	Future

some fundamental aspects of the interplay between our society and the current direction of the global economy.

As we have said repeatedly, to remain sustainable through the next cycle organizations must become far more agile than they are today. They will need to know how to operate as a real-time enterprise with daily, or even hourly, business processes supporting parallel operations constantly focused on the future.

Agile corporations know how to staff up (and down), not only over the course of the annual budget, but overnight. They know how to partner with others for technology support, and how to move from offering a desk and a workspace for everyone to providing the workforce with just what they need at a given moment, whenever and wherever they need it. Further, they know how to integrate those assets and how to develop innovative ways of measuring the return on investment they get by embracing new ways of working, and new ways of organizing work.

All talk of collaboration aside, human capital is still a business's most precious strategic asset—this one thing, at least, has not changed. Right now, in this period of economic consolidation, there appears to be an excess of talent. Unemployment rates hover around 6 percent in a static business climate. What will happen when we enter the next phase of the business cycle? Will unemployment go to 4 percent? 3 percent? Unemployment was at 4.2 percent at the height of the dot-com craze (2000), and that was probably the lower limit for the kind of talent that will be in high demand in the future.

As we go to press, the unemployment rate in the United States is 4.4 percent, a five-year low.

Enjoy the talent surplus while you can, therefore, because as we made clear in Chapter 6, it won't last long. By 2010, we and many others predict that there will be a net shortage of around 10 million creative workers in the United States! Now put yourself in the shoes of a CEO in that environment. If your firm is not a talent magnet, or an *employer of choice*, or located in a place the emerging workforce finds attractive, you won't be able to compete for that talent. You can have the capital, you can have the product, and you can even have the process of product development under control, but without a plan to attract new labor you are doomed.

If you wait until the talent demand equation is inverted, you will be about eighteen months behind the curve. What can your competitors do to you in eighteen months when they have the talent and you don't? It is an ugly, ugly picture. Will you depend on growth through acquisition? Don't count on it. The rapid deflation of the equities market has left most companies with little trading equity for that strategy to succeed.

Now look where the talent is. It's global, which means there is an even higher premium on integrating support infrastructures that rely on information technology to connect work and workers across the globe. Salaries outside the United States range anywhere from 10 percent to 20 percent of U.S. equivalents, and therefore it's pretty clear that your new workforce is going to speak English as a second language. No, that isn't back-office tech workers, either. The point is that for U.S.-based companies, the talent they need for growth will in many instances *not* be located in the places where they currently have a physical presence. They will have to integrate their work support infrastructure in new and innovative ways if they want to remain competitive.

WHY NOW? BECAUSE THE
CLOCK IS ALREADY TICKING

Organizations that thrive in the future will have to plan for several kinds of cycles, not just the obvious general business cycle. There are waves of change ahead of us, from longer ones like the overall lifecycle of a product, to shorter ones like product enhancement. You will need to learn how to operate effectively within these intertwined, shifting cycles. In order to achieve business sustainability, you will need to expand your planning beyond just one cycle to take in a longer, multicycled perspective.

Our experience shows that it takes anywhere from eighteen to thirty months for this kind of large-scale organizational change to go from planning, testing, and revising, to actually implementing and rolling out effective new programs and processes. Some portions of this time scale can be compressed with great effort, but a minimum scope of two years is very reasonable. So you need to act *now* in anticipation of renewed volatility in business cycles and an increased demand to develop corporate agility.

Now, let's consider the futurist perspective.

WHY NOW? TECHNOLOGY IS RESHAPING OUR WORK WORLD

There is much more going on today than the "Make things more efficient" focus of the office automation era and the "Oh, Gee Whiz" of the Internet bubble. We take our lead here from our friend and colleague Rex Miller and his book *The Millennium Matrix*.[1] Although Miller's focus was on technology and the organization of our spiritual life, we choose here to dig a little deeper into the way he sees technology changing the ways we work and communicate.

Miller's basic thesis is that our dominant communication technologies profoundly shape the way in which we perceive the world, make meaning of it, and behave accordingly (making Miller a modern-day Marshall McLuhan).

Over the centuries in human history we have moved progressively from a literal world without books, to a print world, and then to a broadcast world for the last sixty years. Now we are entering the digital era, in which communication has shifted from the one-to-many paradigm of broadcasting to a many-to-many mode enabled by the Internet and all its associated technologies. By the way, this perspective corresponds quite neatly with what we have been predicting for technology itself—but that is a digression.

The digital era introduces some very basic changes into the work world: the focus of work; how we build wealth; how we manage the processes of work; what we value (and how value is added); how production is carried out; and, finally, what we use as a medium of exchange. The changes from the broadcast era to the digital era are summed up in Figure 10-2. This transformation is clearly a sweeping set of changes in how we work and provides, yet again, another motivation for agility.

Finally, let's also consider the perspective of senior executives.

LEADERSHIP AND STRATEGY

If the 1970s, 1980s, and 1990s were the decades of management, the 2000s and beyond will be the decades of leadership. We really don't have the vocabulary to talk about these things yet. Peter Drucker brought us the language of management beginning in the 1940s. We await the next guru with that kind of sweeping power to describe an important emergent phenomenon.

We are convinced that the days of Jack ("Neutron Jack") Welch are gone. And perhaps even the day of Bill Gates is also gone. We believe there is a basic requirement to match strategy with leadership style and ability that has become far more important today.

A feature article in the *McKinsey Quarterly* in November 2005 struck us as a first salvo in this development.[2] Let's start, as the article did, with a question: "What do we mean by leadership?" Whereas good managers deliver predictable results as promised, as well as occasional incremental improvements, leaders generate breakthroughs in performance. They create something that wasn't there before by launching a new product, by entering a new market, or by more quickly attaining better operational performance at lower cost, for example.

We also like the more folksy way of putting it: Managers do things right. Leaders do the right things.

The authors of the McKinsey article point out that if your strategy is to deliver breakthrough performance, you need a different type of leader to make that happen. Seems logical enough; but the problem, we believe, lies within existing workplace structures and business processes that are constructed not for breakthroughs, but for predictable performance. Simply put, successful leaders of the 2000s will not be cut from the cloth of managers of old. Can't you just see General Motors recruiting Richard Branson as its new CEO (as if he would want the job)?

So therein lies the rub. How do companies that recognize this fairly simple truth—that new leadership is required—prepare for the future? Certainly

Figure 10-2

Feature of the Work World	Broadcast Era	Digital Era
Nature of work	Service: Information about customers is used to develop products.	Federation: Both production and consumption is organized around flexible networks.
Wealth building	Distribution and debt: Efficient distribution and financing of debt build wealth.	Creativity and community: The ability to create and organize in groups creates wealth.
Management	Leader: Lead, not control.	Interweaver: Connect, not control.
Value	Quality is most prized attribute.	Creativity in interaction between producer and consumer.
Production	Creating want: People take what they want.	Creating fulfillment: People design what they want.
Medium of exchange	Credit: The use of credit accelerates transaction speed.	Techno-barter: Electronic markets such as eBay, or other on-line auctions creates a new medium of exchange.

not by staying inside their own boundaries. That's too confining, too stuck in the old ways.

This recognition leads us to predict that, with M&A activity picking up and private equity firms on the hunt for new targets, we will begin to see radically new types of leaders emerging. We may even see the development of a *talent agency* pool of leaders—sort of a central casting for leadership. What exact form it will take we don't know—but certainly the old systems of succession planning won't suffice. We believe that traditional executive recruiting and the like is passé.

QUESTIONS YOU SHOULD BE ASKING

Let's start at the top and then dive down into a set of eight specific areas of inquiry. Imagine flying an airplane. What are the absolute basic things you need to know?

1. Which direction you are headed

2. How fast you are going

3. What obstacles are in your way

It sort of looks like Figure 10-3. Notice that's it very foggy in the view through the windshield.

The compass at the center of the dashboard symbolizes your company's direction and strategy. You need to know where you are going. That is why

Figure 10-3

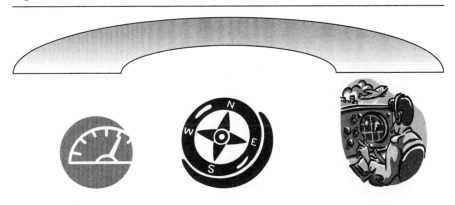

we emphasized linking the collaborative strategy management process to your business strategy. The speedometer captures your speed: Speed is basically a measure of resource expenditure. How fast do you want to get there? The return-on-investment (ROI) calculator we described in Chapter 7 can give you a rough gauge of what it will take in terms of the resources needed to meet your goals. Looking for hazards—as represented by the air traffic controller on the right—lies at the base of the organizational analysis system. What are the roadblocks, and what can you do to overcome them?

QUESTIONS FOR AN AGILE ORGANIZATION

We have identified eight major categories of questions that you should be asking—simultaneously and continuously. There is no magic or best way to sort these questions, and of course, there is always some overlap. But if you are devoting resources to continuously investigating these areas, you will be well prepared for the next wave of change.

1. *Meta forces of change.* What are the global sociopolitical forces that impact how we work? What are the possible alternative futures, given those forces? The scenario-planning methodology used so extensively by Royal Dutch Shell[3] illustrates the power of this question.

2. *Public policy issues.* What are the workplace/workforce effects of trade policies, employee benefits requirements, environmental laws, and labor laws? Today our world is dominated by questions of free trade, immigration policies, environmental impacts, and energy use. What will these public policy issues be in five years, and how will they affect your business and your customers?

3. *Demographic dynamics.* What are the multigenerational dynamics of demography, especially in underdeveloped countries? What factors influence generational cultures and values? What are the long-term trends in educational funding, in the United States and elsewhere?

4. *Geography of talent pools.* Close on the heels of the demographic questions, where will the most desirable talent be living in five, ten, twenty, and maybe even fifty years? Why? What is the psychology that underlies mobility?

5. *Work process and collaboration styles.* We really don't yet understand very well what motivates humans to collaborate, or how compensation and reward systems affect work behaviors. Much more basic research is needed here.

6. *Social and intellectual capital metrics.* How should we measure and audit workforce performance in a distributed work environment? How do you capture increased social capital on your balance sheet? What is that social capital worth in the marketplace?

7. *Challenges and difficulties of managing a distributed workforce.* What are the specific competencies required to manage distributed workers successfully? What do leaders of the future look like? How do they develop these competencies?

8. *Deeper understanding of barriers and sources of resistance to the new models.* What are the cultural barriers to the fundamental changes that the future of work will bring—and demand? What kind of change management processes must be put in place? How do we get senior management on board?

PROCEEDING TO ANSWER THE QUESTIONS

This is our last point. How should you organize yourself to answer these questions? We believe there should be a special, identifiable group of people within the organization who are tasked with answering these questions, over and over again. There are basically two options. Either do it internally or do it externally, relying on outside experts.

Most companies choose a blended solution, where internal R&D groups partner with external groups (e.g., research firms and consultants) on a special-project basis. However, that isn't uniformly effective because most organizations don't have agility embedded in their DNA, so that often new knowledge gets buried down at the activity level rather than at the policy level, where it belongs.

We close with one final set of ideas about organization design to promote corporate agility.

A NEW WAY OF LOOKING AT ORGANIZATIONS

We believe an effective, simplifying heuristic is to view organizations as containing three levels—or, more appropriately, *spheres*—of work. In the activity level, products or services are produced and distributed. In the *administrative* level, different activities are coordinated. In the *policy* level, general direction is set. The point here is to locate the forward-looking role, the futures group (if you will) at the policy level. Perhaps a detailed look at each of these levels will help clarify our recommendation.

Each of these three spheres has a core issue, a characteristic set of processes, and a system of organizing. These processes and systems form unique patterns of action and have optimal functions associated with them. Further, as shown in Figure 10-4, each sphere has a set of communication tools that most effectively promote its functioning.

This figure is a conceptual diagram of the relationships between the two factors—sphere of work and defining characteristics. We believe this simple model provides an organizational map that the practitioner can use in organizational design. Before discussing each block within the model, let's look a little more closely at the spheres of work.

The basic trend in organizations today is to decrease the number of hierarchical levels of power relationships. The three spheres of work—activity, administration, and policy—represent a minimum set of necessary levels of an organization in the traditional sense. Executives set policy, middle managers coordinate action, and nonmanagers do the work of the enterprise. You have to know where you are in the organization to understand how you fit into the overall scheme of things and how and what you can do to increase the organization's agility.

Core Issues at Each Level

The core issue for the activity sphere is, "What are we doing?" These people are concerned about efficiency, resources, and getting things completed. Administrators are concerned with, "How will we get it done?" They are characterized by control issues, methods of work, and maintaining the status quo. Administrators are interested in survival. Policy makers look at the question, "Why are we doing this?" Their concerns center on issues of direction, effectiveness, the creation of new abilities for the organization, and renewal.

Figure 10-4

Defining Characteristics	Sphere of Work		
	Activity	Administration	Policy
Core Issue	• What are we doing? • Efficiency • Resources • Tools • Completion	• How do we do it? • Control • Methods • Status Quo • Survival	• Why are we doing this? • Effectiveness • Theory • Creation • Renewal
Process	• Present • Fast • *Cooperation*	• Past • Translation • *Coordination*	• Future • Slow • *Collaboration*
System	• Facts • "*Intra*-networks" • Informal networks	• Rules • "*Inter*-networks" • Formal networks	• Context • External • "Meta– network"
Pattern	• Circular • Teaming • Heterarchy	• Vertical • Task Force • Hierarchy	• Horizontal • Family • Molecule
Optimal Function	• Activating • Analysis • Work	• Nurturance • Restraining • Heart	• Unify • Harmony • Synthesis • Spirit
Tools to be used	• Productivity • Words • Numbers • Graphs	• Database • Publishing • Communication • Workgroup-based	• Models • Simulation • External links • Enterprise

Process

Activity is about the present, is fast-paced, and seeks cooperation. Administrators engage in a work process that looks to the past for guidance, translates information from policy into activity direction, and tries to coordinate activities. Policy makers look to the future, are usually slow to react, and foster a sense of collaboration.

System

Activity systems are based on facts—knowable and observable. Within this system, group communications are key; the informal social network manages power and status relations. The next sphere (administration) works from historically based rules, across-group communication occupies most of the time, and the formal network structure is used to shape behaviors. At the policy level, systems center on the context of linking the organization to larger wholes, such as communities and markets. The meta network of business and professional associations or community service dominates.

Pattern

The basic pattern of action at the activity level is circular, with people being organized as teams with hierarchical power structures. Examples are sports teams, military platoons, and religious dioceses. Administrators tend to organize around vertical power dimensions, group into cross-disciplinary task forces, and rely on hierarchy to establish order. Policy makers form up around horizontal principles, with equality a goal. The ideal type here is the family or kinship model, which seems to be emerging into a molecular formation.

Optimal Function

The optimal function of the activity sphere is action, or initiating action; it is very functional and results-driven. Administration is a restraining force that tends to impede action but is concerned with nurturance. The policy sphere functions to unify the others, activating and restraining forces through a process of reconciliation, looking for synthesis. This level is the spirit of the business enterprise.

Tools

Productivity tools are found most prevalent within the activity sphere. Examples are software products that manipulate numbers, words, and graphs. Administration uses databases and boundary-spanning communication tools, such as electronic mail. Policy makers use modeling and simulation tools emphasizing linkages across organizational boundaries.

FINAL THOUGHT

An agile organization is one that strategically integrates the management of its real estate, human resources, and technology assets. It does that in a collaborative fashion that requires a change in decision-making processes and styles from what most organizations rely on today. Finally, an agile enterprise organizes itself into three (and only three) levels that center on completion, survival, and renewal.

A F T E R W O R D

As we continue our journey in search of corporate agility, several things have become abundantly clear. First, agility is a relative thing—and the more dynamic the world you live in, the more essential agility becomes. For most of the organizations we've worked with over the past five years, agility isn't a luxury; it is the key to survival. Or, in the words of Lord John Browne, the former chairman of British Petroleum: "We've got to move from *being* surprised by change, to surprising our competitors." That sentiment perfectly frames our message: Agility isn't just a key to survival; it's actually a critical source of competitive advantage.

Our second insight may be even more important: Agility isn't something you do once and then forget about. It's more like breathing: Agility is what you do to stay alive.

Which is to say that the ideas, experiences, and perspectives we've offered here, and all the stories our clients and friends have generously shared with us, are only a fleeting glimpse at the continually evolving future of work. We fully intend to continue observing, chronicling, and interpreting this saga, as long as we've got the energy and the market has the interest. It's our way of staying alive ourselves.

That's our way of telling you that we are committed to turning this book into a living, growing knowledge base—supplemented by a Web site (www.thefutureofwork.net), a blog (www.thefutureofwork.net/blog), a wiki (www.corporateagilitybook.com), and whatever other new collaborative technologies we can harness to create an ongoing global conversation about the future of work. A conversation is a two-way exchange of ideas and information and a community is a multidimensional version of a conversation spread out over time and space, so we need your help, and we encourage you to participate as we lurch forward.

The *Future of Work* community that we've mentioned (and chronicled) so often in these pages is, of course, a living, breathing consortium of active business and public-sector executives who meet several times a year (both physically and digitally) to share experiences, articulate lessons learned, and chart the future of work.

We also utilize an interactive Web site[1] that will provide anyone with an opportunity to contribute to the conversation and become a member of the community at a level of engagement and intimacy that works for you. We'll be compiling your stories and your lessons about creating corporate agility, and we look forward to learning from you. The road to the future will be a bumpy one, filled with potholes and unmarked obstacles, so it's safer to travel in a group. We hope that after reading *Corporate Agility*, you'll think about joining ours.

N O T E S

CHAPTER 1

1. General Electric Press Release, www.ge.com/en/company/com panyinfo/quality/culture.htm.

CHAPTER 3

1. 2005 Spherion Corporation Emerging Workforce® Study conducted by Harris Interactive®, www.spherion.com/press/releas es/2005/Emerging_Workforce.jsp.

2. http://www.usgbc.org

3. 2005 Spherion Corporation Emerging Workforce® Study conducted by Harris Interactive®, www.spherion.com/press/releas es/2005/Emerging_Workforce.jsp.

4. Ibid.

5. Ibid.

6. Ibid.

CHAPTER 4

1. Ken Dychtwald, T. J. Erickson, and R. Morrison, *Workforce Crisis: How to Beat the Coming Shortage of Skills and Talent* (Boston, MA: Harvard Business School Press, 2006), page 9.

2. United Nations Department of Economic and Social Affairs, "Population Ageing 2006," www.unpopulation.org

3. Ibid.

4. Ibid.

5. The 2006 Annual Report of the Board of Trustees of the Federal OASI and DI Trust Funds, www.ssa.gov/OACT/TR/TR06.

6. Centers for Disease Control and Prevention (CDC); NVSR Vol. 51, No. 1

7. Ibid.

8. U.S. Census Bureau, International Database, www.infoplease .com/ipa/A0004395.html.

9. Littler Mendelson, P.C., *Strategic Initiatives for the Changing Workforce, 2004–2005.* Internal white paper.

10. National Center for Education Statistics (U.S. Department of Education); Digest of Education Statistics (2005), http://nces.ed .gov/programs/digest/d05.

11. Alan Wagner, *Measuring Up Internationally* (Washington, D.C.: National Center for Public Policy and Higher Education, 2006).

12. Ibid.

13. Alan Wagner, *Measuring Up Internationally* (Washington, D.C.: National Center for Public Policy and Higher Education, 2006).

14. Ibid.

15. See http://www.wm-alliance.org/Brix?pageID = 57 for details of one program.

16. 2003 Spherion Corporation Emerging Workforce® Study conducted by Harris Interactive®, www.spherion.com/press/releas es/2003/Emerging_Workforce.jsp.

17. http://www.nextgenerationconsulting.com

18. This notion of "live first, work second" is supported conclusively by a study recently completed by "CEO's for Cities" that found two-thirds of 25–34 year-olds selected where they wanted to live

well ahead of who they hoped to work for. http://www.ceosforci
ties.org/rethink/research/files/CEOsforCitiesAttractingYoungEd
ucatedPres2006.pdf

CHAPTER 5

1. Robert Probst, *The Office—A Facility Based on Change*, Business
   Press, Elmhurst, Illinois, 1968.

2. Ibid.

CHAPTER 6

1. http://encarta.msn.com/encyclopedia_1741500823_21/United_
   States_History.html.

2. C. Grantham and A. Campbell, "Organizational Assessment in
   the Distributed Work Environment: Using Measures of Intellectual Capital in the Planning Process," in *International Perspectives
   on Telework: From Telecommuting to the Virtual Organization*, Paul
   Jackson (ed.) (London: Routledge, 1997).

3. Richard Florida, *The Rise of the Creative Class: And How It's Transforming Work, Leisure, Community and Everyday Life* (Basic Books;
   Reprint edition, December 23, 2003).

4. Garry G. Mathiason, Esq. et al, *Strategic Initiatives for the Changing Workforce, 2004–2005*, Littler Mendelson, 2004–2005, p 3.

5. Ibid, page 16.

6. Spherion.com, June 8, 2006, Kip Havel, www.spherion.com/
   press/releases/2006/EW-hiring_process.jsp.

CHAPTER 7

1. "Corporate Real Estate 2010 Synthesis Report," CoreNet Global
   Research Report, Atlanta, 2004.

2. Bureau of Labor Statistics, *American Time Use Survey*, 2005, p. 1

3. Ibid., Table 1.

4. Ibid.

5. Charles Grantham and Judith Carr, *Consumer Evolution: Nine Effective Strategies for Driving Business Growth* (New York: John Wiley/Gartner Press, 2002).

6. Ray Oldenburg, *The Great Good Place*, Paragon House Publishing, 1989.

CHAPTER 8

1. Robert Probst, *The Office—A Facility Based on Change*, Business Press, Elmhurst, Illinois, 1968, p.9.

2. Ibid., pp. 4–5.

3. Ibid., p. 49.

4. Ibid., p. 43.

5. U.S. General Services Administration, *Leading By Example*, 2005, www.gsa.gov.

6. Ibid.

CHAPTER 10

1. Rex Miller, *The Millennium Matrix* (San Francisco: Jossey-Bass, 2004). See also http://www.millenniummatrix.com/

2. Tsun-yan Hsieh and Sara Yik, "Leadership as the Starting Point of Strategy," *McKinsey Quarterly*, 1 (2005).

3. Peter Schwartz, "The Art of the Long View," *Currency* (1996).

4. See http://www.thefutureofwork.net/community_benefits.html

for membership information, and e-mail at corporateagility@
thefutureofwork.net to begin the conversation.

AFTERWORD

1. www.thefutureofwork.net

Index